THE

SCIENCE OF EVIL;

OR

FIRST PRINCIPLES OF HUMAN ACTION:

TOGETHER WITH

THREE LECTURES;

SALVATION AND DAMNATION BEFORE BIRTH, OR THE SCIENTIFIC AND THEOLOGICAL METHODS OF SALVATION COMPARED.— SUNDAY;—ITS HISTORY, USES AND ABUSES.— PRAYER;—THE TRUE AND FALSE METHODS COMPARED.

BY JOEL MOODY.

TOPEKA, KANSAS:
CRANE & BYRON, PUBLISHERS.
1871.

Printed at the "COMMONWEALTH" State Printing House.

INTRODUCTION.

The Science of Evil the author places before the public That Evil should claim the dignity of Science, will, doubtless, appear absurd to some; it will startle others, and a few will start back in holy horror at the thought. But we would caution the reader to suspend a judgment till an investigation is begun. That the title is no advertising dodge, will be made strikingly manifest before he has mastered its pages.

Evil has long bewildered the thinking world. Why Evil is? has long been a complex question. Since the dawn of history a theological notion has embraced a scientific fact; and the myths of the ages have added to the complexity. It is thus, many hypotheses have been put forth to account for it. The early mind struggling for truth, seized a fact of Nature, and dressing it in a mythical garb, passed it down in song to the world. The explanation has come from the imagination, and has been strictly theological instead of scientific. Yet every explanation has had some truth in it. Myths are by no means devoid of truth. They are the harbingers of Science; the nursery songs of the world's infancy.

The true relationship of Theology to Science, we have endeavored to point out.

Something has been said upon definition, and the author's method is one which must commend itself; for it aims to destroy the wrangle so deploringly prevalent among writers on Ethics and Philosophy. How often it is, that two persons or two schools of philosophy will dispute for years, when at last it is found, the only difference between them is in the definition of words. They agree about the substance, but fight over the shadow. This is the whole story of the controversy between the Idealist and Materialist; the whole story about Fate and Freedom. There is truth in both; and the one is dependent upon the other. THE SCIENCE OF EVIL aims to throw light on this controversy.

We would caution the reader about the word *Law*. As words are only symbols of thought, they cannot be entirely divested of a figurative sense. Most frequently we talk about a law of Nature as an active force; whereas, a law is only an effect of the action of Force on matter. Strictly speaking then, a law of Nature cannot be violated. Yet how frequently it is said: If we do not violate a law of Nature it will be well with us. As well say, however, that we can violate an eclipse of the moon as a law of Nature. There is no way by which we can get rid of this figurative sense, without circumlocution. It is in this way, scientific precision is frequently sacrificed to the idioms of speech; for example, we say: "The sun sets," and "Nature's Laws are broken." With this caution the author will be understood.

Particular attention is called to Chapter V, on the

"Origin of Morals and Science;" and to Chapter VI, "How Theology Evolves Science," for a complete exposition of the author's method. That the world is in a continual transition, that it is forever "a becoming," and never reaches any special goal, which can be clearly defined; that Theology must precede Science and is typical of it; and in fact that the whole religious history of the world is only typical of Science, and all the god-names are only symbols of Force, he has endeavored to make quite plain. *Force personified in the god; is only Force made real in Science.* The tyranny of a monotheistic worship, and the comparative freedom of apolytheistic one, is strikingly manifest throughout the world. The latter is conducive to the advancement of Science; the former is inimical thereto. Forcible illustrations of this fact are given in the Jewish god-thought and the early Catholic church on the one hand, and in Grecian theology and Protestantism on the other. Science must be strangled by the hand of the ancient Jew and Catholic, while it was nourished by the Greek and Protestant. Conclusive reasons are given for this, which the facts of history support. That the freedom of Science will one day take the place of a theologic tyranny, and that the scientific lecture will take the place of the Sunday sermon, is a fact shortly to be realized. It is a fact already knocking at the door of the Church.

The Chapter on "Special Evils," answers many complex questions, and throws some light on the mystery of a world's villainy. The tyranny of man over woman, producing in the latter a prostitution of her body, is briefly treated in. the Chapter on "The

Social Evil.' That Prostitution in woman obeys a law of Nature, and ought no more to be punished by man than a man for saying his prayers, may at first seem destructive of good morals. But, when it is known that man demands of woman a submission to his own lusts, and she only obeys through the stern commands of Want and Worship, he may be led to reverse this judgment. By getting a glimpse at his own hidious guilt, the crime of woman disappears.

The author has aimed in THE SCIENCE OF EVIL, to give a connected and logical view of the *First Principles of Human Action.* That it is a full and complete view, he by no means claims; but if he has opened the way to a deeper research into the causes of crime, so that it can be dealt with upon humane and scientific principles, and not according to the caprices of ignorance; if he has given an impetus to the search after Truth, though he may have erred in his own conclusions; or if he has in any way directed man to a higher life, he has gained his object.

It pains the author to find that a few typographical errors have crept into the book. This reminds him of the world's most self-evident truth, that: *To err is human.* He would therefore caution the reader to read "Plato," not "Pluto," on page 134, and "god-men," not "god-man," on page 123. Other minor errors are left to the disposal of the intelligent reader.

JOEL MOODY.

TOPEKA, Kansas, January 1, 1871.

CONTENTS.

CHAPTER I.

CHAPTER II.

CHAPTER III.

CHAPTER IV.

CHAPTER V.

CHAPTER VI.

CHAPTER VII.

CHAPTER VIII.

LECTURES.

CHAPTER I.

THE ETERNITY OF EVIL.

§. 1. Lord Bacon said: "Sciences are facts generalized." There are many facts in the world called evils; collectively they may be termed Evil. These facts generalized, and their common meaning found, constitute the *Science of Evil.* Evil is, and therefore means, something. It has been doubted that Evil is,—but this is only a matter of definition; the facts called Evil have not been denied altogether; another name has often been given some of them, yet the same facts remain. It will be our task to treat of these facts, under whatever name they may have borne, to find their meaning. What Evil is, it were foolish enough to attempt to answer. Force and matter are, yet no one has ever told us *what* they are. We have become cognizant of certain effects of the action of force on matter, and have designated these effects by certain names, expressing quality, quantity or condition. We say certain effects are good, and certain other effects are bad.

So also of men, laws, institutions, actions; they are good or bad. Definition becomes impossible when we ask: Was Feudalism and the Inquisition good or bad, as political and religious institutions among Christians? was slavery good or bad, as a biblical and Jewish institution? were Nero, Jesus, and Lincoln, evils as men? For we find mankind divided in opinion on all these questions. There is a no, and a yes, to greet us at every turning. The North and the South answer yes, and no, in regard to Lincoln. The Christians and the Jews who crucified Jesus answer yes, and no, in regard to him. Is Mahometanism, or Christianity, good or bad? The Christian and the Moslem give adverse answers, and have often fought over this question. Were the wars, which resulted in regard to opinion, evils or blessings? Now, as when waged, the public is divided in opinion. Is war an evil? Opinion is divided; and thus definition of Evil is impossible. There is no common consent to establish a definition. The reason will soon be made manifest. A living author, a deep thinker and close reasoner, Herbert Spencer, has volunteered an answer in his "Social Statics:" "All evil results from the non-adaptation of constitution to conditions." And he says, "this is true of everything that lives." About the same time Theodore Parker, in nearly the same language, defined Evil to be "The non-fulfilment of the conditions of animal life." The former is less restricted, but it still lacks comprehensiveness; and while *true*, may define a *good*, as well as an evil. It would be quite as true sometimes to say, evil results from adaptation of constitution to conditions; for "What is pleasure and life to you, is pain and death to me," as the hare said to the hound. The adaptation of the rabbit's constitution to the conditions of a dog's stomach, brings a good, as well as an evil. It makes the dog happy, but the rabbit has to die for it. If an evil to the latter, it is a blessing to the former. Nor can it be argued that the evil to the rabbit is the non-adaptation of its constitution to the conditions which devoured it, for such animals as rabbits are made for carnivorous animals to live on, and to be deprived of them would bring death to a large class of animals. True, its life was shortened; but this may be a good or an evil. This may be said in regard to death in general. Death is not always an evil—as when an aged man, ripe with years and experience, goes down to the grave—yet death may be said to always result from the non-adaptation of constitution to conditions. Here the definition would include a great good to man, and not an evil. As well define a circle to be always the result of a curved line; so are an ellipse, parabola, hyperbola, and infinite other curves, all radically different from the circle. The definition lacks definiteness, and, while true, may therefore define a good as well as an evil. The terms of which it is composed are variable quantities, as conditions and constitutions may both admit of an infinite number of modifications, passing from the extreme of good to bad, and from the finite to the infinite, as a curve may pass from the finite circle to the infinite hyperbola. But let us bring another element into the case of the dog and the rabbit. The rabbit eats the young apple tree in the farmer's orchard; this brings pain and annoyance to the farmer, blighting his hopes, and rendering his labor useless. Here is an evil to the farmer; yet there was a perfect adaptation of the tender little apple tree to the stomach of the rabbit, which, serving for food, doubtless gave it pleasure. The truth is, the apple tree is adapted to more uses than one, and the stomach of the rabbit to more kinds of plants than one. The rabbit wanted it for food; the farmer also wanted it for food in its fruit time; and in the *conflict of desires* there was pleasure to the rabbit and pain to the farmer. He now hunts it with his dog, who devours it; whereupon the farmer rejoices, and the dog has a fine meal. The apple tree might as well cry out against the rabbit, as the rabbit to cry out against the dog, evil! or, "Non-adaptation of constitution to conditions!" or, "Non-fulfillment of conditions!"

Here is a fable: A lamb was caught by a wolf, and not killing her at once, after the first fright was over she began thus to the wolf: "Ah, me! How cruel you are! What a terrible evil has come upon me, of which I am entirely innocent! How wicked you are! My constitution is not adapted to this state of things! How dreadful to die thus! There must be a fit punishment in store for you at the hands of God!"

To whom the wolf responds: "You little, impudent wretch, you deny the wisdom and goodness of God! Has he not made me as I am, and you as you are, and the grass as it is? The grass to grow from earth, you to eat the grass, and I to eat you? You chide God for his providence. He has provided food for all his creatures, both differing in kind; grass for you, and flesh for me; yes, lamb's flesh occasionally. You talk about evil to you! Your soul will go to the paradise of sheep, when I eat your body. It would be truly a terrible evil to me, could I not get lamb's flesh occasionally; in fact, I should die outright of starvation, and God's wisdom be turned into foolishness, and his government come to naught. How was this you defined about this state of things? Your 'constitution not adapted to these conditions?' Why, you little scouting and blaspheming atheist! Your constitution is perfectly adapted to all the conditions—death and my stomach; therein I will assimilate you, and you will be made bold and wolfish. Your death is no evil. God designed, in his eternal plan, that you should die as food for me. I feel the gnawings of hunger now, his commands writ in my stomach to eat you. Besides, were the world's great Carnivora, who roam the wide world, and soar in its air, and swim in its sea, to take the advice of one little silly sheep, that has been out to grass all its life, in a narrow and short pasture, entirely undeveloped in head and body, saying: 'Oh! ye great Carnivora, stop your eating flesh, thus making misery in the world; eat grass, as we do.' Why, we would all be dead in a month's time. You fool! A spear of your food would make any one of us vomit. You have to assimilate it for us. Then, if we should all die, very soon the world would be filled with pestilence, from rotten carcasses which ought to have been devoured before they decayed. Shortly after we died, you would die of disease, so I might as well eat you now, for your kindred's sake, and the good of the world. Besides all this your constitution, physically and mentally, is entirely adapted to me. Physically you are good to eat; mentally you are a coward, and don't dare to fight me. God Almighty made you so, for which I give him thanks daily, and now especially. You cannot bite—you have no canine teeth; I have. Look here! God made me so." And he opens his mouth and displays a dreadful state of jaw; and the lamb, trembling in fear, had just time to gasp out, "The Devil, not God, made you," and it was torn in pieces.

Now the farmer comes in, and is greatly pained to find one of his fine lambs devoured by a wolf; and he hunts many a day to kill him; whereas, it was but yesterday he hunted with dog and gun to kill the rabbit which had eaten his tree. The wolf, and the rabbit, he calls distressing evils, which ought to be hunted down. Man reasons from selfishness and ignorance. The lamb will give him wool, and it is an evil for the wolf to kill it. The rabbit will eat the young trees, and it is a great good for the dog to kill it. Yet the rabbit has the same right to life that the sheep has, and the wolf to food that the dog has. The evil comes in the *conflict of desires;* the conflict to obtain that which is adapted to different uses and conditions.

Now there are carnivorous and herbivorous men. There are men whose constitutions are as widely different as the wolf and the lamb; and the conditions of happiness are as widely opposite. A Carib delights in a roasted captive; a Feejee Islander prays to obtain the wife of his enemy, that he may eat her; the Dyaks of Borneo, to secure the services of a slave in the next world, waylay their enemies to bring home their heads. They say, "White men read books; we hunt for heads instead." Let a refined young lady of our highest civilization fall captive to a Feejee, and it would be the fable just repeated of the wolf and the lamb. The gentle and timid poet Keats, lamb-like in disposition, was torn to death by wolfish critics—a death more cruel than by engines of wood and iron, with which Christians used to torture the life out of each other for opinion's sake, and who could look upon these death tortures "reveling with joy."

Because men are adapted to the varying conditions in which they live, they often hunt each other down like wild beasts; war becomes not only their amusement, but means of livelihood. Nay, it became the religious duty of a Christian king, near the close of the seventeenth century, to drive out the Scotch from their native heaths, with ruthless barbarity, not unlike a western wolf-hunt. For like crimes, Christian bishops gave him their support, and called him the darling of Heaven, and prayed "that God might give him the hearts of his subjects and the necks of his enemies." In a community of wolves and sheep, or dogs and rabbits, the sheep and rabbits die first, and when food becomes scarce and difficult to obtain, then the weakest wolf or dog; and the strongest perishes last. All those who have to perish first will set up their complaints against the survivor; and the weakest of all is the most to complain; not because the most injured, but simply because the most imperfect; not because of its "unfitness to the conditions of existence," but because of its lack of force, to change these conditions in its own favor. A child does not die because unfit to live, but because too weak.

Yet, because Evil cannot be defined, from the fact that conditions and constitutions are continually changing, both in earth and man, it is not therefore meaningless. Even the conflict of ideas which itself precludes definition, gives it a meaning, terrible as well as significant. What, then, does it mean? It will be the object of this volume to partially answer; and which is meant only to prepare the way for future labor and thought.

§. 2. Does Evil exist in accordance with natural law, or in violation of it? or both in accordance with and in violation of it? For example: A man is killed in the prime of life by lightning in the harvest field; or, a Lincoln is killed by the hand of a Booth; or, Uriah is slain in battle by the command of David; or, a man is stoned to death, by the Lord's command, for gathering sticks on the Sabbath; or, a man is murdered for his money in the highway, or for jealousy in a house of prostitution; a man betrays his friend, for money, that he may be made a victim to the religion of his countrymen; a priest of the Hindu religion cuts off the head of his mother, she consenting, that her ghost may torment and pursue to death a man who had stolen forty rupees out of his house; or, a minister of the Christian religion roasts the feet and heads of women, to extract a confession of hidden gold, or whips his son, less than three years old, to death for not saying his prayers in a manner contrary to that taught him by his own mother before she died. Are these cases in accordance with or in violation of natural law, or both? Wherein is a law of Nature violated in the lightning's stroke? In other words, can Nature act unnaturally? If not, then what law of Nature did the man violate who was killed by lightning in the harvest field? If any, what? But further: Is Evil the penalty attached to violated law? If so, is it intended to teach or correct the person violating it? And is this the sole object of such penalty? How much is the person taught, corrected or benefitted, who is killed by lightning? If none, what is the meaning of it, when no other human being on earth is or ever becomes cognizant of it? And this is a quite probable case.

These questions elicit thought. They are accouchers of ideas. Let us follow them into Nature, for it is there the man of thought wanders, and if often lost as in an endless forest in which he was born and is to live, it is therein he must return again to his domicil, or find a new home.

§. 3. Quite as much, in regard to definition, might be said of morality, wisdom, perfection, and the like, but as these terms are intimately connected with Evil and human conduct, let us see what part Evil performs in the conception of these terms; let us inquire into the relationship and age of Evil, that we may get clearer conceptions of their meaning.

Did the whole universe act in perfect harmony, then there would be no Evil, nor Morality.

For, if there were no Evil, there would be no bad act, and a good act would never have had a name, for goodness and badness are correlative terms, as day and night, father and son, etc. Goodness would be, if at all, a necessity of fate, and man would be but a mere machine, incapable of pain or pleasure, driven by a blind and unfeeling force. But this is not true of man. He is a conscious force on earth; he is quickened with sensation; he feels pleasure and pain; his actions are often partially free; he often designs his actions, knowing that he acts; and he becomes cognizant of the good and bad effects which follow his actions. It is the bad effect which awakens him to the consciousness of its opposite in Nature, and thus morality is born of Evil.

If this be not so, then will some one tell us what morality is, and how it originated? "It is," says one, "the observance of the perfect law of God." But, we ask, how expressed and how given? However this may be answered, there is no truth evolved; we must deal with its essence and treat of first principles. This assumes a law designed for man to obey. But, if it be possible for him to obey a law, it is also possible for him to disobey it; and the possibility of Evil is involved in the command—Obey! But the command to obey would and could never have been given without a knowledge or a belief that evil effects would follow its violation. Whence came this knowledge of evil which would result by disobedience? It is quite evident that a knowledge of Evil must precede any law designed for the good of man. In fact, no rule of right action could ever originate without a tacit or expressed knowledge of Evil to precede it. This is true, whatever may be the source of the law—Nature, God, legislature or parent—or whether the law be perfect or not, if the law be given with a design and is not a mere evolution of blind force. But if Evil precedes the perfect law, and the law is to warn against Evil, then Evil is the prime cause of the perfect law. That is, imperfection must precede the perfect law, and be the cause of it, which shows there can be no perfect moral law of God. This conclusion is either true or false. But if Evil does not precede the perfect law, there would be no object in ordaining the law; for a law without an object is no law at all. If Evil, on the other hand, be considered as an evolution of blind force, it must be treated of under the phenomena of Nature, governed by established laws.

§. 4. It may be objected to this reasoning that, pushed to its furthest limit, from world to world, in its application, supposing other worlds to be inhabited, and from time to time back into a preceding eternity, it makes Evil precede any law of the Infinite God. But this objection carries the seeds of death within it. It is another phase of the argument in reasoning backwards from consequent to antecedent to find a first cause which is called God. But if God be the *first* cause, there was a time when there was no God, for the first had to begin; and it is useless to say there was a God before he acted, or before he was wise enough to act. All we can say of God is to posit the Absolute, and confer such attributes as a finite conception may think best. It would perhaps be best to say God is the Infinite Force. There are reasons for considering this Infinite Force a conscious force, which will be treated of hereafter.

But when we keep within the realm of the knowable, we may define and discriminate. Herein we find a distinction between a natural law and a moral law; for while a moral law is a natural law, all natural laws are not moral laws. Natural law is the genus of which moral laws are species. Oxygen and nitrogen combine in definite proportions to form air and other substances. This is a natural law, but it is not a moral law. But all human laws are in a wide sense moral laws, even that one which says man shall be the chattel of another. This, however, may not be the *best* moral law. The moral law has to do with *finite intelligences*, not with unconscious matter or infinite intelligence. All that can be affirmed in the objection is, that Evil may co-exist in time with the Infinite Force, which always must precede finite intelligences, or the finite expression of Infinite Force.

But it is again argued, that God may fore-ordain something which has never before existed, and thus a perfect law may be given long before Evil exists as a fact. This arises by confounding action and fact: Action is progressive; Fact is eternal. There is a difference between existence and taking place. The knowledge of a fact can never be without the fact *exists*. It may have transpired, or is yet to come. In either case it exists and is known, as is the past or future—as an eclipse of the moon. If you are to die to-morrow, and the knowledge of it were as perfect as infinite wisdom could make it, the fact of your death would be as real to you to-day as to those who should witness it to-morrow. Were this not true, there would be no science, and in fact nothing known beyond our immediate and present action. There would be no such word as to-morrow. It is the sole object of science to fore-tell events, and, were there no *facts existing* before they transpire, science would be but a phantom of thought.

We thus come at the Eternity of Evil another way. If infinite wisdom is, then it is all *now* to Omniscience, and the knowledge of Evil is an infinite fact. For it matters not when a particular evil begins—last night, last year, last age, or last eternity, or at any time in the future it exists as a fact in the universe, forever known to Infinite Force, and must be co-eternal with infinite knowledge. It may be set down then, as a conclusion of sound reasoning, that moral law has Evil to precede it, and is a necessity thereof, or has been evolved from it. Whence we may affirm, were there no Evil in the universe we would know nothing of morality; for there would be none.

An argument which leads to the same conclusion may be drawn from man's own nature. It will not be denied that man is endowed with a faculty called benevolence. It is the function of this faculty to dispose us to alleviate suffering; to prompt us to gentleness and kindness towards each other and inferior animals; to make us charitable and solicitous for the welfare of all; in short, it is the mental finger-board pointing toward Evil in the world. Whenever, therefore, you prove that man has benevolence, you prove also that Evil preceded the creation of such a faculty in man, the sole function of which is to warn us against it. This, however, only proves that Evil was in existence before the existence of benevolent man, and that the cause of evil is independent of man. But, should we confer benevolence as an attribute of God, then we must affirm that Evil is co-eternal with such an attribute. But, arguing solely from man's nature, we find him endowed with many faculties which could never possibly have originated without Evil to precede them. Let us apply the same rule to other faculties which we have just applied to benevolence.

It is the function of a certain faculty to desire property. This desire is independent of the manner of acquiring it, and of the uses to which it shall be put. But, how is this desire created or made known? What is the cause of the function? Simply the bodily want of subsistence and the means of comfort. The body has been deprived of food, or felt the pains of heat and cold; the limbs have been torn, and the feet bruised. Hunger has driven man to provide for the morrow; the pains of the flesh to cover his body; the bruises of his feet have given him shoes; the heat and cold shelter and fuel. Here is one of the noblest faculties of our nature developed and stimulated by Evil to precede it. If it be objected that this ought to confer upon the lower animals this faculty, it may be answered it cannot be affirmed they have it not; and further, the actions of animals would lead us to conclude they did possess such a faculty, yet unaided by man's superior scientific prevision. The dog, when he buries a bone, and the squirrel, when he fills his nest with nuts, are cases in point. What seems to strengthen the conclusion still more than these, is the fact that when animals are provided by man for long periods of time they lose this faculty of provident thought, and often die of starvation; and even further, lose the instinct of a proper selection of food, and so die. If the miser should be brought forward as a fatal objection to the foregoing conclusion, inasmuch as he is not impelled to accumulate the means of subsistence solely by a view to consequences, it may be answered: The abnormal use of a faculty cannot viciate or destroy the cause of such faculty, and proves nothing. As well say, because now and then a man is a glutton, or because frequently people eat too much, hunger is not, therefore, the cause of our eating. But without the desire to eat awakened by hunger, no one would search for food; yet hunger is pain, and if prolonged soon develops into secondary evils.

The faculty of caution prompts to common prudence; it anticipates harm; it is the sense of fear. Fear is the ruling mental element in man, as well as all other animals; without it, life would be a thousand-fold more in danger; and from this comes the first law of life—*Preserve thyself.* Yet, without Evil, it is impossible for it to have originated, if man is governed by law, and his faculties have evolved from primary conditions; and if they were not thus evolved, but were given by a wise Creator; then man was thus endowed because of Evil, which existed as a fact in Divine knowledge, so that either hypothesis brings us to the same conclusion.

Evil also as a pre-existent cause in the world, may be seen in all animal action. It is finite, and at best cannot be perfect. And while all imperfect actions are by no means evil actions; yet all evil actions are imperfect actions. From this very fact arise the questions, "What is good?" "What is right?" "What is proper?" "What is just?" Yet none of these questions would have been asked without Evil to precede them in the world, and to accompany them in human action. No notion of justice, of propriety, of right, of goodness, could ever possibly have existed or come into existence without Evil to precede such conception or knowledge, because each of these terms is correlative with Evil. Hence what is called the "Moral Sense" has its basis in Evil.

And herein we come upon a term which itself shows there can be no definition of morality. For if morality exists it is the result of those deeds prompted by some faculty of man. This faculty may be called the "Moral Sense;" although we cannot use the word sense as meaning a blind mental force, it must rather mean a conscious knowledge, for without knowledge there is no rational action; and the "Moral Sense" must arise from a plurality of faculties. But this faculty, however we may define it, never acts the same in any two individuals, it is common to all, yet leads all to different conclusions. In other words all have the knowledge of right in the abstract, yet no two would agree as to what right is in the concrete act. As millions have the abstract idea of God, yet no two would agree as to what God is in *being*. All disagree in the concrete conception. What one man calls the moral law another one would deny, or amend in many ways; a third would deny the conclusions of both, and a fourth would select from each and cast much away that he considered rubbish. The moral code of Moses will not do for Jesus, and the code of Jesus will not do for any Christian of this age. The Christian code will not do for thousands of the most civilized and intelligent of the world. Whereas many select from Moses and Buddha, Jesus and Mahomet, Paul and Luther, and cast aside from all these much they consider rubbish; others discard all men as binding authority, taking no man for master, not even Jesus of Nazareth, living up to their own highest convictions, as did Jesus himself. To make this statement quite clear, let us make some of the world's moral teachers, ancient and modern, expound their own ethical doctrines, as though face to face in convention.

Jesus—What is this you say, Moses, about loving your neighbors but hating your enemies? do you think that right?

Moses—Yes, that is according to the perfect moral law of Jehovah. It is recorded, (Deut. xxiii:6,) never make peace with an enemy; an eye for an eye, and a tooth for a tooth; this is the law. Remember Amalek; blot him out. Thou shalt not forget what he did, (Deut. xxv:19.)

Jesus—That is by no means the perfect law. I speak as one having authority; I say, love your enemies; bless them that curse you; do good to them that hate you; and pray for them which despitefully use you, and persecute you, (Matt. v:44.)

David—You are certainly mistaken my son; Moses is right. If the Lord pronounces a curse it is most assuredly right for his servants to follow his example. You are wrong about prayer also; I have no hesitancy in praying the Lord to curse my enemies, and that right soundly, (Ps. 109th.) This is, I think, in accordance with the perfect moral law.

Luther—You are quite right King David, this is a law found in human nature as well as the Bible; I can preach and pray best when I am quite angry.

Protestant Christian—Yes, King David; you, and Moses the Divine law-giver, and Luther the great reformer, are right. We are so beset with evil in this world, that it is only a vale of tears to those who cannot get right down and pray to God to curse this whole infidel crew, who are flooding the whole world with irreligion and atheism under cover of the words morality and science; trying to overturn God's government and establish the kingdom of Satan. Pray, too, with faith, the assurance that he will blot out the iniquity,—yes *blot out*, that is the language he used of old,—and blast the memory of all who preach infidelity.—Oh! for thy fervor King David,—and damn the fool who says in his heart there is no God. Yes, he is a fool who denies Jehovah, the God of Abraham, and Moses, and David, and our good and blessed master Jesus Christ. This is according to the perfect moral law of God.

Jesus—Not too hasty; you evince a zeal which lacks thought. You are mistaken; I never worshiped Jehovah,—it was God, the Father of all, who adorned the lilly and took charge of the sparrow; not the God who would rejoice to destroy people,—besides you must not call me good, there is none good but one, that is God. I believe in the Fatherhood of God and the Brotherhood of man,—not in cursing and revenge; and you have no moral right to call me a fool for not believing in the special god of my countrymen; nay, verily, when you say "*thou fool*," you are in danger of hell-fire, (Matt. v:22.)

Universalist—Oh! oh! Jesus, you didn't mean that. You are a little provoked at that orthodox fellow, I know; but you ought to have control of yourself. You are to save us *all* from that; one extreme leads to another. You ought to have more charity for weakness and error. It is really not

Christian to talk about hell-fire when you believe in the Brotherhood of man, and the golden rule.

Moses—This quarrel arises from forsaking the *law.* Jehovah is the Lord, and he has a chosen people. The rest of mankind are idolators and will be blotted out. He has given us his *law*; this is perfect, and applies in all the relations of life.

Jesus—That law says, when a man has found something unclean in his wife (and this something means anything) he may give her a bill of divorcement and send her out of his house, (Deut. xxiv:1.) There is no law to generalize this, and give the wife the same right when she has found something unclean in her husband. But, *I* say, whosoever shall put away his wife saving for the cause of fornication causeth her to commit adultery, and whosoever shall marry her that is divorced committeth adultery, (Matt. v:31-32.)

Christian—Then you would make out this Christian age to be most adulterous and perverse.

Whittier—Yes, and the Christian ages ever have been; you resist evil;

> Where Christ hath spoken peace, his name hath been
> The loudest war cry of contending men;
> Priests, pale with vigils, in his name have blessed
> The unsheathed sword, and laid the spear in rest—
> Priests wet their war banner with the sacred wine
> And crossed its blazing folds with the holy sign!

Jesus—Yes, and you swear; you call mankind, who do not believe your doctrine, fools; you pray in public; you pray in anger, and for the Father to curse your enemies, his children; you commit adultery under sanction of *law*, and by lust in your hearts; you are continually solicitous about the morrow; you are laying up treasures on earth, all the very contrary of what I teach. And, furthermore, your moral law is a professed hypocrisy, inasmuch as you do the very reverse of what you profess,—you profess to follow, to take me for a master, and oftener disobey than follow my instructions.

Moses—They profess to follow my instructions also, but come infinitely short of it. All this arises from forsaking the *law*. You despise my statutes, saith the Lord; you keep not my Sabbaths; witchcraft goes unpunished; your children are disobedient and ask for rights; your wives are rising up and demanding votes, when I have classed the wife with property in the tenth commandment, placing her in the Divine schedule above personal property, but below real estate, and she ought to know her sphere; you have abolished slavery in the blood of your fellow; verily, thus saith the Lord, I will rejoice to destroy you, (Deut. xxviii:63.)

Spiritualist—I suppose by witchcraft you mean Spiritualism; but thank God we live in an age of light and knowledge; in America, not Jewry; and your command 'Thou shalt not suffer a witch to live,' falls on dull ears in these times. Moses, this section of your god's moral code is obsolete. It belongs with your law to give forty stripes for civil offenses, (Deut. xxv:3;) your morals of selling unclean meat to aliens, (Deut. xiv:21;) of stoning children to death for disobedience, (Deut. xxi:21.) This belongs with your barbarous law of taking women captive and parceling them out to satisfy the lust of a brutal soldiery, (Num. xxxi:17-18,) and stoning men to death for gathering sticks on the Sabbath (Num. xvi:-32-36.) We have a new code of morals suited to this age, and a world's higher civilization.

The foregoing discussion cannot be said to be unfairly represented, which shows how useless it is for one amidst such a complexity of opinions to define morality. Even just now we find in a journal especially devoted to the cause of Christianity the following sound reasoning: "For what does Christianity amount to, if the man who accepts it, and the man who spurns it, may be alike 'good.' Christianity is a superfluity and impertinence. It has no indispensible mission. For by goodness of character much more is meant than mere external virtue and amiability." Then speaking of a certain ethical teacher, who disclaimed the name Christian, presumes him to be "a man of virtuous impulse and habits, who would scorn to do what the world calls wicked and dishonorable;" and says: "but the standard of the world and the standard of Christianity are infinitely wide apart. 'That which is highly esteemed among men is abomination in the sight of God.' Thousands will be condemned as sinful and guilty in the sight of God, who were accounted 'good' in the sight of men." * * * "Christ is the source of *all real* goodness." Now by this is meant, a *belief* in Christ is the source of all morality. Yet, there are thousands of people of this world who do not profess Christianity simply because they live up to their highest convictions of knowledge, belief, and duty;—in other words because they are *honest* in matters of belief and profession;—so that the very essence of morality in the Christian religion is to believe in a god who will in some instances damn an honest man because he *is* honest.

By Christianity it is here meant, that system of religious belief and practice most widely known as such, and includes both Catholic and Protestant. There must be eliminated from this some of the minor sects known as Christians, were we to test them by ethical or theological doctrine; such as Unitarians and Universalists. These merely call themselves Christians and are counted out by the vast majority of Protestants. Neither can we include many eminent moralists and teachers of religion who have been called Christians. As Moses, Confucius, Socrates, Jesus, Parker, Emerson, and others. For, while Theodore Parker called himself a Christian, and Socrates has been called such by eminent Christians; and Jesus has the honor of being worshipped as a Christian god, yet these persons have in their teachings *very little* in common with the Christian religion, and *very much* that is radically different therefrom. This shows how difficult it would even be to define Christianity; how much more difficult is it then to define morality.

§. 4. The reason of the foregoing complexity is because of *conditions.* These are ever varying in time and place, and to sustain that harmony which is ever prominent in Nature, man is so constituted that he changes also with the varying conditions, yet, perhaps never establishes a perfect harmony, as entire harmony would result in that mental disaster, known as satisfaction. It is by bringing greatly varying or adverse conditions together, which produces such varying actions and opinions, as illustrated in the fable of the wolf and the lamb, and in the discussion between eminent moralists. Evil and morality are both variable quantities; they are finite in expression and admit of comparison, because dependent upon conditions and finite action. This can be made mathematically evident from the following illustration with regard to ignorance and wisdom. Absolute wisdom is the entire absence or zero of ignorance; and conversely, absolute ignorance is the entire absence or zero of wisdom. But, between the two absolutes, of wisdom and ignorance, there are the two finite and variable quantities which take the unqualified expressions, wisdom and ignorance. In other words absolute wisdom and absolute ignorance are the two poles of a progressive and finite knowledge. In the life of man wisdom is the increasing quantity, while ignorance is the decreasing one. But man is not omniscient, and the only correct conclusion is, that he starts from absolute ignorance and progresses towards absolute wisdom.

With the least increment of knowledge he must be wise in a degree, and yet almost absolutely ignorant. With each increment of knowledge he travels on towards wisdom. We say of a child, it gets larger, stronger and wiser; but we can affirm of the wisest man, he is ignorant; and we measure his quantity of wisdom by the infinite measure of his ignorance. It is when a man becomes somewhat wise, he may gain sufficient force of thought to conceive in some small degree how profoundly ignorant he is. Surely, when compared with omniscience, the wisest man who ever lived, or lives, would be in quantity but the infinitesimal part of an atom compared to the earth. By ignorance, then, we mean not wise ; but this by no means defines ignorance. We say the babe is ignorant, the school-boy is ignorant, the middle-aged and the old are ignorant, but by this we do not mean they have no knowledge whatever, we simply mean they are wise or ignorant as compared with some standard of measurement, established by common consent, and which varies in times and places. That which falls short is ignorance, that which is equal to, or exceeds is wisdom. But in the progress of the race one age establishes the standard of measurement a little greater than the age immediately preceding. This change is by an insensible movement as though the standard were an elastic rod susceptible of being made longer but never shorter; and it is only by comparing one age with another, or many others, that any change can be observed. But this may be still further differentiated by admitting the standard of each individual to figure in the question; and we have a quantity varying from the Hottentot to the Humboldts of the world. Now, when one age says, this man is a fool, that man is ignorant, and the other man is wise, it uses these terms as compared with the standard of wisdom of that age; and when the individual affirms that this, that, or the other man is a fool, ignorant or wise, he compares the man usually with himself.

It is just the same with morality. It is a variable quantity, and passes onward from imperfection, as the starting point, towards absolute perfection. The standard of individuals and the ages are all different, and must necessarily be so, else there would be no varying conditions. And thus it has come to pass; the ages of Moses and Socrates, and Jesus and Luther are widely different and can be distinguished. What was considered morality in one of these, would not in the others be a true conception; as what was meant by wisdom in one of these ages would not be meant in either of the others. So also of great religious teachers; the standards of Moses, and Socrates, and Jesus, and Luther, and Parker are widely different. Yet, it is the standard which the age sets up; which is accepted and rules public action. So in morals; we have existing on earth the notions of the Caribs as well as the Beechers of the land. Morality is a word of comparison or degree.

In the progress of man the human race does not equally advance. All do not go on with measured equal pace. Some races far outstrip others, some individuals far outstrip the race, tribe, or family, to which they belong; so that we have to-day from the highest to the lowest every phase of intellectual and moral development. This age is not superimposed upon the past, burying it entirely away from the sunlight of to-day; but, like the geologic strata, all the formations of past ages crop out on the surface of this age somewhere, showing us the changes which time has brought about. We study the past in its fossil remains, both in earth and man. And as there are living representatives of animals which predominated in past ages, so there are living representatives of moral doctrines which predominated in past ages, but which are now looked upon as barbarous and out of place.

This law of varying conditions is organic, and perhaps inheres in the ultimate atom. Some generalizations upon this fact may not be out of place.

The first great law we find in the world is, *Nature, distributively, never repeats herself.* No two men, no two women, no two children, can be found exactly alike, either in physical features or mental organization; no two animals of the same species alike, no two animalculæ nor insects which swarm by the hundreds of millions can be found exactly alike. They may appear alike to the natural eye but not to the eye of science. No two plants alike. Nature seems to be so prodigal of varieties, that no two flowers nor blades of grass, nor seeds are alike; and we presume no two ultimate atoms of matter alike. The different states of carbon, as the diamond, charcoal and graphite, would lead to this conclusion, as also to explain isomerism in chemistry supposing the atomic theory to be true. Not only in the individual is this law of variety to be seen but there are great class and family distinctions. Thus the race of mankind has its great typical distinctions, as the Caucassian or white race; the Indian or brown race; and the Negro or black race. These typical distinctions are founded in Nature, and a general law governs them. They bear not only marks of physical variation but great mental differences as types of mankind. Not only this, but each type has also marked characteristics as a nation of men. Thus, in the great historic race, the Caucassian, we find marked mental characteristics—the Romans, the conquerers; the Grecians, the artistic; the Hebrews, the devout. The Romans were the most combative, ambitious, acquisitive people on earth; they were a nation of Napoleons without his knowledge. The Grecian mind was metaphysical, elegant, highly literary. In this soil sculpture, architecture, poetry and philosophy all flourished. The Hebrew mind reveled in its barter and fervent worship. To trade and to pray, became a Jew. The Hebrew government even was a theocracy. Jehovah, in a miraculous manner, according to their own history, chose the leaders.

He annointed them with holy oil, breathed into them the "spirit of God," fought their battles, preserved them as a chosen people from the rapacity of surrounding nations, or sold them into slavery for their lust after other gods. Thus, in the life of nations, in their great mental characteristics, a general law is proclaimed in individual variation.

We are now able to see the immediate cause of so many conflicting opinions, and why people are engaged in an endless discussion of rights, privileges and duties. The true cause of an opinion lies further remote, and depends on the degree of knowledge.

CHAPTER II.

PERFECTION IN MAN FOREVER IMPOSSIBLE.

§. 1. If the foregoing conclusions are true, it follows that perfection in man is forever impossible. For, suppose, starting from absolute ignorance, as all are compelled to at birth, having inherited no knowledge, but at most only a certain tendency or capacity to know, and perhaps certain instincts which are irrational, and can never rise higher than a manifestation of transmitted habit, we progress in a given ratio towards absolute wisdom; it would be impossible to reach the infinite quantity for two reasons. In the first place, we would have to progress by increments of finite knowledge, and finites added to or multiplied into finites never produce an infinite. And, in the second place, it would require infinite capacity to acquire and retain absolute or infinite wisdom. Neither can we in a finite or restricted sense become perfect. Some further remarks on this conclusion of man's unlimited imperfection will not be out of place; for the assumption of attainable perfection has always led to failure in ethical teachings. Upon this false hypothesis it is argued, and that truly, that man should have a perfect code to govern him, and that to the command given in accordance with the perfect law there is neither variableness nor shadow of turning,—that the law, which was meant to govern him, has no exceptions. From the false assumption of attainable perfection has grown up what is called the perfect law, which has never had that perfect expression, which would make it applicable to man. If the command be given, simply, as Jesus gave it, "Be ye therefore perfect,"—this leaves the question a nullity if literally construed, as it is absolutely impossible to be perfect; but, if it be interpreted to mean "aim at perfection," then it is left open for each fallible person to aim as he sees fit; discharging the forces of action, regardless of consequences to others; aiming at the empty air; the mark in the midst of a multitude; or even shooting around the corner of some great sin; in either case he may *think* he is aiming at perfection.

§. 2. The mistake of concluding that a perfect law is applicable to man arises from the tacit or expressed assumption that man is perfectly free and can be just as good or just as bad as he pleases. Prospectively it assumes, that ideal perfection is an attainable real from such perfectly free action; and retrospectively it is a theological dogma that our first parents enjoyed a "perfect estate." This gave rise to the belief in a "Golden Age," common to all Eastern mythologies. In the Christian theology it is held that the Devil was thus free, and instead of freely being good, freely made himself bad; that Eve and Adam, instead of freely being good, freely made themselves bad, and so of all their posterity.

In answer to this, it may be affirmed, mankind are free to the extent of their capacities, abilities, or circumstances; in other words, that conditions govern the direction of their free activities. Hence, some persons are less free than others. The slave, who toils under his master's lash, is not so free to travel, acquire knowledge, amass wealth, in short to call out all his mental activities, as is the master. The man who is locked up in a jail is not so free to steal or murder, as he would be at large among people. Hence, what is often popularly called goodness may be the result of restraint, and badness the result of more freedom. Again, the person who has inherited a mania to steal and murder is not so free to live without committing these crimes, as one who has no such mania. The idiot has not the freedom to become wise; he is mentally chained to ignorance. The "virtues" and "vices" of people are often born with them, and the *will*, instead of governing the conduct of people, is governed *itself* by the mental condition; so that, given such a birth and education, a certain character, which *guides the will*, is the product. State the kind of a man you want, and science, under the conditions, will produce him. This is why the Catholic is a Catholic, the Protestant is a Protestant, the Mahometan a Mahometan, the Infidel an Infidel. Under ordinary or normal conditions a mother is not free to stand and look calmly on, without wondering whether it were hurt or not, should her child fall from her chamber window. She is only free to run and gather up her child. Neither is she *free* to hate or love it. Love is a normal necessity of mankind. Nor is there such a thing as love, hatred, or belief, freely produced by the *will.* None of these are *free.* No one, by *willing*, can love or hate an other, nor believe or disbelieve anything. These are governed by the necessities of his condition. The condition he may in a measure, though quite limited, change or control.

There is a good illustration of human freedom in the flying of the kite. You bind it to the air by means of a string. You restrain it with a string and it soars aloft. The conditions of the kite are then fulfilled. But remove the restraint by breaking the string and it careens madly to earth. So man is free to act virtuously, only because of his restraint. His passions must be restrained by a knowledge of the evils coming from their abuse. He ought to have the freedom to use well the materials which are given him in greater or lesser abundance. Yet, knowledge has the right to control ignorance at all times. This gives the parent a right to control the child, the master the pupil, the overseer the workman, within their relative spheres.

But, if man has inherited weak or rotten materials, he can only build out of them a weak or rotten life. If he has inherited strong and sound materials, he may build, if he applies wisdom thereto, a strong and sound life. Thus, if we have poor materials to work upon, we are mostly what we are made, never what we would wish to make ourselves, even within the world's present attainment; and, if we have good materials given us, we are in part what we are made, and in part what we make ourselves. Man comes into life unbidden on his part; seldom bidden on the part of his parents. His acts are the budding forth of a germ within, nourished by outward circumstances, and the resultant of these two forces, called the conditions of his being, gives him character. If he is born a Negro, Indian, White man, or idiot, he lives and dies such. The physica and mental conditions of all these are engrafted into their very being, and it is these which distinguish us as Negro, Indian, White man, sensible or idiotic.

§. 3. To live in accordance with the perfect law, or even to fulfill his ideal, man must have the power to make himself whatever he desires. But his desires may far exceed his natural capacity, and capacity is a condition bounded on all sides by his desires. Education may increase the capacity, this elevates the standard of intellectuality, but a particular intellectuality soon reaches its limit. In the mental, as well as in the physical forces of the animal, there is a certain limit, beyond which it seems impossible to pass, and this is called the natural capacity of the animal. The physical capacity of man increases by education to a certain extent, and then stops. Milo might run the whole length of the Stadium with a four year old bull on his shoulders, having carried him daily from a calf up to that age; but this does not prove that Tom Thumb could ever possibly have done the same; nor, that Milo, himself, could ever possibly have carried a full grown elephant on his shoulders. So also in mental culture in a particular direction, and by a life of study upon any one thing, a person may become an adept, far transcending in this his otherwise occupied neighbor; but it will be found he does not progress beyond a certain degree, far this side of perfection, or even his own ideal. He stops at the natural limit of his powers, and when he has gained his utmost, he is farther this side of his ideal than when he began; for his ideal moves also on in an increasing ratio. This is the testimony of all who have accomplished great things. It is the testimony of all who can grasp in memory, their own life.

Mentally, as well as physically, men are not created equal. Equality lies in the right to use, according to their best knowledge, their unequal powers of mind and body. As one star differs from another star in glory, so one person differs from another in mental or physical capacity. Yet both, stars and persons, have the equal right to dispense their own quality and quantity of light, and if obscured by the dazzling brightness of others, they must submit.

One person may have the taste and ability of the writer, another of the orator, another of the blacksmith, or farmer. One may be a linguist, mathematician, or musician, and some, with great capacities, may succeed in much, while others succeed in nothing. Could we possibly become whatever we wished, simply from the "freedom" of our will, and our capacities to grow, we might all of us become Shakspeares, and Miltons, and Bacons, and Newtons. But there was one Hamlet, and one Iago to be created, and but one Shakspeare to create them. There was but one "Paradise Lost" to be written, and but one Milton to write it. Byron could apostrophize the Ocean; Longfellow could write "Hiawatha;" Burns hold conversation with "Auld Nicky Ben;" but it takes a Milton to speak like Moloch, and a Shakspeare to cut the pound of flesh for Shylock. There was but one Oliver Cromwell for the greatest of English events; but one George the Third for her smallest event. There was but one Diogenes with the cynic pride of meanness, to tread on the academic pride of Plato. There was but the one Philip to call forth the invectives and eloquence of the one Demosthenes, and but one Aristotle to educate the one Alexander. If Sir

William Hamilton had been born an Osage indian, Scotland would boast no philosopher the greatest in the world. If Archbishop Whately had been born a Hottentot, Ireland would have produced no one to give us a logical effigy of Aristotle. That is, to suppose other conditions, is to suppose entirely different persons; and the freedom of the will and the ideal perfection are swallowed up in the conditions. In other words, there is no way to arrive at perfection but by progression, by bettering the attained present in the attainable future. But we would have to progress infinitely to reach the ultimate. Like the curve of the hyperbola, which continually approaches its asymptotes and does not touch them till space ends; so man, in his progressive nature, may continually approach that divine attribute which reaches out from the Absolute, but at which he will never arrive. Verily, were we perfect we would be *gods.*

True, man may progress till he knows all about this earth, perhaps to its very centre; till he knows every element of the sun, and can tell its coming effects on the earth for thousands of years; fore-tell every adverse current of air, for weeks, and get such control of the forces, which act with such awful energy in earth and air, as to make the winds and waters obey him. Yet, this would come as far short of physical perfection, as the earth is less than the whole bulk of infinite orbs. Moral, physical and intellectual perfection is forever impossible.

§. 4. In the Ideal world, man by no means makes to himself a perfect ideal. The ideals of men differ, as do their beliefs and actions. The ideal of a Michael Angelo, would not be that of a Phidias, for the body of a god. They would differ as widely in conferring mental attributes. The ideal of an Emerson and a Christian, would differ widely for both God and man. There is a vast abyss between the ideals of a Caffre and a Shelley. The finest ideals of men, in their loftiest flights of thought, fall far short of true conceptions, either of God or the Ideal Man. A perfect man, has never yet been conceived in thought. There is imperfection beyond all possible conceptions. The Jesuses of the world all fail. We grow up to, and pass on beyond them. There may be finite intelligences in the universe, far greater, in reality, than earth's loftiest ideal. Why not? It is the most dwarfed egotism to affirm, all finite intelligence is produced upon this mote of a world. And, if other worlds produce their intelligences, those intelligences may be as much superior to us physically, morally, and intellectually, as it is possible for conditions to be as much superior to ours, as we can imagine; and those intelligences may have their ideals after which they are struggling, as much superior to our ideals, as it is possible for *them* to imagine.

The prime cause of the worship of Jesus to-day, is this struggle and longing after the ideal in manhood. The world has painted its Golden Age in the past, and looks forward to the Millennium. The Jews looked forward to a temporal reign of the Messiah, who would restore the Lost Tribes, and deliver the people from the hand of the oppressors. He is yet to come. The Christians claim that the Messiah came in the person of Jesus, but did not stay. The disciples believed he was to return, as he himself told them, within that generation. He did not come. The early Christians said he would come in the next generation, and the next, and the next. Now, the time is postponed to the ideal fulfillment of the "Good time coming." The perfect man and the perfect time are still in the future. Science and sound reasoning teach us they will be forever there, the ever sought, never obtained. The Ideal is the reflection of the great fact of the world's history within the consciousness, *that the human race is passing on to the better.* This gives to each one the Ideal Manhood and Womanhood. That is, the better man and woman, but in no wise the perfect. And it is a necessity of the endless difference of mental capacity in the human race, that each being must have a particular ideal. The Ideal Manhood varies as do people's conceptions of a personal god. In fact the two methods of conception are similar. Man projects his own image on the infinite back ground, and calls it God, or Ideal Manhood. The personal god, and Ideal Manhood are identical. The god Jesus is but an ideal man; he even falls below the ideal man of some. This is all that gives intensity to worship. That the personal god and the Ideal Manhood, are but reflections of self, is proven from the fact, that sex has to enter into the conception. The Catholic is not alone contented with Jesus, he must have his Mary,—the Shaker his Annie Lee,—the Spiritualist his Father and Mother god. The Protestant church fails in the feminine conception, and what deductively must necessarily follow, proves true. This wing of the Christian church is composed largely of women; Jesus is the ideal man whom they worship. There is no ideal woman for man, and he seeks his god elsewhere. Too much stress is often placed upon this worship of the Ideal, whether as a god or an exalted man. It is not this worship which makes the world progress. It is the progressive fact of human nature, which creates within us the Ideal. Yet, among the vast millions of earth, this order is reversed, and an effect substituted for the cause. Mankind does not progress because of laws and religions. Civilization does not arise from these; but progress which is only another name for change, is the eternal law of Nature which produces them all. It is *Dissatisfaction*, rooted in the soil of Evil, which is the cause of all progress. Man is dissatisfied with his lot. He labors to better it. Physical conditions thus grow better. These re-act upon him mentally, and tone down, and soften, and refine the feelings. The god he had conceived of in a ruder state, he becomes dissatisfied with, and he mentally changes his god, conferring other and more exalted attributes. This changes his form of worship. He breaks his idols of wood and stone, casts aside his cross, and ascends to the soul's highest Ideal; and having forgotten what he once was, wonders how those he has left behind, can still be

"Pagans suckled in a creed outworn."

§. 5. We often hear it asserted that man will some day reach a perfect estate. This conclusion is doubtless drawn from the constantly increasing rate of progress. It is often asserted, man progresses in a geometrical ratio; and in a geometric series the limit is soon reached, which, if not absolute perfection, is so near it, that it would be folly to try to conceive of the difference; and, that in practical results they would be so near perfection they might be considered as such.

But we deny the conclusion founded upon any geometrical progression. For the sake of any argument which may be founded thereon, we assent to the geometrical progress of man; and affirm: man may progress in a geometrical ratio, but only advance in an arithmetical one; and relatively he does progress towards perfection, but absolutely he does not progress at all. For the purpose of illustration, we have constructed the following diagram: Let K. K. etc., represent the indefinite plane of man's activities;—I, the point of ignorance from which he starts, and K. K. K. K. etc., the indefinite points

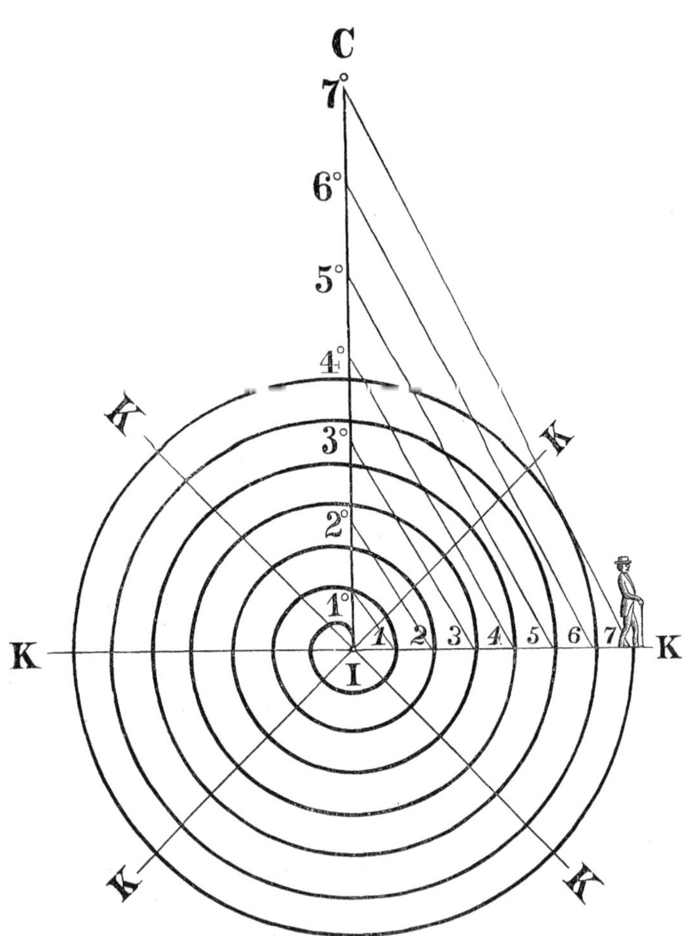

C
7°
6°
5°
4°
3°
2°
1°
K
K
K
K
K
K
1
2
3
4
5
6
7
I

of knowledge towards which he progresses. To cover the whole plane of his activities, he must pass spirally outwards from the pole of his ignorance towards knowledge. Let now these spiral revolutions about the point of his ignorance on the plane of his activities, be represented as circular, and the distance between each be represented by a constant number, say unity. Then the diameters would increase in an arithmetical ratio. But the ratio of diameter to circumference is 3·1415926=p. Now suppose that man completes each revolution in the same length of time, and we have one half of 1, 2, 3, 4, 5, 6, 7, for the rate of his advancement, but p, 2p, 3p, 4p, 5p, 6p, 7p, for the rate of his progress. That is, he may progress in a geometrical ratio but only advance in an arithmetical one.

But again: Let any point on I C represent the Ideal Conception; and suppose that man's Ideal Conception, increases in the same ratio of his advancement. Then at 1 he has the mental power of 1°, and at 2 of 2°, and so forth. But the distance between the points of his attainment and the Ideal Conception is always increasing. Now, really this is true of man's conception in regard to his knowledge; for at the point I, he is so profoundly ignorant that he really thinks he knows everything; at 1, there are a few things he does not know; at 2, quite a number; at 3, very many; at 4, the knowledge of his ignorance becomes quite annoying to him; and thus he goes on, till at 7, he has sufficient knowledge to comprehend how profoundly ignorant he is; and thus the perfect at last, only gets farther away from him. But what he loses in the direction of C, he gains toward K; so that relatively he advances, but absolutely he does not.

Now, this is perhaps as good an illustration of progress, and the real facts in the case, as the history of man and his own feelings would warrant. We may, therefore, safely conclude: that man may progress in a geometrical ratio, but only advance in an arithmetical one; and that relatively he does advance towards perfection on the plane of his own activities, but absolutely he does not; for there are infinite other planes he can never touch, both above and below him.

§. 6. By force of the same fact of impossible perfection in man, it follows that a perfect law can not be given, and were it given could no be obeyed. A perfect law has never yet been expressed. For, if we try to give expression to the law of human freedom; that is, the liberty of each, limited only by the like liberty of all; and say with Spencer: "Every man has freedom to do all that he wills, provided he infringes not the equal freedom of any other man," then, it is no wrong for him to injure himself nor any animal belonging to himself; whereas, it is the chiefest of all chief wrongs to injure one's self. It is a sin against the first law of life. This law cannot be applied to children. It neutralizes parental rule. In fact, there could be no government of family or state; for it supposes a perfect man who is to will and to do perfectly. But, on the other hand, if we should restrict this perfect liberty, by saying: do what you will so long as you injure not yourself, nor any other person or animal; we would bind him down to inaction and death.

The Golden Rule comes as near as it is perhaps possible to express the Ideal Law; yet it comes far short of perfection, and can never be obeyed. It tells you to do nothing less, nor more, than you would wish or desire others to do towards you. This supposes you to be perfect to insure good results; and, furthermore, supposes an absolute equality in individuals, not in rights alone, but in conditions. The Golden Rule can not always be obeyed with good results, from the fact it is a sympathetic ideal, devoid of a penalty. At most, it only sets up *yourself*, a very imperfect creature, as the standard of action. Your *desires* shall be the test; all actions shall square with your desires. Perhaps no one desires to be punished. Even when one has transgressed, the desire is to shun the effect, to flee the punishment. It matters not how villainous or exemplary the transgressor, the desire always is, to shun the penalty. The Golden Rule applied would thus pardon every transgression, rather than inflict a punishment. The Golden Rule expresses *pardon;* it is not a law with a penalty. It cries out: "Forgive!" From it does not come that merciless cry:

"Oh, transgressor, now suffer!" It grows out of sympathy for weakness and ignorance, which are ever leading people into error and sin. It binds up the wounds of satisfied law, and would stay the arm of Justice, which alone can bring health to a people. It preaches the sermon on the Mount. It is an angel of love in the midst of vice. It blesses always and curses not. It would destroy a world with kindness, never save it by a single act of justice. It pets and sympathises with the villain whom Justice holds with a vice-like grip.

The Golden Rule does not come to us as a law. It may be obeyed or not, in thousands of instances without bad results to us, and with good results to others. Unflinchingly carried out, no wayward child of the family or state would ever be punished. It would not only mar the exalted beauty of sympathy, but entirely destroy it, to put the Golden Rule in the form of a law; thus: Do unto others as ye would that they should do to you, or pay a fine of —— dollars and costs, or serve —— years in a state penitentiary, or hang by the neck on—— Friday till dead. Yet, this is the blank form in which all our statutory enactments aim to be written. Beautiful, as the Golden Rule is as an ethical flower in the gardens of civilization, it would be but a noxious weed yielding the seeds of death, if applied to an Indian savage, who thinks it the chiefest of all human glory, to adorn his buckskin shirt with the hair of women and children, he has killed for their scalps. The Golden Rule is an ideal thought, which cannot be conceived of by such a savage, whose head is only a battery of cruelty and death. Among such, the Golden Rule is simply oil added to the fierce flame. Among men, it never has worked, and must forever fail. Its language is: "If a man compel thee to go with him one mile, go with him twain;"—it matters not, whether he is going to heaven or hell. "If he take thy coat, give him thy cloak also;"—if he steal thy horse, hunt him up and give him thy cow. "If he smite thee on the right cheek, turn to him the other also;"—if he outrage and scalp thy wife, offer him the scalp of thy child also. In short, be a lamb, and enforce a lamb's ethics in a den of wolves.

The great mistake is, those who can appreciate the Golden Rule the most, and see its transcendent beauties, forget that the low and the vile have no appreciation of it; and there are races of men, we presume, so low in the scale of developement, that the Golden Rule has never yet been conceived of by them; for it is the highest development of sympathy, the fairest flower of the Ages. That it has not worked, we only have to open any page of the World's history to find true. It does not prevent slavery; for the Wolf's logic to the Lamb, is ever in the mouth of the slaveholder, as thus: "If God Almighty had made me like a negro, or other barbarian, I should think it a great kindness, nay, a righteous act, to enslave me, and treat me as well as slaves are treated physically; and besides, morally, it would be an infinite blessing to me, to bring me within the fold of Christ, and save my soul." It is thus the Golden Rule is self-destructive, amidst Evil. How could a half nation of Christians ever defend Southern slavery with the Golden Rule on their lips if it prohibited it? Applied to the common school system of this country it will not work. Does a man see no value in an education, never having learned to read and write, and thanks God for it, he prohibits his children from going to school, and votes and works against common schools. The bliss and villainy of ignorance the Golden Rule can never disturb. Ignorance has to be torn out of man by the roots; the operation always accompanied with pain and bleeding. Does a man whip his child to death in obedience to a religious obligation, his Golden Rule tells him he has done no wrong; it even sustains him in the awful work of death. Does he burn heretics at the stake, his Golden Rule only says he ought to be treated in the same manner *if a heritic*, which he assents to. Ignorance, glutted with brutal indulgence, always folds the Golden Rule about itself and goes to sleep. The Carib eats his captive, and the American indian decorates himself with the scalps of babes and mothers; Lovejoy goes down under the heel of a mob, and a Parker is lampooned in the prayers of Boston; and yet, the Golden Rule is as dumb as eternal silence. Not that it is in itself wrong, but because the mainspring of all our actions does not lie in moral codes or any rule of conduct. We act independent of all these. *Action* is not the result of moral law; but this is the result of our development—our imperfect state—our *condition*. Our actions are the effects of causes lying back of, and beyond, all moral codes; and were we possessed of the knowledge of the constant forces which ever evolve actions we could predict them with that certainty with which an astronomer predicts an eclipse.

From what has already been said on the conflict of opinion, in regard to moral law, this is made apparent. But let us once more illustrate the false method of definition in regard to morals. It is an oft repeated maxim: "*A person has no right to act wrong.*" It is safe to say a thousand people would call this a truism, to one who would question its truth. Yet, nothing could be farther from a just law of action than this maxim. It at once supposes the actor to be possessed of full knowledge of what and how he is to do; and the exact result of all his actions. Let us rob it of its subtlety and say: "A person has no right to act unless he has a perfect knowledge of what is right." This at once says a person shall never make an experiment because of his ignorance. Because he does not know how, he is never to learn. Yet experience is the school in which people gain knowledge; all art has sprung out of it; all science; all self-government; all civilization. The child politic or the child human has a right to act though it often stumbles and acts amiss. In fact it cannot help acting. If it acts wrong it will soon know it, and the right is only thus made known; and generalizing its actions, it has the science of its life. That maxim, if enforced to-morrow, would result in human inactivity, poverty, ignorance, and, in a few years, entire extinction of the race; yet it is the very essence of the Golden Rule. Science reveals to us punishment as the inexorable law of Nature. The Stomach and Back both say: "Do or die." Nature does not merely say: "Work or go hungry or cold." Hunger and cold often come at best. But it is "do or die." "Ho!" cries the drowning man to his fellow in the water, "help, or I perish!" "I gladly would," responds the more fortunate, "did I not have to save myself." This is the response which the first law of life forces from us all. Seldom do we find a person who will willingly lay down his life for another, save his own child, whose weakness demands his aid. Here, sympathy sways the parent into entire obliviousness of his own life. It is the demand which weakness always makes upon the strong; that inevitable tendency in all nature to equilibrium, though the strong have to suffer for it. All that can be laid down as a rule in regard to human action is: "A person has no right to do that which he *knows* to be wrong."

CHAPTER III.

DIVERSITY IN UNITY.

§. 1. We have said that diversity is a fact of Nature. But Nature is an infinite Paradox. It may be as truthfully asserted that unity is a fact of Nature. This is seen both in the development of plants and animals, and in the secondary action of physical and mental forces. The unity of Nature proclaims its constancy, its precision of action. The force which binds worlds together in harmonious action, is no freak of God's will, for a special purpose; but an infinite and universal force for a general and infinite purpose; and science proclaims, as they go plunging through space with a seeming reckless velocity and momentum, sufficient to burst each other into chaotic fragments should they collide, they are so governed, that no unforeseen accident can happen them; attracted by each other their orbital aberrations are part of their predetermined movement. The earth in going round the sun from year to year keeps such time to the "music of the spheres," that she swings round no millionth part of a second too late, nor no hair's breath of space gained: and though her orbit may intersect the path of a comet, Infinite Intelligence, has promised safety alike to earth and wandering star. The constant forces of the Universe are no more disturbed by comet or moon's nod, than is the earth's mass by the falling of a sunbeam. The earth was created and is sustained by a fixed law, and will so continue to exist while an Infinite Force sustains her. The stars look down upon us and "have us to bed," through fixed laws, bringing "tired Nature's sweet restorer, balmy Sleep," like an angel of mercy to aching brain and weary muscle. The sun shines by a fixed law. No motion of light which reaches this dusty globe but reveals in scientific truth, the universal Providence, and the stability of the Universe. The grass grows and withers, in accordance with an everlasting covenant. So every material thing connected with this earth declares the unity and harmony of Nature. The air we breathe, in entering the lungs, or driving the cloud of thunder, or in the sweeping cyclone, or gentle zephyrs' breath, fills all its offices and makes all its varied manifestations through fixed and general laws. The simple elements of which it is composed mix in accordance with a fixed purpose. Two parts by weight of nitrogen to one of oxygen is the "breath of Life;" reverse this order—two of oxygen to one of nitrogen, and it becomes the breath of Death; and this air we breathe, and which gives us life, carries in its wings the vapor to water the earth, and from which the dew is distilled through laws which are as fixed and constant as those which keep the earth in its orbit. No drop of water that comes from the cloud but is formed and falls by immutable laws, and in infinite Providence it is made and sent for the comfort and life no less of Judas than Jesus. It falls on the good and bad alike, the just and the unjust.

§. 2. Naturalists, observing that members of the same class resemble each other in the general plan of organization, tell us of their "*unity of type.*" This "unity of type" has been called the "soul" of Natural history. "What can be more curious," says Darwin, "than that the hand of a man formed for grasping, that of a mole for digging, the leg of the horse, the wing of the bat, and the paddle of the porpois should all be constructed on the same pattern, and should include the same bones, in the same relative position." Of the relative connection in homologous parts Geoffroy St. Hilaire says: "The parts may change to almost any extent in form and size and yet they always remain connected together in the same order. We never find, for instance, the bones of the arm and the fore-arm, or of the thigh and leg transposed. Hence these names may be given to the homologous parts in widely different animals." Owen also tells us that "the skeletons of animals whether modified for aquatic, areial or terrestrial life, will show that whilst they were perfectly and beautifully adapted to the sphere of life and exigences of the species, they adhered with remarkable constancy to that general pattern or archetype, which was first manifested on this planet, as geology teaches in the class of fishes, and which has not been departed from even in the most extremely modified skeleton of the last and highest from that creative Wisdom has been pleased to place upon this earth." This he tells us is no transcendental dream, but the fruit of inductive research.

We see the same unity of plan in the construction of the mouths of insects. "What can be more different," says Darwin, "than the immensely long spiral proboscis of a sphynx moth, the curious folded one of a bee or bug, and the great jaws of a beetle; yet all these organs, serving for such different purposes, are formed by numerous modifications of an upper lip, mandibles, and two pairs of maxilæ. Analogous laws govern the construction of the mouths and limbs of crustaceans. So it is with the flowers of plants."

That Nature works upon a general plan is seen in the growth of vertebrate animals, however widely different. This is strikingly manifest in the embryos of animals. Thus Von Baer, the eminent Russian naturalist, for many years professor of zoology in the University of Konigsberg, says, "The embryos of mammalia, of birds, lizards and snakes are in their earlist states exceedingly like one another, both as a whole and in the mode of development of their parts; so much in fact that we can often distinguish the embryos only by their size. In my possession are two little embryos in spirit whose names I have omitted to attach, and at present I am quite unable to say to what class they belong. They may be lizards, or small birds, or very young mammalia; so complete is the similarity in the mode of formation of the head and trunk of these animals. The extremities are still absent in these embryos, but even if they existed in the earliest stage of their development, we should learn nothing, for the feet of lizards and mammals, the wings and feet of birds, no less than the hands and feet of man, all arise from the same fundamental form." It is thus that science is revealing the unity of Nature, and the harmony of her action. At every step, of physical science, there comes the evidence that nature has but one mode in which she acts, and that *Diversity is swallowed up in Unity.*

§. 3. But shall we say that nature only proves constant in physical action, never in her mental forces? Surely not. She is as constant in the one as the other. Let us reason from what we know in the animal world. As man's body was typified in all vertebral forms below him, so was his mentality. His passions, appetites, instincts, reason, and most of his habits are all typified in the animal world below him. There is a unitary law running through the mental world. Many animals of the same species eat one another. Thus the male aligator eats his young till too big to gorge at a mouthful. This typifies cannibalism. Hogs will eat their young often, and man will eat the flesh of this hog cannibal. If man will eat man, deeming it a dainty morsel, it is not shocking to find the like done by the inferior animal. Men have wondered how man could have fallen to such a depth as cannibalism. The wonder is how he has risen above it. Human theft is typified in every domestic animal, having brought it, no doubt from their wild ancestors. Many of them, as the cat and the dog, will often hide what they have stolen, if too much to eat at once. Robbing is a sort of mental glory to the eagle. He will soar for hours high in air, or sit perched on some lofty hight, watching the active and unwearying fishhawk, hunting his prey; and when the hawk has obtained it, and is fluttering off through the air, that old robber will pounce down on him with a scream and gather up the fish before it can fall to the ground or water again; and thus carry off the hard and honestly earned food of his neighbor, never expecting to give a valuable consideration therefor. The English cuckoo, and some other birds, will go buccaneering, lay their eggs in other birds' nests, and all unmindful of their own young make other birds bring up a foreign progeny. The young cuckoo, it is said, with a wonderful selfishness, will cast out the legal heirs of the nest to perish of cold or hunger. In imitation of the cuckoo's selfishness and lack of maternal love, how often do we find mothers belonging to the race of man, to forsake their own children, sell or give them to others. How often do we find some basketful of infantile flesh left at some one's door. It is difficult to see the distinction in animal morals between the animal that eats its own offspring, and the parent who kills the child either before or after it is born. If public opinion or selfishness demands this of the parent, how low and sensual must be that public opinion or selfishness. The seeds of prostitution are sown in the animal world far below man; creating an insatiable demand in the male, which no refinement of life or moral codes can remedy. The fire is shot up from the hell of the lower world into the veins of man, and there has yet been nothing distilled in the laboratory of morals that can extinguish the fire.

Human slavery is typified in the red ant enslaving the black ant. We are struck with wonder, and almost horror after having been so long engaged in getting the black man liberated, through that bloody means—death, which is forever to cure the diseases of nature, to find one ant enslaving its fellow; and so helpless have the slaveholders become that it seems Nature, in her eternal plan, has ordained slavery as a fact in the life of these ants. This fact was first recorded by Pierre Huber in regard to the ant *Formica rufescens.* "It is absolutely dependent on its slaves; without their aid the species would certainly become extinct in a single year," says this learned naturalist. "The males and fertile females do not work, they are incapable of making their own nests, or of feeding their own larvæ. When the old nest is found inconvenient and they have to migrate it is the slaves which determine the migration and actually carry their masters in their jaws." "So utterly helpless are those masters," says Darwin, "that when Huber shut up thirty of them without a slave, but with plenty of food which they like best, and with their larvæ and pupæ to stimulate them to work, they did nothing; they could not even feed themselves, and many perished of hunger. Huber then introduced a single slave, and she instantly set to work, fed and saved the survivors, made some cells, and tended the larvæ, and put all to rights." But the naturalist might have taken this fact as an act of life-long benevolence in one ant towards its feeble fellow had he not run across the slave-catching *Formica sanguinea.* These ants are active, pioneering, courageous little fellows, and capture the black ant as the Spanish and English captured the black man in Africa, for the purposes of labor.

Thus we might go on, and we would find in the animal world, which many moralists have called so innocent and pure, all the vices to which man is addicted, typifying these vices in him. There we find murder, the most relentless and cruel; theft the most cunning and secretive; robbery the most pitiless and daring; slavery the most abject and perfect. There we find all the horrid vices which arise from the sexual instinct:—incipient prostitution, rape—in short, Lust. There we find the minor vices of a refined selfishness; pride, vanity, jealousy, coquetry, There we find also the vices of dishonor:—deceit, lying, treachery, fraud, and, lastly, war. We find all Nature has a dark ground, an obverse as well as reverse face. Name a crime, to which man is addicted, and its roots can be traced far down into the animal world.

This dark side to all nature surely looks devilish; it is slimy with the slippery embrace of monsters of the land and sea; it is putrid with the festering vices of humanity. We look into natural history, and there we see reflected as in a mirror of hell, held by fiendish hands, the image of man's dark nature struggling in the coils of the fabled serpent. We are thus forced to conclude that physically and mentally, Nature has a unitary universal root, which runs through the whole animal world.

§. 4. The assertion that "only man is vile," science bluntly contradicts; in fact the good and pure are pre-eminently found there. This leads us on to ask: what is the great distinction between man and inferior animals? In other words: how shall we define man? Shall we say with Carlyle, he is a forked radish with a head fantastically carved, or that he is created in the image of God? The one is about as scientific as the other. Both are expressions of utter failure at definition. Yet, the two combined will bring us nearer the truth than any definition we have hitherto seen. He is a combination of the vegetable and the god. There is mind and matter wedded. He is an illustration of universal polarity, rooted to earth, yet stretching out towards conscious existence hereafter. He draws his nourishment from the earth like the vegetable, yet is quickened with sensations produced by an infinite Force. Nor do we arrive at further truth by trying to distinguish man as a genus, and say herein he is radically different from all other animals. Huxley tells us, the difference between man and the monkey is the anatomist's difficulty. There is no such anatomical difference as the hands and feet indicate to the natural eye. Science looks closer and finds none. Mentally we are at a farther loss to distinguish. Agassiz says he cannot say in what the mental faculties of a child differ from those of a young chimpanzee, and he thinks, as did Theodore Parker, that the argument for immortal life will hold for the animal as well as man. Professor Huxley says, "No impartial judge can doubt, that the roots, as it were, of those great faculties which confer on man his immeasurable superiority above all other animate things, are traceable for down into the animate world. The dog, the cat, the parrot, return love for our love, and hatred for hatred. They are capable of shame and sorrow, and though they may have no logic, nor conscious ratiocination, no one, who has watched their ways, can doubt that they possess that power of rational cerebration which evolves reasonable acts, from the premises furnished by the senses—a process which takes fully as large a share as concious reason in human activity."

It is safe to affirm the difference between man and the monkey is only one of growth, not one of Nature's plans which would make us radically different. For example: the initiative faculty and reason have grown into what is termed the *inventive genius*. This is the perfection of the rudimentary instinct of other animals. The bee makes her hexagonal comb to store away her winter's food, but goes no farther in art. For ages, perhaps, the young bee has made no improvement on the mother's work. Yet, the perfection of the hive-bee's work is one of physical growth. The beaver builds his dam to deepen the water to add to his commissary of provisions; but the young beaver makes no perceptible improvement on generations past. The birds build their nests just as the mothers of their kind built for ages before them, and if any changes have come in these instinct arts, they have been produced in change of conditions, imperceptibly in long periods of time. There is nothing progressive in *design* in all this. But there seems to be no limit to the constructive and inventive genius of man. He builds things in the head before he puts them in material shape. He goes forth and takes beams, and plates, and polished wood out of the oak which grew for centuries uncared for and unthought of only in the farreaching thought of the Infinite, and builds houses for himself, and barns for the companions of the plow. He builds ships, and guides his course on sea by the stars and the magnetic needle. He builds houses for transporting vehicles, driven by steam; makes hoes and plows to cultivate the soil, to perfect tree and grain and vegetable, that else could not have been perfected. He talks over land and under water—speaking across a continent or through an ocean, magnifies his eyesight a thousand fold. All the happy arts of life which go to add comfort and and ease, to give pleasure and secure peace, spring directly from the inventive genius of man, each and all being first formed in the *ideal*, the mind creating, the hand fashing. In this he is superior to all other animals. In intelligence, accumulated by *design*, he is also far superior. The knowledge of most of the lower animals is confined to transmitted habit, called instinct, and a limited accumulation of facts through reason and experience; but man grasps to all else, hidden truths of the world of matter and of man. He not only discovers the simple truths of Nature, but deduces others from known premises by process of abstract reasoning. In this field of knowledge there seems to be no end to his attainments, digging the truth out of the ideal soil of the world. The facts of experience he stores away in the laboratory of his knowledge, and when he wants a lesson of wisdom to give to others, he tells of like results from like causes, and foretells coming events by reasoning on the fixed purposes of Nature. It is in the Ideal world where some men rise immeasurably above the animal world, and the degarded and barbarous of mankind. It is here necessary to particularize and qualify. In using the term man as distinguishable from the animal we mean the man who is capable of *ideal conception.* The Ideal is the highest attainable conception, though in itself it admits of degrees, and forever varies. It is the transition from the concrete sensation imaging the real, to the abstract conception imaging the ideal, which seems to make the crowning distinction between man and animal. It is the transition from the imitative to the creative thought. We see no work of animal which cannot be explained upon the hypothesis of imitation, even when they better their own works. But, man has ideal patterns which he tries to put into material form, whether of tool house, animal, or man; and the highest act is to aim to create the ideal man. This does not violate the assumption that the ideal is the ripened fruit of the imitative faculty. In other words that Imitation and Ideality are opposite poles of the same faculty.

§. 5. Before we proceed let us sum up the foregoing conclusions:

1. It is assumed that Evil is.

2. It cannot be defined.

3. It precedes all finite intelligence.

4. Imperfection is a perpetual fact; because, an expression of finite force.

5. Morality and special evils are the result of it.

6. Morality cannot be defined.

7. The Infinite is, but cannot be defined. It is only posited as the Absolute Force.

8. There are reasons for affirming the Absolute Force to be a conscious Force.

9. Man is a progressive finite intelligence.

10. He must be forever imperfect.

11. No perfect law can be given.

12. If given, it could not be obeyed.

13. Condition determines volition.

14. Self-preservation is the first law of life.

15. Variation is universal, and this fact of endless distribution, is swallowed up in the infinite unity of all. Nature expresses Diversity in Unity.

16. Dissatisfaction is the mainspring of Progress. This evolves the Better.

17. Laws and religions are the result thereof.

18. These express development do not produce it.

19. The Ideal is the crowning thought of man, but is necessarily limited and imperfect.

20. The Golden Rule is the law of sympathy and will never work because devoid of a penalty.

21. Punishment is an inexorable law of Nature.

22. Justice is scientific and will work, because it punishes error, sin and ignorance.

The foregoing conclusions, it appears to us, are founded in the nature of things. Viewed in the light of the Infinite on the one hand and the finite on the other, they come with axiomatic weight. But as the human mind is prone at times to doubt the authority of axioms, and even to question the truths of experience, we must grant what the mind requires —the benefit of a doubt. We do not feel authorized to affirm that man a fool who questions the truth of an axiom, but we are warranted in affirming that man not wise who sets no value on the facts of experience. We will therefore present some further considerations which may rise to the dignity of *First Principles*, before we evolve the Science of Evil.

CHAPTER IV.

MATTER AND FORCE.

§. 1. Nature is dual. That is, there exists *Matter and Force.* These two things are real and distinct, and never can be in any sense identical in nature. The one *acts*, the other is acted upon. There is the actor, and the medium of action. But the two co-exist and cannot be separated. As manifestations of Force we may mention light, heat and electricity. These manifestations of Force, are often called *forces.* These, however, are only the *effects* of Force acting on Matter. For brevity we call them forces, but must all be considered as one force. They are all finite expression of the infinite and one Force, as the atoms of matter may be distinguished as oxygen, hydrogen, carbon, etc., yet all finite expressions of Universal *Matter.* If the Universal Force were called Mind it would answer just as well. But these separate kinds of matter are known or distinguished only by the kind of motion which Force produces by acting upon them, as the chemical affinity between unlike elements. The attraction of gravitation, acting upon like masses, would not thus distinguish different elements. So also of forces; the affinity of chlorine for the metal sodium to form a salt is different from the affinity of oxygen for the same metal to form soda. Soda and salt express a compound of different chemical elements and forces, yet both forces are called affinity. So the force which keeps the moon in its orbit around the earth, is a different force from that which keeps the earth in its orbit around the sun, yet both are of the same kind called gravity. Now, if you go to the top of a tower, and cast a stone horizontally, the force, which makes it fall to the earth, is the same kind of force which keeps the earth in its orbit around the sun. Yet the motion of the stone is partial and incomplete, describing a part of an hyperbolic curve and not one which would keep it going.

So, also, of mental force, this is quantitative and qualitative; secondary and original; that which is produced and that which produces, at the same time the effect and the cause.

§. 2. The most peculiar characteristic of Force is that which is termed *Polarity*. Here we must particularize. It is the function of Force to move matter. Force expresses itself in the motion of matter. Matter is in perpetual motion. There is perhaps no atom of matter in the universe that ever came to *absolute rest.* This earth has several motions; three upon its axis, one accomplished in twenty-four hours, one in nineteen years, and a third in about twenty-six thousand years. It also has a yearly motion around the sun, and one with the solar system; and doubtless other motions we know not of, motions of aberration, caused by the disturbing influence of other celestial bodies. There are motions produced by Force acting on celestial bodies, which may be called Celestial force. But matter is made to assume many motions, so made by Force, from the atom or molecule to the celestial body, and is known in its solid, liquid, gaseous and etherial states. Thus, we have the motion of matter called light, the motion of matter called heat, and another motion of matter called electricity; and we affirm there is still another motion of matter called thought; governed by the same general laws. What is called mind we assume to be Force.

When Force acts, it is found to be in certain definite ways. This is termed the manner of its action, or its *law.* Thus it acts equally in opposite directions; and, in mechanics, we say action and re-action are equal. Herein we have evolved a *law* of equality. This is when the force has a fixed centre of action. Thus equal weights will balance on the two equal arms of a lever. This is a definite force in equilibrium. Or drop a pebble in still water and waves will radiate in every direction. These, however, are but partial manifestations of the law, as the wave is only seen in latteral or horizontal motion: and in the scales the wave of motion must be perpendicular. But if we should say, the sun radiates light, it is a complete centre of motion, and the radiations would be as from the centre of a globe, continuous in all directions; and each wave would represent the increasing surface of a sphere. But again we may say, motion decreases inversely as the square of the distance from its centre. This is another *law*. But these laws are deduced as abstract. That is, no disturbing force is allowed to figure in the premises. They are abstractly true, and are called general laws, but in the concrete they are not true, for there is constant interference, in the finite parts, and one centre of motion may conflict with another: As when light radiates from the sun in accordance with the general law, the earth breaks the wave of motion, at a certain point in the radiating sphere, and makes a cone of darkness,—the earth as its base and the vertex reaching far into space. So that really it is not true that light continues in all directions. What is meant is, it would if not interfered with. Nor can it be said it diminishes inversely as the square of the distance from the radiating centre; for it may be entirely neutralized at a given point by counteracting forces or augmented by other forces. Now, when we say, motion radiates equally from a common centre in all directions, we express the polarity of force, which is true in the abstract, but not truly expressed in action when a force is disturbed. The magnet is a good illustration of the polarity of electrical force; and from this we use the terms positive and negative as expressing *one* force acting in different directions.

It is quite evident, if Force acts on matter to move it, then Force and Matter must either be universally diffused or have some great centre. It is, perhaps, the only safe assumption to affirm Infinite Force to be universally diffused and inheres in the atom. But, if so, each atom must move and express *polarity*. The atomic motion must then be the basis for other motions which are *derivative* and dependent on this. But derivative motion must partake of the parent form, which has evolved it, and so we have two great laws to express Force, which we may combine, thus: *Force ever evolves its own like, and acts in polarity.* But this again, expresses *Diversity in Unity.*

§. 3. Inductively we may be led to the same conclusions. If a magnetic needle be divided into two parts it is found there are two magnetic needles made by the division; and it matters not how many times it be divided, polarity still exists in each part, whence we may conclude this property inheres in the atom. But again, if we now take two magnetic needles of equal force, and place them together, with poles reversed, the forces of both are neutralized, so that the compound needle will not exhibit polarity. It cannot be said the forces are destroyed but merely balanced, for polarity is at once evoked with the slightest disturbance in the equilibrium. In fact, it is from its disturbance that we gain knowledge of Force. Now this is true of forces, it matters not what the conditions. One will disturb its fellow, and cause some change therein, when brought into proximity; and it must necessarily follow, the stronger force will prevail; yet weakened in its inherent power by the quantity of conflicting force, till the prevailing force has conquered the weaker and brought all the atoms into the same kind of motion. It then may have an increment of force from the one which at first opposed it. If this reasoning be true, then it is possible that sound opposed to sound will produce silence; light opposed by light will produce darkness; mechanical motion opposed to mechanical motion will produce rest; and chemical energy counteract chemical energy. All of which science has proved true by experiment.

It is in this way Force may be rendered latent, put to sleep as it were, for it can never be destroyed; and at the same time be so bound, that the individual atom may be replaced by others, and so continue active yet apparently inactive, till other forces set it free again. For all forces, which are *derivative*, contain primary forces within them which do not cease acting while the *derivative* force is asleep. Secondary force, which is thus at rest, is said to be in a *statical* condition,—when active in a *dynamical* condition.

For example: The tree accumulates force from the atmosphere and earth, storing it away in the wood. To liberate this, great force is evolved *in heat.* The whole vegetable world is a great storehouse of force. The earth itself is a vast reservoir of force. The coal beds are force in statical condition. The force of coal is unlocked and set free by chemical action. These are examples of forces balancing or neutralizing each other, or force in equilibrium.

But on the other hand force in action begets its like and this may be called *impression* or *induction.* This must be true of both original and derivative forces.

§. 4. We are now enabled to distinguish abstractly and scientifically between organic and inorganic bodies, and this solely by the play of forces within their parts. To do this, we assume, the ultimate atom or molecule is in motion. This motion is peculiar to each atom; as we assume no two atoms are exactly alike; yet, very many may nearly resemble each other, and their motions would be almost alike; which would distinguish atoms into *elements.* As, for example, we assume no two kernels of wheat or corn are alike, yet they so nearly resemble each other that they may be classed as corn and wheat. It is in this way we also may class the *elements* as oxygen, carbon, etc. The motions of the elementary atoms are each as elements different and original, and never cease. *Like atoms have like motions*, and these atoms may be aggregated in kind, or diffused through each other. The atomic motion is the most powerful. It would be easier to stop the rotation of the earth than to stop the motion of one atom of oxygen. But now these atomic motions must conflict, as they are different in kind, yet have no power to destroy one another; all they can do at most, is to *oppose* and by equality, as it were, place each other in equilibrium, or by *union* produce a new kind of motion. It is the like kind of motions which produce equilibrium, but unlike kinds which produce a new motion. This new motion we call a compound motion; as for example oxygen and carbon combine to form new substances, but the new substance only expresses a new or compound motion in its parts. This we call a *derivative* motion, or new expression of force. It is not a new or different kind of force, but merely a new expression in matter; yet we will call it a *new force*, meaning always thereby a new *motion*.

But it is plain this new or *derivative* force may be again compounded with an original or compound force and produce one differing from either. Now this last derivative force may be opposed by another of the same kind, and so neutralized or balanced, that it may be said to be put to rest, but at the same time the original or atomic force or other derivative forces within, mav still be active:—which is only saying the atoms of the whole are in motion; but the compound body does not change. But if this be so, then the atoms may pass off, and their places be filled by like atoms. That is the compound body, force or motion would remain; but the atoms of which it is composed may also remain, or partly or wholly pass off. This is the legitimate conclusion deduced from atomic motion which can never cease. But this, we affirm, is the basis for a distinction between inorganic and organic bodies. In the former all the atoms are retained with their forces; in the latter, some of the atoms or all pass out, to be replaced by other atoms with their like forces in kind. Only a partial transmission is, perhaps, common to all vegetable and some animals; but just where, in the animal economy, all may be said to pass off in the life of each it is difficult to tell. But one thing must be evident, the change of parts, the development and reduction of all bodies whether organic or inorganic must be due to forces, their constancy and precision of action, not on the variable and constantly moving atom. To the atom is due the variation, the diversity; to the force, the likeness, and constancy expressed in the universe. Force and Matter then express the law, Diversity in Unity.

§. 5. But again, Motion is transferable; and by this we mean that like begets its like. This is peculiarly the property of Force, which ever tends to this, and it could not express variety were it not for the unlike atoms. As simple and common illustrations of this we say laughter begets laughter, weeping begets weeping; sympathy, love, hatred, anger; these beget their like. This is only transferable force, or like atoms induced into like motions, when coming within the vibrating wave. Fear also begets fear. A panic is induced in a regiment by the intense and uncontrolable fear of one soldier. Bravery is also, transferred from a commander to his army, as has often been shown. Sheridan at Cedar Run is an illustration of this. Napoleon was a peculiar illustration of this characteristic of Force. He was conceived when his father was grasping the sword; his mother carried him to battle in her womb; and he was born upon tapestry embroidered representing the battles and heroes of the Iliad. The forces of war were all centred within him. He was born a magazine of war-forces; and from himself radiated their waves throughout France. This force was strong and permanent within him, and he induced or begot its like temporarily within all who came near him. It was not only a man or an army he inspired with war; it was a whole nation. It was not Cambronne, nor the Guard, but Napoleon, who spoke when they returned to the Allied Forces: "The Guard dies, it never surrenders."

It is thus, also, thought induces its own self. How often two persons begin to speak after a protracted silence the same thing, however remote from the subject of conversation when last talking. That it was not a train of logical thought, has often been proven in two ways; tracing back the thought through two entirely different and conflicting routes, and by the persons at the same instant speaking the *same words*. Some persons, also, looking at the diseased part of another, will often feel a like pain or uneasy sensation in the like part upon themselves.

We have frequently seen a man read the characters of persons by simply holding a letter from them in his hand, without looking at the writing; and a man who would answer any written question by placing it in his hand, however securely folded or kept from his vision.

But this is not alone a peculiarity of mental force; there may hundreds of illustrations be taken from other sources; as, for example, the "Singing Hydrogen Flame." By lowering a glass tube over a burning hydrogen jet a short distance, and securing it there, while in this position no sound is emitted. But if now a person begins to sing the scale, when the proper note is struck the tube begins to sing the note, and continues it. This is an illustration only of transmitted motion in the atmosphere. But it is the motion of matter, produced by force, which makes all impressions of whatever kind. These impressions are universal wherever force acts; and it is only a very small part that are made on, within and around us, that we ever become conscious of. These impressions are lasting, as well as instantaneous. It only wants science to bring them out and read them. Says Youmans in his chemistry—

"If we cover a board with powdered sulphite of calcium, (made adherent by a previous coating of gum arabic), lay a key upon it, and expose it for a few minutes to sunlight; on bringing it into a dark room and removing the key, a dark, well-defined image of it is seen on a white ground. The surrounding phosphorescent glow gradually diminishes and the image disappears. Now place a pencil on the surface and expose it again, and when the image vanishes repeat the exposure a third time with a ring. When all traces of the last image are gone, heat the board and the images will reappear in reverse order,—first the ring, then the pencil, then the key. And they have been thus evoked weeks and months after they were formed." * * * "It would moreover seem that one object can hardly touch or approach another without impressing a change upon it which is more or less lasting. If we lay a wafer or small coin upon a piece of clean, cold glass, or polished metal, and breathe upon the surface, upon tossing off the object after the moisture has evaporated, not a trace of it will remain. But if we breathe upon it again, a spectral image of the coin or wafer comes forth, which as it fades away may be again, and again, recalled by a breath, even months afterwards. Objects also impress each other without contact. Engineers have noticed that the near parts of machinery visibly impressed each other. By exposure over night, a very distinct image of the grain of wood has been obtained, when placed more than half an inch from the receiving surface."

All these facts are simple illustrations of the one law of Force, that it ever tends to produce its like, and expressing this law only in the motion of matter.

This beautifully solves the mystery of *Inheritance*, as we will now briefly notice in a few objections to the Darwinian theory of "Gemmules," as stated in his chapter on Pangenesis.

§. 6. The great work of Darwin has laid the world under lasting obligations for that vast collection of facts which he has brought together in his book on "Plants and Animals under Domestication." "Every one," he says, "would wish to explain to himself, even in an imperfect manner, how it is possible for a character possessed by some remote ancestor suddenly to reappear in the offspring; how the effect of increased or decreased use of a limb can be transmitted to the child; how the male sexual element can act not solely on the ovule but occasionally on the mother form; how a limb can be reproduced on the exact line of amputation, with neither too much nor too little added; how the various modes of reproduction are connected, and so forth." To which we would add, how the image of an object may be imprinted on the body of a child, or how a permanent characteristic may be given to it before birth from temporary mental excitement or desire of the mother.

Darwin presents the following Provisional Hypothesis: "The whole organization, in the sense of every separate atom or unit, reproduces itself. Hence ovules and pollen grains,—the fertilized seed or egg, as well as buds,—include and consist of a multitude of germs thrown off from each separate atom of the organism." This multitude of germs thrown off from each atom he terms "gemmules," and he further says they must be thrown off during all the stages of development. These gemmules are matter and transmitted in substance. We would substitute in place of this the following hypothesis: Each organism is a union of compound forces. Each separate compound force begets its own like motion in each cell of its structure. These cellular forces are continually modified by new conditions, which will render in *time* the organism more complex. The atoms of each cell are in progressive motion; that is, new atoms of the same kind are continually taking the place of the old atoms which pass away. But as it is the constant attribute of Force to express polarity, each separate compound force must express polarity in the organism. Hence each separate faculty, muscle, nerve and bone must be dual. In other words, each entire organism, however simple or complex, contains within it both sexes, *in cellular duality.*

The crowning difference between this theory and Darwin's is, we assume that it is Force which begets itself, while he assumes that it is matter which begets its own like. By Darwin's theory, each atom throws off a multitude of "gemmules" during all the stages of development. To make the theory work and fulfill all the conditions of each supposable case, this would have to be true. But this is not all; these "gemmules" would *all* have to be transmitted in substance. It may be objected that, however minutely divided, these gemmules are nevertheless *matter;* and if thrown off, say during a period of sixty years, they would have to be retained in the body that time. It is moreover necessary that each atom should throw of its gemmules at each minute subdivision of time, which it is impossible to compute, for no one can tell how rapidly development takes place, if at all, by known subdivisions of time. So that while the "gemmule" is indeed minute, the time in which it is thrown off is correspondingly short. The number, therefore, of such atomic births for one hour must be immense; and if multiplied into a life of sixty years, or more, must be quite materially perceptible. But when all these "gemmules" are transmitted, either in a latent or active form, there must be an accumulation of unchangeable matter at some point of time, say in ten thousand years. But in living organisms we find no such fixity to matter; not even that a single atom remains in the cell for a day. The body of man changes so rapidly that perhaps no individual atom of matter is retained in it more than a month. But if a "gemmule" could remain unchanged, an atom could; and if an atom a cell, and if a cell a whole structure. Biology seems, therefore, to negative the hypothesis.

Again: How shall we account, upon this hypothesis, for acquired characteristics, transmitted drunkenness; transmitted mania to steal; bodily and mental impressions, directly from the mother, while the child is in the womb; or for *variation* in any form? Simply by modified cells, which implies modified atoms and "gemmules." This, the author of Pangenesis asserts, must be the case. But "gemmules" are matter,—and how is matter modified? Not in the structure of the ultimate atom, for chemistry negatives this; but simply in its combination with other atoms. But this is only chemical change. In other words, a "gemmule" can only be *modified* by chemical action. *But this is a modification of Force, not matter.* Why not say, then, there is a modification of forces in the living organism, which is induced in each atom, with which the modified force is related, and which must be transmitted to the offspring, therein to act with regularity and precision, to be again modified, controlled or counteracted by other forces with which it comes in contact? This modified force may receive increments of like force, and so be enhanced or intensified, or it may be neutralized, and so lie dormant.

Upon this hypothesis the force perpetuates itself in the line of the least resistance; and leaps from atom to atom as soon as brought within the circle of its influence. The atoms of the body may be replaced by other atoms, in the "wear and tear" of the same body, or in the building up of a new body in reproduction. It is in this way a force may be lying *latent*, as it were, by action in a living and changing organism, and may be perpetuated from generation to generation, and only become visible when some favorable condition will bring it out. It is not necessary to perpetuate force, that the cell or the gemmule should remain in the living organism, any more than that the raindrop which goes to form the rainbow should halt to perpetuate the image. As the rainbow is reflected from millions of different drops in a shower, and at no two seconds is reflected from the same drops, so a force may continue for years in the same body instantly changing its atoms, or for ages in the reproduction of its kind. The functional or structural modification of a cell must lead inevitably to the structural or functional modification of an atom or "gemmule," which must be retained in the body in multiple form to perpetuate itself in the offspring. But, on the other hand, if it be force which is modified, its modification will at once produce structural and functional modification in the organism. But we find secondary force can be and is modified daily and hourly. It may be increased or diminished, or entirely neutralized. It may be put to sleep or awakened. It may be changed in form, quality, quantity, intensity, but never destroyed, while the atoms of matter in which it acts or sleeps may, by an original motion of their own, pass away from this secondary active or sleeping force. Force may come in the sunlight and reappear in the coal a million of years after, having locked up the atom perhaps in mineral form; or it may appear in the thought of Peter the hermit, and inoculate nations of men with a religious zeal which shall last two hundred years, as a single atom with distructive force would spread pestilence throughout a nation; example of force acting in mental or physical form. Or as a combination of both, it may appear in the erratic course of a drunken man, and reappear in the mad course of vicious offspring. Nay, the force which played such wild freaks in the bodies of extinct animals, may be living to-day in other bodies somewhat modified, while the cells and gemmules of matter in those extinct animals upon which this living force acted may be now bound up in solid rock.

Man is not a storehouse of matter, for this constantly changes and passes away from the body, but that which is constant and remains is Force. Matter cannot remain latent in man, or it would thus accumulate and obstruct the action of the many busy housekeepers, the forces within. But we can readily understand what is meant when one speaks of a latent force coiled up like a spring in this bodily temple of ours; and when some ancestral feature or habit speaks out in us not known to our parents even, it is made plain enough when it is affirmed 'the long bound force has been set free.' It would obscure the mental vision and confound the understanding, to speak of latent matter in the body, residing in our ancestors for a thousand years. Man is rather a storehouse of vast forces. These are stored away in muscle, nerve, bone, brain, ready for use when called into action, and he is not like the plant acted upon by external conditions for a manifestation of force, but he can in some measure invoke the forces within him, and *compel* them to act. He can guide their action and bind them up again. The theory of latent material "gemmules" it appears to us is akin to the old theory of latent fluid heat.

But again: How can it be said that matter begets its like? Matter we assume is increate and unbegotten. It then has nothing to beget. Every atom that will be is already begotten. *Changed*, it is said, into new forms, which new forms resemble the parent forms. But how *changed?* Not by itself, for it cannot itself act. It is *Force* then which acts in, through and upon matter, Force only it is which may lie dormant, Force only can be evoked. It is only Force which begets its like. That is, induces like motions in material atoms. When the son at maturity resembles his father, we do not mean then, that the son contains in his body some original matter in multitudinous "gemmules" which his father actually once carried about with him in his body, which by multiplying produced the son in the image of his father; but we mean, the force which generates its like in action, has aggregated like, yet entirely separate, elements into like features, which force forces like features into like expressions, at corresponding ages; moving the nostrils and lips the same; modulating sound from the throat the same; drives the flesh into like habits, of gesture, gait and labor, and the mind into like channels of thought and disposition. It is Force, not Matter, which does this.

Inheritance is a law of the mind as well as the body. What aggregation of material "gemmules" can be set off for theft begotten in the daughter, drunkenness in the son, insanity in one, lust in another? What aggregation of material "gemmules" which shall in these same persons oppose in mental conflict all these vices, and cause contrition and remorse. This would indeed be a strange warfare of transmitted "*gemmules.*" May it not better be said it is a conflict of mental *forces*, and that man can in a measure control these forces, guide or subdue them?

But mental inheritance is displayed in *society* on a far grander scale than in the animal alone. The aggregate world where there is inter-communication inherits the mental forces of the past. To-day is mentally begotten of yesterday, and the variation only comes in the new conditions of to-day producing new or evoking latent forces; which are again transmitted in worldly mental function to *to-morrow*. These are the mighty mental forces which act as States or Nations, the aggregate of many separate centers of forces. Here we also see the great law of Induction, or Force begetting its like in what is called *public opinion*, or *public conscience*, guiding each separate individual, the atom of the state, in thought and action, appearing in dress and literature, and in habits of all sorts. There is no hypothesis of transmitted "gemmules" which can explain this.

Every animal which has preceded man has had a mental as well as physical life which has been transmitted to the world. As two cells of matter enlivened with Force may multiply a million-fold, evolving from the homogenious cells a complex organism which passes into being of different form and habit, evolving now a caterpillar, and then a flying moth; the one crawling on the earth and eating its substance, the other a winged psyche living in the sunbeam and extracting the nectar of flowers; so mental action ever passes from the lower to the higher, from the simple cell of one idea to the complex logic of science; from the low and barbarous instinct of savage life to the far-reaching and refined thought of civilized man. This earth is older than we have been accustomed to think. Physically and mentally its foundations lie deep in time. The softer strata which lie super-imposed upon each other, all have a granite bed, lying close upon the central fire, and the alluvium of our fields tells a story older than mountain or continent of to-day. So the close reason, the quick perception, the intuitive inspiration, which give rise to all human mental phenomena of to-day, lie super-imposed on the mental grantite of the stone age, and are older than the Herschels and Newtons; the Aristotles and Platos of the historic period. It is just as necessary that Thales should precede Socrates, as that Socrates should precede Aristotle. Just as necessary that these should precede Copernicus, as that Copernicus should precede Galileo and Newton. Without the Indian and Egyptian mind, there would have been no Greece. Without Greece no science to-day, any more than there could be to-day without yesterday.

So also of Religion.—The Protestant church has numberless branches to-day; and it is itself a branch of the Christian Catholic Trunk, whose roots penetrate the Roman, Grecian, Egyptian and Indian soil for nourishment. The Cross of the Catholic is descended from more self-sacrificing and superstitious times than the Christian age and many a god was crucified on it before Jesus of Nazareth. There is not a rite in the Christian church that does not date back of Christianity a thousand years. And there is no man, who says his prayers to-day, who does not take hold of the hand of every worshipper on earth; whether he kneels to Fire, Sun, Image, Hero or Spirit. The origin of our worship is as humble as the lowest type of man, and the religions and faiths and creeds of the world are all brothers and sisters to one another. No Spiritualist would be to-day without Protestantism; no Protestant without Catholicism; no Catholic without the old Roman religion; no Roman religion without the Polytheism of Greece and the Monotheism of the Jews; no Grecian or Hebrew faith, without Egyptian Idolatry; no Egyptian worship without the countless years of religion lying hid beyond.

Just so also of Law. The lawyer of to-day in this country takes hold of the hand of Kent; Kent repeated Blackstone; he repeated Coke; Coke, Lyttleton; Lyttleton the Pandects of Justinian; and he Numa, Solon and Lycurgus; and so on back to song and traditional story, when the people obeyed the verbal command of some hero, who was once followed and reverenced as a man, but became, when dead, worshipped as a god. In short, the mental story of the world is one of inheritance, the ever begetting of Force, and not by any means a transmission of material "gemmules."

§. 7. The known laws of Force will explain, so far as we have investigated, all the phenomena of reproduction, whether by fission, gemmation, or sexual generation.

In fission the animal is a simple illustration of polarity manifested throughout the whole organism; like a magnet, which must reproduce the whole in all its parts. The animal represents one compound animal Force, the sexual cells being in contact, and when divided it matters not how often each part must reproduce the whole animal. It is a simple case of Force inducing like motions in all the cells of the animal. The bud of a tree is more complex; for each bud is an orginal centre of motion, which begets its own like in buds, however numerous on the same stem or trunk; but as they are original centers, each center is subject to separate modification, and is only sure to reproduce itself in bud form, never from the seed, as the seed may be a compound of many forces different from the original bud. In sexual reproduction, there is a compound or *double* union of sexes; two female and two male forces, mingled in cell form. These forces play upon each other, and represent every force in both sexes, at the moment of their mingling. These may blend and produce an offspring unlike either parent force; one may entirely neutralize the other, and produce nothing; one may shade into this, that or the other, producing the mother here, the father there; or they may evoke some latent force by the combination. Or, again: the male force may be so overpowering, that the offspring not only will most resemble him, but the embryo offspring may induce a corresponding reproductive force in the mother which will be permanent. The sympathy between the embryo and the mother, must be great; the one more or less impressing the other. This must be the seat of permanent changing conditions in the offspring, and sometimes may be induced in the mother. The embryo represents the weaker forces, and hence are the more easily conditioned.

There is a misnomer in the terms male and female, as there is in the terms positive and negative. They do not represent two forces, but each of them one force; neither is it a difference in the atoms, but only a condition of the force, in finite expression. Each male and female are both separately male and female. The one condition of force predominating in one more than the other. So that man, for example, is more male than he is female; and woman more female than she is male, and by this we mean, not really, and in fact, but that each has the other sex latent, which under conditions may be developed, as is recorded of a certain hen after laying and bringing up her brood, assumed the whole male dress and disposition, ever after.

But it is useless to dwell on the application of this hypothesis; this we leave for the reader and student. We only wish to indicate the principle for application hereafter. By applying this principle: Force acting on unlike atoms of matter; Force ever begetting like motions therein; its instantaneous and irresistable effects thereon; its correlation and conservation, must not only explain all inheritance, but all phenomena of whatever kind. It is the *union* of matter and Force—not matter alone, nor

Force alone, which produces effects, and is the cause of all effects. But it is the peculiar function of Force to beget its like, and of matter to produce variation. For the atom is variable *in being*, and Force is the *Infinite Unit.*

§. 8. We are now prepared to apply the foregoing principles to Evil, and evolve therein a science which will evoke its meaning. But first let us see how man is himself an expression of Force. We find this in his bodily and mental activities. The muscles express bodily force; the brain, head force. These forces lie coiled up in muscle and brain. But it is the universal law of Force to express polarity, however it may be divided or cut up. The mental force may thus be divided into faculties, and each faculty in its functional activity will express polarity. Thus we have as purely mental expressions, right and wrong, happiness and sorrow, hope and despair, love and hatred, knowledge and ignorance. These are correlative terms, and each pair expresses one force. The one brings the other as a necessary consequence; the one implies the other, as the positive pole of a magnet implies its negative pole. But either pole may act—nay, both poles must act. These may be converted, the one into the other in action, as right may be pushed into wrong, happiness into sorrow, hope into despair, love into hatred; nay, knowledge into ignorance, when expressing feeling. It is perhaps true that the wisest *feel* the most ignorant. There is no hatred or jealousy which has not a love basis. Those who love the most can hate the most. Those who can pray the most fervently, can curse the most bitterly. The purest can be the vilest. This law of polarity forces itself upon us everywhere and at all times. It is thus we speak of pain and pleasure, virtue and vice, heat and cold—in short, good and evil, only as opposites, and cannot conceive of the one only as in contrast with the other. The animal and vegetable world we distinguish as male and female. We speak also of the centripetal and centrifugal forces, action and reaction, and that antagonism which is everywhere prominent in Nature. By all this we only mean the polarity of Force. In a theological point of view, we see the same manifest polarity in God and the Devil. People taking a purely personal view of Force in Nature, have projected the one pole on the infinite background and called it God, and the other in the same way has been called the Devil. All of which results from the inherent and necessary antagonism expressed in the *atomic* forces of which a body is made up. Wherever there is a center of force there must be polarity expressed, or there could be no force. *To find the polarity is to disturb the force.* In fact, we can learn nothing of Force only from its disturbance.

We have then as the expression of the universe:

The Infinite Force and the finite atom.

The Perfect and the imperfect.

The Unity and the diversity.

The above duality leads to the following conclusions: The infinite whole is made up of its finite parts. Nature is one divisible unlimited whole. The Infinite could not exist without its finite parts. The Infinite universe of matter is absolutely dependent on each one of its atoms. If one atom could be destroyed the whole could. So of the Infinite force; it is made up of finite forces, because of the variable atom; and the Infinite could not exist without each finite force. If the smallest possible force could be destroyed the whole could. If the force which evolves the thought of a mosquito could be once destroyed, and the thought lost, so also could Infinite Force, and Infinite intelligence be blotted out. As no particle of dust can be lost, so also, no thought can be lost from out the universe. But the mosquito's thought is an imperfect one, because finite. The mosquito doubtless acts amiss quite often in the sphere of its own operations. We say then of each mosquito it is finite, imperfect, and different from all things else. Yet the Infinite and Perfect Unity, could not exist without this finite and imperfect diversity.

CHAPTER V.

THE ORIGIN OF MORALS AND SCIENCE.

§. 1. The first command given to the animal was ACT. This was compulsory and arbitrary. To make the animal act it is first constructed to act, and then forced into action by being acted upon. This beautifully illustrates the play of forces, their correlation and persistence. The creative forces we have discussed elsewhere, and we will now treat only of the active animal.

We will suppose that when Nature had formed her animal and enlivened it with sensation, she spoke and said: "Now my little animal act." To whom the little animal responded: "No, mother, I like rest, I shall obey Statics rather than Dynamics." Here is the first disobedience so often expressed in the world. Nature then responds: "But I will compel you to act." She then breathes into its nostrils the breath of life. In rushes the foe to its organism oxygen gas. This begins to tear down its body, burning and consuming the structure.

Sensation now cries out, "Supply your loss." This is known by the animal saying to Nature: "Mother, I am hungry." Ah!" says Nature, "I told you I would make you act." "How pitiless and cruel you are," says the animal, "why can't you just as well feed me and let me rest." "I know no rest," says Nature, "neither shall any of my children." "But why torture me with hunger, have you no sympathy, no love for your child?" "Much indeed; I have provided what I think necessary," responds Nature. "But you would sleep always, and be nothing in the universe did I not torture you while in the embrace of Statics. I have sent Dynamics into every cell of your body to war against Statics. When Dynamics overpower Statics, then you will obey me; for I always act." "But, mother, *how* shall I act?" "Ah! that is a great moral question," responds Nature, "which I shall never discuss with you nor enlighten you upon *till you act.*" To whom the animal responds, "This is adding insult to injury, cruelty is no name for this. You are burning me up with oxygen and will not tell me how to extinguish the flame." "Fool!" says Nature, "I have but one way to teach you. This flame shall never be extinguished while an animal lives. I will make hunger gnaw at your vitals and thus drive you into the jaws of Death, or into paths of wisdom. All you can do at most is to add fuel to the fire, for a few years or hours; but so long as you gather fuel fast enough to feed the flame, and act wisely, I will temporarily suspend the pain of Hunger. I shall drive you out of your garden of Rest, and guard the gate with a flaming sword, that you may never enter therein. You shall never eat of the tree of knowledge but with pain." And the animal with a desire to live, goes out with Nature's blessing pronounced upon it. "Do or die." This has often been pronounced a *curse* by theological teachers. Nature has driven it out hungry and ignorant. But is there any relation between Hunger and Ignorance? Hunger is a physical active force, purely dynamical. Ignorance is a mental state. It is mind at rest. Force asleep: Statics. But Hunger is a sensation; the effect of Force acting on matter; the first conscious thought of animal life. Thought is then not a force; it is not mind; but an *effect* of Force acting on matter. Thought we make universal, and special. The former is any effect of Force acting on matter; the latter is conscious in the individual.

In the universal sense thought is stamped upon the face of Nature. Nature talks; she has voice and motion; an articulate and silent language. The landscape which the eye gathers in, is thought saluting thought; the me calling to the not me; the echo of a god-thought beyond and without, back to the conscious thought of man within. The world we tread is a thought of the Infinite Force. The verdure of Spring; the gorgeous Summer; the sear and yellow Autumn; Winter with its fleece of polar ice and snow, are yearly fractions of the universal thought earthward. The longest life of man is but a thought of God raceward. And how like the two thoughts are, the year and the life of man; the Spring time of youth, its tenderness and verdure; the Summer with its strength and fullness and honor; the Autumn storing up the fruits of labor; and Winter bringing the winding sheet of death.

That sensation precedes hunger we do not doubt. Sensation is the speech of a disturbed organism, and tells of waste. It is common to all animals and some plants, but just where it passes into consciousness it is impossible to tell. Perhaps when food has to be obtained by locomotion or slight movement of parts. The plant expresses rest rather than motion; as a whole it is in a statical condition, yet not entirely so; as the animal expresses motion, yet not constant. In other words, Statics preponderates in the plant, Dynamics in the animal. And it is necessary that the plant should not feel pain, and that the animal should. For the plant is a mechanism of construction; whereas the animal is a mechanism of reduction: the plant supplies oxygen to the atmosphere; the animal withdraws it from the air; the plant deoxidizes, the animal oxidizes; and thus the former absorbs heat and electricity, while the latter produces both; and hence motion is necessary in the latter and unnecessary in the former. In other words, pain must move the animal that it may live. This is only another illustration of the unity and conservation of Force. It would be an unwarrantable assertion, however, to say all plants are devoid of all conscious thought. It is, however, asserted by many that no animal has thought but man. This is by confounding thought with a high expression of mind. But when we consider mind as mental force, thought is only the effect, the record of the action of this force, and may be conscious or not. Consciousness is secondary mental force; the image, as it were, of an active force which it itself beholds, as a man looking at himself in a mirror. If this image be retained, it is experience; and man reads in his experience the record of conscious sensations only as images of effects of active force on matter.

Unconscious force is that which acts without reflecting its effect upon itself. This may be either a material or mental force, which acts unconsciously; as in sleep there must be unconscious mental thought. But a purely material force is always unconscious, as the steam which pushes the piston rod in an engine. That is, it is unconscious to self, but may not be to other forces with which it is connected, as the engineer. In this manner it is easy to see how Infinite Consciousness may be an attribute of Infinite Force, made up of its finite conscious and unconscious parts. Each man who is capable of affirming consciousness of himself, and that he is only a part of a posited whole, must come to a conclusion that consciousness is an attribute of the whole. But if consciousness exists as a high or complex phase of force, as force it can never be lost; it may be counteracted for a time, and so sleep or rest unconscious, but can be evoked again; not only may be, but perhaps must be.

§. 2. But hunger we have said is the first conscious thought, and is one of sensation, and that sensation pain. But we have just stated that there is a great antagonism between the animal and vegetable forces. Taking a broader and more comprehensive view, we will see that the animal and vegetable kingdoms illustrate the action of but one force, in its positive and negative expressions, and may be illustrated by placing the two poles of a galvanic battery in water; the one will liberate oxygen, the other hydrogen, in definite ratio. It is thus by electrolysis we have the elements divided into their antagonistic or opposite states. In the animal we see the play of the positive part of the force predominating, and in the plant the negative. It thus also becomes evident that there is not only a relation between the animal and vegetable, but that the one implies the other, in origin as well as subsequent development, as they are but different expressions of the same force. Now, when the animal first said, "I am hungry," it only told that the force positive was predominating in it, *sufficient to produce motion* in its parts to supply the waste. That is, it becomes a self-acting force, capable of connecting the circuit between the vegetable and the animal, or connecting the positive and negative poles of this force. The break produces hunger; the connection satisfies. That is, when the animal is hungry it lacks food; but all food comes from the vegetable world. Hunger is therefore true, unmistakable speech, and may be illustrated by the telegraph. It is by a break, or combination of breaks, in the passage of the electric force, to complete its circuit, which constitute the words in telegraphy. Without these breaks there could be no speech. Well, Nature talks to her little animal in just the same manner, precisely on the principle of the telegraph. She breaks the circuit between it and the vegetable, and this break is the first sensation, called hunger.

§. 3. But now see what is the result. The first sensation is the first knowledge. It is the first blow given upon the head of sleeping Ignorance. Oblivious, negative, statical Ignorance is now disturbed; a few more blows awakens him, a greater number makes him complain, a still greater number moves him. That is, the animal is moved to search for food only through pain. How otherwise could it be moved to act? No one can imagine or guess. It had refused to act because held tightly in the arms of Rest, perfectly enamored of Statics, a senseless, unfeeling thing. The only way was to disturb it; to breathe into it the foe to its organism; to make it writhe with pain; to inaugurate Evil as a fact of its life. Here is the positive, the moving force. But where is the negative pole? How beautifully this manifests itself. Did not the little animal ask, when commanded to act, "But *how*, mother?" Here is the birth of morality, which comprehends knowledge. The world's morals are all bound up in that little word "how." It comprehends the word "ought." The "ought" is partial, and dimly visible to the scientific moralist; the "how" expresses all. "Mother, how shall I act?" What sympathy arises for the *hungry*, *ignorant* animal, asking that question to a parent, who responds: "I shall not tell you till you act." Here is the birth of sympathy. It goes forth in ignorance, driven by Pain, to find out not so much how to do, but what to eat. But the one implies the other. (We will not stop here to trace the animal in a developental sense, in which it is necessary that it should obtain food without locomotion, brought to it by currents of air or water, and then that the first locomotion must be in a buoyant fluid before land life, but pass to consider it only in a mental sense; and we will take the land animal, man, for the illustration.) If food is not immediately at his mouth, movement becomes necessary. But the first movement is accompanied with a fall, perhaps; the fall with another source of pain. Here he cries out "how?" How does Mother Nature tell him how? First she has tortured him into action, and then she begins a process of torturing to teach him how to act. "Step on this thorn and suffer; this will learn you to provide against it," expresses the whole command of life, from the cradle to the grave. Here we are driven to conclude that knowledge, as well as morals, are born of Evil. And it is because Nature withholds knowledge till it is obtained in the experience of Pain, yet compels us to seek it, that the questions how and why are asked; and the fear of pain is the beginning of wisdom as well as of morals.

§. 4. The Necessity of life compels us to act. This is force *compulsory;* we cannot evade it, change it, nor annul it. But Moral law is one of restraint. This is force discretionary. We may change, evade or annul it, till the *how* is obtained. It is one of trial and experiment. It only says, "Do nothing that you know to be wrong." It could not say more. It is negative, the force of restraint, and born of Evil; as is the command "Do or die!" on the other hand, positive—the force which impels onward—also born of Evil. And thus we return again to the one force of Evil, with its positive and negative expressions.

§. 5. But force must express itself. This we call its language. The meaning of Force is both moral and scientific. The word "how" expresses moral action; the word "why" expresses science. "*How* shall we act for our own good?" is the ever-repeated question of morals. "Why is this so?" is the ever-repeated question of Science. Morality, then, comes first, and applies to the individual force. Science comes later, and applies to the universal; and thus many may learn the moral of life long before they can comprehend its science. The law of morals, in fact, runs far down into the animal world; but doubtless few of the lower animals have ever asked "why?" And the question: "What is the cause?" is perhaps confined to but few men. The question "How?" is the incipient reason—the half-born question "Why?"—which may develop into "What is the cause?" Science is, therefore, preceded by Morality, and must be born of Theology, as will be fully shown hereafter.

§. 6. But Hunger, which is waste in the animal, evolves a universal law; or, rather, is a partial expression of such, namely: Waste must be restored, or what is consumed must be supplied. It is the law of *Supply and Demand.* This is plainly a polar force. Waste creates a demand; the demand calls for a supply. The waste is always accompanied with pain, the supply with pleasure. But first there must be Pain from Waste. But Pain is only the cry of Waste for more materials, and when the supply comes there is feasting, and merriment, and joy. How beautifully this illustrates every joy of life, every blessing, every pleasure, on the one hand, and every sorrow, every curse, every pain, on the other. With loss comes sorrow; with gain comes joy. When a child is born there is rejoicing; when it dies there is sorrow. And why? Birth and Death are opposite poles of Life. The one expresses waste, the other supply. It is the same law of Demand and Supply. Pain and Pleasure, then, are the two poles of this force, which expresses the law of Demand and Supply, and it is Pain which precedes Pleasure. It is the antecedent, the cause, and expresses the positive pole. And thus it must be concluded there is no pleasure in this world or the universe that does not come primarily in this way. All our pleasures lie superimposed upon pain, as the finer and softer earths lie superimposed upon their granite bed, and this upon the central fire. In fact, no one can trace back any pleasure of his own experience without finding some waste, some loss, some pain, for a starting point. The first sensation of the child when it comes into the world is pain. If we can judge anything from the actions of children, we must draw this conclusion. With the first breath is a cry. In rushes the foe, oxygen, to disturb the sleeping, statical lump of flesh which had been built up from other sources than that one which would ever force it to act. Till it breathed it was like the plant, unconscious. The cry was the echo of the first sensation, and doubtless conscious, but too feebly registered to be long retained, and so lost to memory. Memory is only a process of reading mental impressions, retained in the brain, which often, by injury, may be completely destroyed. Even the school education of a person has been obliterated by a blow, and when healed he had to relearn everything from the alphabet up.

§. 7. We will now readily understand how sensation will produce a mental faculty. Here we must define, but to define we must trace the origin of a faculty. Hunger, we have endeavored to show, is the first sensation, which means action and knowledge. But action involves the "How?" and the "Why?" as well as the Demand for Supply. How many faculties are included in these three words, How, Why, and Supply? Let us answer this question before we proceed to consider whether or not hunger would create them, and how it is a child is born with faculties before it experiences a sensation. We care not how many separate faculties may be attributed to man or how few to other animals, they may all come within his Intellectual, Moral, and Selfish nature. We wish to make the analysis apply to all animals, and we have thus used terms to suit all classifications. But "How?" expresses all sympathy and morality, as we have already seen, and "Why?" expresses all science and knowledge; and "Supply" generalizes every selfish desire, even our hunger and thirst after knowledge, righteousness, and future life. These three words all arise in the same fundamental cause; the result of one force Hunger, with the ever accompanying polarity, conflict and antagonism. "Now, my little animal, act!" "No, for Rest has bound me." "But I will *compel* you!" Now Waste enters upon its work, and the animal cries out in pain, "How?" and afterwards "Why?" We will briefly illustrate.

It is said man has acquisitiveness. Why so? To supply waste in the system. How caused? By primary sensation. And so has come those faculties, his love of food and property. But obstacles oppose him on every hand; he has to meet with difficulties and dangers; his food grows high and he cannot reach it; low in the earth and he has to dig for it; or in some place unknown to him and he has to search for it; and if not obtained in season he finds it is destroyed. Here are called into play new forces. To obtain food he finds life a battle; a continual war with the elements, and seemingly all Nature. He has to combat and destroy, step cautiously and secrete. And he evolves here the most selfish of his faculties, and writes over against them an "*instinct*" called the first law of life, "*Self Preservation.*" But again: another effect of the same law of Demand and Supply not coming from waste among atoms in the individual body, but from waste in the race, by death, gives rise to an irresistible passion to multiply. That is, Death implies birth. Here arise those faculties which imply the union of the sexes and the care of offspring. They are the result of an irresistible force, with its polarity of death and birth.

The author of a "New Theory of Population," has called attention to a remarkable feature of this law of Demand and Supply; namely, that the forces destructive and the forces preservative perpetually tend toward equilibrium, and vary inversely. That is, the lower the organism and the less capable of providing the means of subsistence, the greater the power of reproduction. This he amply illustrates from the vegetable and animal kingdoms. Beginning with the microscopic Infusoria in which the rate of multiplication is beyond compute, we find a constant ratio of decrease as we ascend in the animal world, till we come to man and the elephant, in which it is the least. From this law he concludes that eventually the rate of multiplication will be just equal to the rate of mortality. That is, the approach to equilibrium will never cease until on the average, each pair bring to maturity but two children. This is a view which all perfectionists must take. Those who believe that a perfect law can be given to man and that he will eventually be enabled to obey it, are logically driven to the above conclusion. But the question arises right here: Can man ever have the *power* on earth to prevent all the accidents to matter and man, or will he ever acquire sufficient knowledge to shun them by mental contrivance? It is quite obvious he must not only so perfect himself in science that he can foretell the "falling of lightning," or a meteoric stone, or else have power to control them; but also this knowledge or power must be made universal among mankind, even down to the sucking infant; for how is the young child to shun them but by knowledge acquired? or is the universal knowledge to be born with the child? Will the young child unborn be assured of the fact, that it will live out its full number of years, and that it is so provided for in wisdom that it is impossible for it to die till the day, hour and second are fulfilled? Shall there be no quarrel among men, no predaceous animal, no drouth or freshet, no railroad accident, no lost mariner of sea or air, no earthquake or volcanic eruption, no "strong wind," no lion to lie down with the lamb in this world? No rattlesnake, mosquito or fly; *no hunger or pain?* It would have to result in this and far greater perfection.

Now, what would be the result of all this perfection? *Perfect satisfaction,* the greatest catastrophe to man that could happen. As well open the earth at every spot on which a being stood, and let the central fire lick him in at once. The only difference would be in the means employed to extinguish him. It would be the embrace of death in inaction to make man perfectly satisfied. It is dissatisfaction which drives every wheel of industry, provides every mouthful of food, adds to the head every increment of knowledge; and it is dissatisfaction which keeps it there.

There are two causes which combine to drive metaphysicians and moralists into the above fallacy, affirming a limit to the perfect, and approaching it as a hound would overtake a hare. These are the causes of failure shown in their reasonings; but we are of opinion there is the crowning reason lying back of and out of which these grow; the failure to comprehend that man is the result of a positive and negative force, and, because finite, can never be in perfect equilibrium and live. A finite force is partial and related to other forces, which may control, influence or neutralize, but never destroy it.

§. 8. Let us now define a faculty, and then trace its development in some particular one, for a clear exposition of what we mean.

A faculty is the capacity to receive and reflect a definite sensation. The *kind* of sensation is its function, and names the faculty. Sensation is the motion of a disturbed organism. The knowledge of it is consciousness. For example: the faculty to distinguish colors is the capacity to receive impressions of the coloring ray of light. These impressions of the ray are the sensation; the kind of ray names the function. It may be said, then, man has a faculty of color, the function of which is to distinguish colors. But this is only produced by force. Intercepted, this force is retained. There is no escape for this motion of light; it does not pass through the organism, nor is it reflected therefrom. The sensation must, therefore, be retained in the organism as intercepted force. In other words, the force of sensation becomes latent. This is how a faculty may grow, or may be evoked, or transmitted. A faculty, then, may become an *organ of force*, which, when awakened or excited, must find *bodily* expression and reflect the sensation in consciousness. Those faculties which arise from the motion of light may be called the observing faculties. The faculty of music must arise from the motion of air. We have heretofore indicated how hunger will produce the selfish instinct, or those faculties which would protect the animal, and how Death would lead to the domestic faculties, evolving from waste in the body and waste in the race a law of *Demand and Supply*.

§. 9. We now pass on to debatable ground, to see if there be any "intuitive" faculty; that is, one which has come in any other way than through sensation. Let us take what is known as the "Religious faculty." And now, a few words of explanation before we proceed.

It is, perhaps, true that the word Religion cannot be defined, as but very few would agree as to what it is. It belongs to that class of words which express varying conditions in human affairs, such as knowledge, ignorance, morality, etc., and must itself change with the ever changing human race. It is one of those words which in meaning keep pace with man's growth, if not with all animal growth. To define Religion by generalizing a certain class of actions of the most civilized people on earth, into one expression, would not be a true definition, any more than to generalize a certain class of actions common to the most barbarous; nor could we stop here and affirm religion as certain actions common to all men, by finding and defining by that which was common to all men; for that which would be stricken off from the highest might itself be the very essence of the most civilized religion, and what would be left after this were taken away would not alone remain with the lowest type of man, but be found common to the ape and dog. To define religion by the superior, or inferior limit, is simply to affirm the utter failure at definition. To get at the truth we must go back to primary sensation; and herein the animal kingdom may not be the limit. Definition is here lost. Nor, on the other hand, can we stop with the highest type of civilized man. We must define so that all religious actions which shall come after may come within the definition. To define we have to circumscribe and limit. We may, however, classify both mentally and physically. As man is both a vertebrate and religious animal; that is he is possessed of a backbone, with its neural and hæmal arches, and he performs acts of religion. Now the vertebral characteristic of the animal is quite changeable, and varies widely in the snake and man; and thus also of the religious act. As there is a typical relation in the bony structure of the two, so there may be in the religious action, differing no more in the mental than in the physical. In fact man has done worse things, more hideous and brutal, in the holy name of religion, than it is possible for a rattlesnake to do, owing to its inferior development. Just where the animal act can be classed as religious, it is difficult to tell, perhaps impossible; as no one can tell just where fear passes into wonder, nor where wonder rises into worship. The religious principle is one of taming and domestication, but this only can come through intense pain and fear. To tame a wild beast you must begin by inflicting the severest pain. This produces an inordinate fear. This subsides into submission, and may develope in the offspring that faithful, confiding, obedient disposition, so manifest in the dog toward his master. The dog worships his master, and exhibits a devotion unparalleled by man to his god. He often defends his master with that ferocity with which Calvin defended his "Triune God." He will suffer and die for his master, and if the master smites, he crouches down and receives the blow with a devotion and submission becoming an ancient Christian, whereas he would rend any other person who treated him thus. He will even die worshipping the master, who in his passion slew the worshipper. If there is anything different from religion as exhibited in man in all this, we fail to find it. It is the nature of Force to reveal itself in animal consciousness, and having thus revealed itself, it compels its own worship. And when the animal acknowledges in action, and assents in reflection, to the existence of superior force, that assent and acknowledgment makes the animal a religious being in thought and deed. This develops into reverence—a feeling of inferiority in self—with its opposite pole of superiority conferred in other beings, or Being. This is worship. The actions which this worship produces is religion. What, therefore, is religion in one community, is not in another; what was religion in one age, was not in another; what is religion to-day, was not yesterday, and may not be to-morrow. It cannot be said that religion is that endeavor or observance which tends to make one better, for religious endeavors and observances often make people worse. Religion, in fact, has been the mighty engine of man's greatest cruelty, oppression and wrong. It has called human devils the servants of God, and mad men saints. The religious sentiment in itself is blind; it is an irresistable feeling; an impulse which may drive mankind into a lust after God. It is the mover of the will, and lies far back of the endeavor or observance. The effort to make one better is the product of Reason. There is design in this: it is action founded upon *cause and effect.* But religion is considered rather a duty toward God, an observance to please him, and any effect which it might have upon the *character* of man, *religion* entirely ignores. Should such consideration ever enter into religion, it is derived from Reason, and not the blind feeling of the religious faculty. The religious faculty is that one which prompts man to worship. But this involves the conception of a Supreme Being. It is thus the moralist who does not discard the word religion, yet who discards the popular notions of Deity, finds himself in conflict with the atheist on the one hand and the popular theologian on the other. The difficulty rests in the fact that *Morals* and *Theology* are as separate and distinct, as is the opinion of the propriety of certain human conduct and the speculations about an unknown being. And this is the real distinction between Morals and Theology. Now, religion may be considered on the one hand purely theological, and on the other hand purely humanitarian; or it may, in the third place, hold an indefinite relation to both. There must, therefore, ever be a quarrel between Morals and Theology in regard to this word religion, till Theology posits the Infinite Force and there passes into science. The faculty which prompts man to worship would still remain. The object of the worship only would be changed. Thousands already worship at no other shrine than Science.

§. 10. We assert that the feeling of fear is the primary cause of worship. We will indicate its mode of development, and then trace it in history.

Before fear there must be something to fear. This is pain. Or, in other words, Evil preceds and is the cause of Fear. The experience of pain produces the anticipation of harm. This anticipation of harm is not alone a sentiment of man; it is common to all animals, and is almost as necessary to life as food. It is the expressed command of Nature to the animal: "*Preserve thyself!*" From this comes every phase of instinct in the animal, as well as the development of far-reaching, provident thought in Reason and Genius. It doubtless sprung up originally with sensation in the demand for food called hunger, with the most inferior animal, and is the lowest or first expression of mental force. This first sensation must have been anterior to the development of ear, eye, or even a permanent mouth, when food might have been taken by absorption. Among the small microscopic Polygastric Infusoria we find, perhaps, the process by which animal mouths were made. The food, coming in contact with the body, sinks into it, and is enveloped by the surrounding mass closing over it, as a ball of tallow would sink into a kettle of soft soap, and be finally absorbed. Thus, Motion brought Feeling, and Feeling every organ of sense. Air and Sunlight brought Ear and Eye. It is said fishes have been taken from the Mammoth Cave without even the rudiment of an eye. These organs of sense are necessary to the body as it passes from the homogeneous mass to the heterogeneous organism. They are developed by external agencies, and produce, in their turn, mental faculties.

The anticipation of harm is perhaps the first reflection in the animal, for life depends on it. To be kept whole it must shun that which would destroy it; it must provide against cold and hunger; it must provide for and against both internal and external conditions. But this implies knowledge of its approach to danger; it implies a knowledge of Evil as a fact of life. It matters not what we call this knowledge—sensation, instinct, reason, intuition—it is simply knowledge, no more nor less: the effect of Force on Matter; and if intuition exists anywhere, it must be in the first sensation, which brings its knowledge; the first *reflection* of itself in the animal, *which is the first experience.* The numerous animals which sport in a drop of vinegar under the solar microscope are found to swim about, shunning each other, sporting with and fleeing from one another. The spider which weaves its web and lies in wait for its prey has the same kind of *knowledge* that the robber exhibits when he strikes down his victim in the wood or highway. The rabbit which runs from the dog exhibits the same kind of knowledge, or anticipation of harm, that the man does when he runs from a band of savage Indians who are pursuing him for his scalp. The cunning of the bear or fox that will spring a trap for the meat which is intended to betray them into it, by striking it with the paw at right angles to the jaws of the trap, exhibit about as much "genius" as a man would in like circumstances; and this act will show a process of ratiocination as full and complete as any abstract reasoning from cause to effect. Thought, and reasoning from effect to cause, will explain all the complex actions of the animal. Without it there is no explanation. Our actions themselves negative the assumption that animals are solely guided by a force which is not a conscious knowledge. The horse and dog receive our caresses. If they have no conscious knowledge, and cannot appreciate and reciprocate our affection, as well caress a stick or stone. The watch-dog at the gate bids his master welcome, and the stranger to wait outside. The wild habits of animals are lost in domestication, whether of man or wolf. Because an animal is very small, is no evidence that it has not much knowledge. The ant is less than the elephant, but we have no authority to say the ant knows less than the elephant, relative to their own plans of operation, any more than the force which makes an atom revolve is less than that which keeps the earth in its orbit. Nay, it may be easier to destroy the orbital motion of the earth than the orbital motion of one of its atoms; and for the same reason we have no more authority to affirm a mental force less strong when acting in a small man than when acting in a large one. The difference is only one of condition. We cannot measure experience with tape lines, nor gather thought in bushels. A very small and delicately organized woman of our highest culture, will experience more pain or pleasure in a moment, than a Hottentot would in a lifetime; and she might acquire more knowledge of science in a day, than it were possible for an Osage Indian to acquire in a lifetime, with head and body twice as large. But what has this to do with the development of worship? We shall see.

Wonder and *astonishment* in man have been produced by the experience of unexpected pain. But wonder is the incipient reason; it is the half-born question: What is the cause? The "why?" is involved in it. This is at first connected with primary sensations, and doubtless long remained closely related to physical pain, the "how?" governing all the animal's activities. *Now*, it is very easy to see, in a train of causes, that one force must beget another, the effect standing as the cause of what must follow. But at first this was not so; the effect was only studied. This, in fact, was all that was thought of, and "How shall I provide for myself?" was the all-absorbing question. But when the animal said "*I wonder*," it became a reasoning being: the cause was here conceived. Wonder is, then, taken from pure sensations of pain, and may be referred to every novelty in nature, from every unaccountable effect which is felt to those which are observed. Thus fear, which, from the primary sensations, was always connected with wonder, and doubtless antedated it in animal life thousands of years, became at last a constituent element in every unaccountable phenomenon; and the question which came so early in the development of man's thought, and which was born of Wonder: "What is the cause?" was answered in the first mental conception of cause by being personified in Being. This Being was the "God," the "Wonder-Worker," the "Hidden," the "Spirit of Fire," the "Sun," the "Air;" and when man had learned the use of the tool he had made, this Being became the "Great Artificer," the "Master Builder," and so on in the catalogue of names. But it could not be otherwise than that this being should be feared, for Fear and Wonder are twins of the same birth from the experience of unexpected and unaccountable pain. See how naturally this comes. The child, enlivened with sensation, is ushered into the world full of external realities. It feels: it knows not the meaning of these startling sensations of pain. Even its first sensation is pain, and whatever of pleasure that shall come after must lie on this bed. It sees: it knows not the meaning of these flitting shadows. It passes on through that stage, when it only asks "How?" till it reflects and asks "Why all this?" As the child passes upwards in years, older ones cannot answer the question. When grown, he looks within, and reflection is bewildered in the strange, and hidden, and awful mysteries of life. He seeks a cause without, and becomes dizzy treading the paths whereunto the imagination leads him. He wonders over a wonderful reality, and then names his god "Wonder-Worker," or "Hidden," or "Fire." But this "hidden" cause must be grasped by the senses. It is a real being, and not only feels and acts, but must have an abode, a real dwelling. The wonder-working god must hide away in objects, and reveal himself to man through the senses. And as man grows in knowledge, his god flits from object to object, ever taking higher forms, passing through terrestrial and celestial forms—ever hidden, yet active, till revealed in man himself; thence passing into infinite spirit, and thence into Infinite Force.

History seems to corroborate the above genesis of the god-thought. The first names of deity which have descended to us in history are those which express wonder, concealment, pain and fear. Ammon, which means hidden, is an old Egyptian god. Jupiter, a very modern god, always concealed himself and dwelt in the highest and most inaccessible parts of the earth. Jehovah never permitted himself to be seen, save in part, by the specially chosen medium of his commandments to man. Thus has come the saying: "No man can see God and live." To see God would be, it was thought, a fearful and most calamitous sight.

We affirm there can be no worship without some hidden and mysterious object to contemplate, and to search after with feelings of awe. Even the worshipers of Science exhibit a devotion worthy of a Moslem or ancient Christian. That the world's first worship came through fear is but an historic generalization. The early bibles of the world command the people to fear God; and as the first worship was Fetichism—the worship of a god in a thing, which the senses could grasp—stone, fire, sun or animal which contained the hidden "Wonder-Worker," those things themselves became sacred and objects of fear. When we study the history of the barbarous races of the world at the present time, we find fear the ruling element in their worship. It is fear which causes the tiger to be worshiped in many parts of the Old World. In Sumatra the people will not kill it, though it commits frightful ravages. It is fear which makes the inhabitants of Kamstchatka and Siberia pay reverential respect to bears. It is fear which calls forth the priest in Abyssinia to pray over the skin of a hyena, and to thus exorcise the enchanter within it. It is fear which prostrates the Guebre of Persia before the fire on its altar.

In the worship of fire there is a prominent religious fact which runs far back into the history of man. The Guebres affirm Zoroaster brought fire from heaven, and they keep it continually burning in temples erected to the *one* god. The Sun they affirm is his eye. The Ancient Druids also worshiped the fire, and like the Guebres, they had no idols, but the human sacrifice often ascended in the *flame.* They had two yearly festivals of fire, the one in May, "The fire of God," and the other in November, "The fire of Peace." But these festivals of fire were perhaps in honor of the Sun.

That fire should have been worshiped is most natural and evident from the genesis of the god-thought. There is the unaccountable thing called fire. It is a subtile foe, or a warming, cheering friend. To the untutored mind it is an object of fear as well as pain. The Hidden cause is the Being of Fire. And this Being becomes at once an object of worship. The early mind reached out in speculations upon the origin of fire, always reasoning upon some theological hypothesis: for so great a blessing must have been bestowed by the god of fire, or else the god was really in it. The Grecian fable of Prometheus, who, with the aid of Minerva, the goddess of wisdom, went up to heaven and lighted his torch at the charriot of the Sun, is perhaps the finest illustration in point. But if we leave the fable to the beauties of that realm whereunto the imagination leads, and descend into the region more of fact than fancy, we might go back to the early time which now lies hid in the unfathomable past, and behold the untutored animal, we may give the name of man to distinguish him from what is still below him in animal life, picking up two flints and striking them together. There now comes flashing from the lips of those stones, the burning words of *Force*,—"This is the revelation of fire to thee, oh, man!" He drops them in amazement, and trembling in wonder and fear, falls down and worships his god—this god of fire concealed in the stone. Here is, perhaps, the true Prometheus of history. What speculations upon the "Hidden," the "Wonder Worker," the "Spirit of Fire," must arise from this simple display of *Force!* What gods may grow out of it! What oft repeated stories! What legends of god-man! What poems of history and theology shall descend from it! The worship of God in a stone is the most natural and irresistable effect of such a display of Force,—when there is not that being on earth who can give the true hypothesis. This worship expresses the first hypothesis of *science.* Without this it is impossible for us to imagine how *science* can come to man. *Fetichism*, the conception of a god in a thing, is the first hypothesis to account for *Force.* This is the parent of every subsequent hypothesis in science; and without this there would be no science to-day. "Why does this fire come from the stone?" asks the untutored savage, little dreaming that this question will shoot its fiery rays of thought far up through the countless ages, culminating in art and science, guiding man's head to knowledge, and his hands to comfort. "Why is this so?" asks the savage. It matters not how he answers this question—he cannot answer it wrong. If he say it is the god acting, the same may be said to-day of *Force.* And if he falls down and worships the god, it is only worship paid to *Science* at its birth.

Is it called superstition? There are the seeds of

science in every belief which rises to the dignity of an hypothesis about God; and time was when they were indispensible. The superstitions of the world have retained within them the germs of all Science. As a walnut, made up of its bitter rind and still harder shell will contain and preserve the germ of a future tree, so also Superstition has been the rind and hard shell which has ever preserved the germs of Science, and in which Science has been transferred from people to people, and from place to place, taking new root in different soils of the world. But let us now ascend from Fetichism, taking one more step.

§. 11. Fear made the mother cast her child a prey to a beast. Fear bent the necks of men beneath the Juggernaut. Fear kindled the fire which consumed the human sacrifice offered to this god of Fire; nay it tore from the hearthstone the nearest and dearest to appease the avenging wrath of this "Hidden" god.

We are told in Grecian story how Agamemnon, just before departing from Beotia to attack Troy, while hunting in the forest, killed a stag which was sacred to the goddess Diana. Whereupon the army was visited with pestilence. Cálchas, a priest who stood as mediator between men and the gods, thereupon declared that the wrath of the goddess could only be appeased by the sacrifice of a virgin on her altar—and none but the daughter of the offender—himself a war-god among the Grecians.

The maiden was brought; the altar prepared; the priest, with knife in hand, was ready to perform the religious rite; when lo! Iphigenia, for that was the virgin's name, was snatched away by the goddess and a hind left in her place. We read a modified version of this story in "Jephtha's daughter," and in the arm of Abraham being stayed and a ram left in the place of Isaac.

But we may come nearer home than Grecian or Hebrew fable, and follow the early religious thought of our own forefathers, the early inhabitants of Western Europe. The same wild and awful god-thought was theirs; the same dread superstition hung over the land; the same fear sent them trembling in the same sacrificial rites before their altars. That beautiful poem by Alfred Tennyson, entitled *The Victim*, describes the human sacrifice to the gods Thor and Odin, who gave their commands to the priest to take the king's nearest and dearest, his only son.

And why was all this? It was surely a higher phase of worship than Fetichism. It is not difficult to tell. Any natural yet unaccountable phenomenon was thought to be the work of Deity. But if it came like a scourge, as in pestilence, famine or the like, it was considered a *special* visitation. But why scourge a people? Not knowing that scourges obey natural laws, and may be provided against as one may provide against hunger, they were attributed to the wrath of Deity. To stop the scourge was only to appease Deity. But why offer up the nearest and dearest? Because the most painful for man to do so. Here is the reasoning, and it is just as conclusive as logic can make it. If Deity sends pestilence, he must be angry at man. But if he sends pestilence because he is angry, he *delights* to see man suffer pain. Therefore, if we inflict the most severe pain on ourselves, and tell him it is to appease him, he will be delighted in seeing us suffer; he will be appeased and stop the pestilence. Newton's reasoning, which affirmed the law of gravity, was no more conclusive than this.

When theology could be brought to the stern logic of human sacrifice, the Reason of man was grappling with *First Principles*. At this stage of man's development, Science was not only possible, as in the incipient "why?" of Fetisch worship, but it was *actual*. It had not only taken root, it had put forth the shoot. Nothing but to destroy all theological speculations could ever root it out of man.

The religion which compels a worshiper to offer up his only child to his god is the most sincere. That man who can do this is a true worhiper of his god. This requires the greatest self-sacrifice, for the tie which connects the parent to the child is the strongest. At this point *Fear* culminates, and must thereafter forever diminish. But at this point also Science is born, in *Logic*. True mental ratiocination shall ever grow therein. This will divide the one person supreme into many parts, and distribute his power. Then will science forever grow.

Now, it was faith in the Reason of man which compelled those early worshipers to offer up the human sacrifice. It was by obeying *Logic*, the stern god of the head which brought those evils of *religion*, so prevalent among the early races of the world, so common among all races of low development, and so general among mankind everywhere when ignorant of the true nature of *Force*. It is Force which has been worshiped throughout the ages, whether revealed in stone or book; and when perceived by the senses and interrogated by Reason, the answer which came back to man as the word of God has ever been the conclusion which *Logic* has given him from the premises supplied by the senses, when trying to grasp the nature of Force. Nor could science have come in any other way than through the god-thought. Nor could it have come without those terrible evils which have so afflicted the world. Science, in fact, has not only been born of Theology, but, like a wayward child, Theology has cradled it in affliction, has beaten it at school, spurned it from her presence when grown, immured it in dungeons, and, in the hope of destroying it in the world, has often driven its devotees to the scaffold or stake. And why must Science be thus scourged? Before we answer this question, let us take one more step in the development of the world's worship.

§. 12. From the worship of the Fire-god which spoke out of the stone, perhaps in the age of Stone, naturally came the transferring of the god, which is only Force, to other objects which are themselves active agencies in Nature. Thus the Sun would be truly a Fire-god. The air would be an invisible Spirit. Hence the Latin, *spiritus*, which means air. This would give life, for the living breathe it, and to be deprived of it is death. Hence it would be deemed sacred, and called *The Holy Spirit.* And then taking a wider range of thought, this principle of Force, which is everywhere manifest, would confer upon each department of Nature a presiding god or goddess. And we have Grecian theology. This is a great advance above Fetichism. It is an advance from the simple to the complex. The homogeneous mass has now become a heterogeneous organism. This must inevitably develop science, and to destroy this theological speculation would indeed destroy the science of this people.

And it is necessary that the god-thought should be thus divided to evolve science; for although Force is an infinite unit, it only manifests itself partially and in a special manner to man. He must become acquainted with the simple and special manifestations of Force before he can understand the complex or grasp the universal. He has to build on a foundation of thought older than his own,—a foundation strong and suitable, yet rough and unhewn; and he can never ascend to the constructing architect till he has passed through the practical mechanic: he can never be a poet till he has been a great sufferer; never a painter till he has been a great observer; never an ideal thinker till he has been a practical worker. And it is when the god-thought passes from the tyranny of one idea to the complex conception of many gods that a genesis of science is possible, inasmuch as this unfetters the mind and renders it less subject to the control of Fear.

From the above conclusion it is easy to see how the stern mandate of Logic, which compelled man to offer the human sacrifice in obedience to his fears, was countermanded in human reason even without a knowledge of the true nature of Force, or without conferring less revengeful attributes upon Deity. See how this came about.

§. 13. The human sacrifice was superceded by the sacrificial beast. Yet man must propitiate the god through his fears in this also.

Among the Grecians the sacrificial beast was decorated with flowers, and the person who offered the sacrifice wore a garland around his head. Here we see the dawn of the esthetic in man's nature, for the love of the beautiful is a growth like all other emotions, as truly as is knowledge itself. Before he begins, he washes his hands in pure water, "typical of washing away the sins of the soul." As the flowers which adorned his head prophesied the coming fruit, so the water prophesied the pure man. In fact, the esthetic is only the prophesy of the fairer, the purer, the better in the world which man feels within him, and he baptizes himself with water and the "Spirit of Fire" as emblematic of the purer man. He now approaches the altar with his offering. Here he has brought the first-born or choicest of his herd or flock. In solemn reverence and implicit faith he lifts the head of the beast heavenward; he applies the knife to the throat, catches the blood in a bowl, and secures a sanctification through *blood.* And why? Because the blood was thought to be the life of the animal, and he has offered a *life* to his god. This notion was common to all ancient peoples who offered sacrifices to their gods. The legs of the animal are inclosed in fat and burnt on the altar with wine and incense, and while the savor of the flesh ascends to heaven the ceremony is accompanied with prayer and music.

That wine should be a necessary accompaniment in the religious ceremony is by no means devoid of meaning. In the early times wine was not typical, as now; but it was thought to be the real blood of a god. Doubtless many of the early Christians thought so; and if not really so when it came from the grape, that the priest had the power to transform it into the real blood of Christ. But among the Grecians the interference of a priest was not necessary. Wine was the blood of the grape, and the vine was the sacred plant of the god Bacchus, whose real blood was in the grape. Now this blood came through the direct rays of the Sun-god, warming, cheering, beautifying and fructifying the earth. Hence, the wine was held sacred because divine in its origin and mysterious in its effects. It was most natural, therefore, to use it upon religious occasions, at first as a real and at last a typical offering.

This also marks an era in the progress of religious ideas. It marks the passage from the real, in the sacrificial rite, to the typical. It was adopted as that article which most resembled blood or life, and at first must have been though to be the *real* blood of life; for it was too bold a step to pass at once from the real to that which is only typical. But eventually, when the nature of Force became more generally understood, and the wonderful and miraculous effects of wine became quite *natural*, instead of the blood this wine would become typical only of blood. At this point the sacrifice entirely disappears, save in the Catholic Christian church, where the wine is thought to be changed into the *real* blood of Christ, who offered himself a sacrifice for a whole world. But with the Protestant this wine is only used as typical. It is thus the sacrificial child, virgin, man and beast are no longer slain nor brought to the altar. This rite passes gradually away, culminating in the typical wine. Thus we see a gradual ascent from the sacrifice to God of the first-born son of the king up to the less favored or esteemed human victim,—to the first of the flock or herd, then to any animal which had blood, till we come to that which only typifies blood, the juice of the grape from the god-plant the vine, which is smiled upon by the Sun-god of the world.

In this gradual ascent we see his fears gradually giving way, and the finer and higher sentiments growing stronger, and influencing the conduct of man.

It is thus the religious world is forever appeasing the stern god of the head Logic, by a continual offering of the "typical" and "emblematic" sacrifices. It must some day see that the whole religious history of the world is only typical of Science, and all the god-names are only symbols of Force.

§. 14. As the primitive conception, like all subsequent conceptions of God, was purely human—that is, conferring human attributes—it was a most natural and easy step from Fetichism to make man a god. This doubtless first transpired in connection with some man—a leader, a brave or strong man—who could perform physical feats beyond the ordinary powers of man; for Force, it must be kept in mind, it is that is worshiped, whether it be of head or hand. He thus became the hero, who was looked up to by those who knew him; was followed and *feared*, and when dead worshiped. He became the mighty man of the chase or battle; when he dies he only goes away to return again, and the funeral ceremony became a religious rite. His memory would be held sacred, and after generations, hearing the story from parental lips, would magnify his powers and works, till at last the story of a wonder-working god, with name and history, descends to the world. The name of the gods would thus become "The Strong," "The Mighty in Battle," "The Man of War," "The Destroyer." The attributes of savage natures would be conferred in the assertions: "Vengeance is mine," "Blood cryeth from the ground," "I will rejoice to destroy you." Even the ancient Scandinavians conferred upon their gods the "sacred duty of blood revenge." Jupiter was the father of gods and men, the great Thunderer who dealt out the lightning to suit his fancy. This was his weapon and the symbol of his strength. Mars drives his chariot of war, and Apollo his chariot of the sun. Vulcan is the great artificer of heaven, and Mercury its swift-winged messenger. Hercules performs physical prodigies, and is honored with a seat among the gods. The ocean has its Neptune, and the central fire its Pluto. Thus the Grecians gave to each department of Nature a presiding god or goddess; but these gods were only mighty men.

The same anthropomorphitic notion is seen in all early theology, both East and West. For example, we read in Genesis how the sons of God saw the daughters of men that they were fair, and from this was born a race of giants; but the Teutonic version is, that the marriage was between the daughters of the gods and the sons of men, which produced the strong men of the world. Pluto says the Etheopians represent their gods with flat noses and black complexions, while the Thracians give them blue eyes and ruddy complexions. The North American Indian has a great Indian for a god. And thus it has ever been; men project their own image on the infinite back-ground, and worship it as god. That is, Force is taken as the god; the attributes of the god are only those of men. Perhaps the true method of the genesis of the god-thought may be summed up as follows: The Promethean savage of the age anterior to the Stone, struck fire from two flints, which he fell down and worshiped as his god; and in after ages, for his discovery, became a god himself, who has been honored in many a fiery name and feast of flame. From these two things came the world's worship. Fire became the symbol of divinity. Its festivals have been many a time honored from of old; the objects it represented manifold,—from sun and moon, and fire of earth, to the red blood of man and beast,—appearing at last in the blood of the vine, the intoxicating beverage of the gods, and symbol of the blood of God to-day.

In all this progress through the countless ages of worship, from Fetichism to Symbolism, it is quite obvious there has nothing been worshiped but Force, the highest form of which has the attributes of man. But the investigation into the nature of *Force* has evolved Science. The theologic thought was only to give Force a Being—to make it a material essence; and this, again, has been the history of Force from Kepler's spirits, who kept the planets in their orbits, down to latent fluid heat, or the spirits of alcohol. The theologic notion has forever hugged the idea of Force. But when Science affirms the Infinite Force, manifesting itself in each atom, Theology must ascent, and posit this as the God; for there can be but one Infinite Force. Theology will then have passed into Science, and the world's worship will have a transmutation as gradual and complete as that of the bloody rite of human sacrifice into the harmless sacrament of the symbolic wine. In fact, it is when this wine religion shall have passed away, that Science shall be enthroned. At this juncture it will be the sole office of the religious faculty to apply Science to human conduct, and evolve from Morals a science of life. This might be truly termed a scientific morality, or religion. But Theology and Morals are separate and distinct. Theology is the incipient science. It is the struggle of the Reason to grasp the cause, the hidden, the nature of Force under its god names. It must pass away with Science. But Morality has to do with the conduct of man; and as man is a growth with evervarying conditions, it must forever remain with man; forever paint its ideals of Beauty, and Love, and Wisdom; forever interrogate Science; forever ask: "How shall I escape this evil?" A true Religion will never come until it thus assumes a scientific form. A worship of the Universal Force, with no other forms and ceremonies than the manipulation and exhibition of this Force in finite expression: the lecture room the church, and the scientific lecture the Sunday sermon.

§. 15. Nor can we escape the god idea in the scientific affirmation of Infinite Force, for the following reasons:

1. Intelligence is a fact in the universe, because exhibited in man. But man is a finite expression of Force, mentally, physically, or any way he may be viewed. Man is a part, then, of Infinite Force. But as man is not the only part of Infinite Force, we may reasonably affirm intelligence, in the infinite other parts.

2. To deny the existence of Infinite Intelligence, is simply to deny *all* human knowledge. *Infinite Intelligence cannot therefore be denied.* But the universe *manifests power.* That is, we *know* there is power in the universe, else it would not be manifested. But this is simply Force expressing itself—literally telling man *it is*, and *he is*, and he *knows it is.* Now if this does not *prove* an acting *intelligence* in Nature, both in and outside of man, then nothing can ever be proved by human reason. And in fact this is above and superior to human reasoning; it is the effect of primary sensation, that which evolves

the first knowledge. It is the germ cells of human Reason. The first experience upon which all deduction rests, and where all knowledge begins.

3. Now the ancients called this manifestation of power in the world the god or the gods. If taken as a unit it was called god, if considered as exhibited in each department of nature, the gods. And what can we affirm to-day in the light of science more consonant with Reason than to say: The Infinite Force is intelligent, and is God.

4. This Infinite Force can only be known by man in part. But the *part* proves the existence of the whole. If we know a part of something exists, we *must affirm* the existence of the whole. But the power of the universe is manifested upon so large and grand a scale, we are lost in the contemplation thereof, and to satisfy the ultimate of Reason we posit the infinite. This is the absolute idea. But all possible conceptions, that is the conferring of attributes, must forever fail. There is infinity beyond all human conceptions. Force is infinitely powerful and Intelligent; *this is God.* The God of Science.

5. The above hypothesis must destroy the long continued wrangle about "Nature and God." If Nature be considered the display of Force acting on matter, the *action* being regular, necessitated, and fixed, this would only be saying God reveals himself in matter, through fixed laws. No other hypothesis of a perfect God is possible. And what has been called the *Power* of God, in the Universe, is only

Force acting on matter. Power of God equals Force. Power of God manifesting himself in Nature would read: Force acting on matter. It is only necessary to give the Force intelligence to make the god idea complete.

6. There is a fallacy afloat, often appearing in popular theological discussions, affirming that we cannot possibly know *anything* of God. This may have come from an entire misunderstanding of Herbert Spencer when he affirms: "the power which the universe manifests is utterly inscrutable." *So it is;* but no one has the right to say, therefore, we know nothing of the power of the universe. The power which moves an atom of oxygen is utterly inscrutable; yet we may affirm many effects of this power. The power which evolves conscious thought is utterly inscrutable; yet we *know* thousands of things about conscious thought. Force is utterly inscrutable; but we can affirm many things of Force, and know its modes of operation. The ultimate atom is utterly inscrutable. Nobody knows *anything* of an atom of oxygen; cannot tell its size, shape, color or motion. Yet, are we compelled to say from this that therefore we know nothing of its effects? When we try to investigate the nature of either Force or Matter—that is, to find out *what* they are—we find them utterly inscrutable. Yet they make known their *existence* in consciousness. *They manifest themselves.* *We* do not make them reveal themselves. We do not fix ourselves

into such a mental condition that we can grasp them and know of their existence. We are not the *actors* in this, but the *recipients* of knowledge. It is *they* who make themselves known. Surely this is utterly inscrutable. So that not only the God of the universe is not only inscrutable, but so also is his revelation in man.

CHAPTER VI.

HOW THEOLOGY EVOLVES SCIENCE.

§. 1. We are now prepared to indicate the method in which Theology evolves Science. We have heretofore shown that Theology was born of Fear and Wonder; that Pain and Evil must precede it. Now, if it can be made apparent that Science has a necessary historic relation to Theology, the scientific meaning of Evil may be somewhat inferred. We have also already seen that Grecian theology was one of many gods; that different expressions of Force were represented therein; and instead of being central and unitary, the god-thought was thus widely distributed. The legitimate result of this is, it must destroy the tyranny of Fear, which leads to theological control; for man may choose the god from among many which he is specially to worship. Religious worship becomes thus divided up, and the mind is at liberty to speculate upon the manifold operations of Force, and thus may assign different causes for the many effects which are witnessed therein.

Perhaps the first great step towards mental freedom was the notion that the gods faught among themselves. This warfare among the gods was plainly derived from that antagonism which is everywhere prominent in Nature. The forces of earth and sky warred against each other; the winds and waters and thunders were seemingly in a tumultuous uproar. Conferring the attributes of men, they were subject to anger, and their anger was not alone directed against men. There might be different opinions held by the gods, and a division in their councils which led to open rebellion. But if the gods could hold different opinions, and go to war over them, surely men would be justified in doing the same. This would open up the way to that mental conflict which must ever evolve Truth, and which it is impossible to imagine could come in any other way. And when this mental conflict was conducted in a measure free from death, it could only be so defended by an appeal to the conduct of the gods. Polytheism must therefore lead to the broadest and most diverse speculations upon all the phenomena of Nature. It is not alone sufficient to say: "And there was war in Heaven, and *one* god conquered and ruled ever after with a rod of iron;" but the battle must be left undecided. The command: "Thou shalt have no other gods before me," if enforced upon a nation must fetter the mind and squelch all scientific speculation in that people. For, we affirm, theologic speculation is only the incipient science, the "why?" being there first evolved. We must, therefore, look for the greatest advance of science among that people whose worship is the most polytheistic, and the least advance among that people whose worship is the most monotheistic. As examples of these we take Grecian and Jewish theology. We will first take up the Grecian thought, and see what that accomplished in one department of science, Astronomy, before we treat of the other and its relation and influence on Christian thought.

§. 2. When Xenophanes, the old Grecian poet, went out at night, and looking into the vast depths beyond, sang to the stars with low chant and four-stringed lyre, he was singing the natal song of Astronomy. Without this song, and poetic frenzy, and zeal of a "speculative madman," perhaps the science as known to man would not have been.

This song was a hymn to the god of the stars, who directed the throng in infinite space, and who was himself the *center of all.*

But primarily the germ cells of astronomy lie in the first contemplation of the stars. That they should have been contemplated is only to say people have eyes and must observe; that sight will produce sensation and sensation thought; that thought will return and reflect its own self and *wonder*, and then ask "Why?" But contemplation alone would not answer this question, nor would song bring the answer. There must be a basis for it to rest on in human knowledge, independent of the star or stellar phenomena. In its broadest sense that basis is Mathematics, which comprises *number and equality*. But this is again only "*Diversity in Unity*," the ever-repeated expression of the Universe, the Infinite Force acting on divisible matter.

But Number was at once thought to be divine. Pythagoras said: "Number is the Infinite, the substance of all things." This was his god. But Equality, we have seen, is only a law of Force—its undisturbed and definite expression. This is not only the basis of mathematics and of mechanics, but we may trace it throughout the whole social organism—family, church, state—and we will find it the basis of all just legislation and government, as it is the basis of all reasoning,—the very substance of *Logic*. But this Law of Equality, this definite expression of Force, was considered *Divine* also, and a special deity made to rule over it.

The peculiar phase of Grecian astronomy was that of the spherical heavens, which at last materialized the stars, which had hitherto been considered either as real gods or the panoply of the heavenly host. The sky, to all appearances, is a concave sphere, and to suppose the stars fixed therein, and the sphere revolving about the earth, turning upon an axis, one pole of which was at or near the north star, would make the conception full and complete. The origin of this notion outdates history. It perhaps took ages to complete this thought. The Greeks inherited this hypothesis, together with the history of the week, the days of which were presided over by the sun, moon, and five planetary gods.* When the course of the sun was traced on the concave surface of this revolving sphere, and the constellations of the Zodiac named, a step was taken in astronomy which insured it to coming ages. It was then, as Pliny remarks, that the gates of Nature were opened. Plutarch says, Pythagoras was the author of this discovery. This was the fact that the sun travels in a circle obliquely situated with regard to the circles in which the other stars move about the poles. This gave rise to all the technical terms used to-day with regard to a globe,—pole, axis, equator, tropics, arctic and antarctic circles, equinoxial and solsticial points, zodiac, horizon,—all having local relation to the sphere, its circles, and the various movements of the sun and stars.

Now, see what this led to. It could not have been otherwise than that the earth should have been pronounced globular. It is said Anaximander, who invented the Grecian sun-dial, held the opinion that the earth was globular. This was six hundred years before the Christian Era. Whether this be so or not, we do know that Aristotle, the great logician and naturalist, the deepest thinker, closest reasoner, the greatest investigator of physical science, the

* We refer the reader to lecture on "Sunday," p. —, for a history of the Week.

the brightest star of the Grecian galaxy, believed it and taught it. Here is his argument, nineteen hundred and fifty years before Copernicus repeated it: "As to the figure of the earth, it surely must be spherical; and, moreover, from the phenomena, according to the sense; for if it were not so the eclipses of the moon would not have such sections as they have. For in the configuration, in the course of a month, the deficient part takes all different shapes: it is straight, and concave, and convex; but in eclipses it always has the line of division convex. Wherefore, since the moon is eclipsed in consequence of the interposition of the earth, the periphery of the earth must be the cause of this by having a spherical form. And again: from the appearance of the stars, it is clear not only that the earth is round, but that its size is not very large; for when we make a small removal to the south or to the north, the circle of the horizon becomes palpably different, so that the stars overhead undergo a great change in position, and are not the same to those who travel to the north and to the south. For some stars are seen in Egypt or at Cyprus, but are not seen in the countries to the north of these; and the stars that in the north are visible while they make a complete circuit, there undergo a setting. So that from this it is manifest not only that the form of the earth is round, but also that it is a part of not a very large sphere; for otherwise the difference would not be so obvious to persons making so small a change of place. Wherefore we may judge that those persons who connect the region in the neighborhood of the Pillars of Hercules with that towards India, and who assert that in this way the sea is *one*, do not assert things very improbable. The mathematicians who try to calculate the measure of the circumference make it amount to 400,000 stadia; whence we collect that the earth is not only spherical, but is not large as compared with the magnitude of the stars."

Long before the Christian Era, also, the earth was said to revolve on its axis, and also around the sun. Upon this point let us transcribe the words of Copernicus: "I found in Cicero that Nicetas held that the earth was in motion, and in Plutarch I found that some others had been of that opinion; and his words I will transcribe, that any one may read them: 'Philosophers in general hold that the earth is at rest, but Philolaus, the Pythagorean, teaches that it moves round the central fire in an oblique circle, in the same direction as the sun and moon. Heraclides, of Pontus, and Ecphantus, the Pythagorean, give the earth a motion, but not a motion of translation; they make it revolve like a wheel about its own center from west to east.'" We also find that Archimedes states that his contemporary, Aristarchus, of Samos, asserted that the earth had not only a yearly motion about the sun, but also a diurnal rotation on its axis. That this hypothesis existed is further proven from the fact that Aristotle argued against it. Ptolemy also argued against the diurnal motion of the earth. Cicero also believed that Mercury and Venus revolved about the sun. This surely renders the work of Copernicus not the first in discovery, and which shows an ancestral foundation on which he stood higher and stronger by far than he was aware of. These Grecian opinions, however, were only entertained by the few, and the astronomical conclusions were that the heavens and earth were spherical—the earth the center, and the heavens and earth revolving about it. This was the condition of astronomical science at the time of Ptolemy, who lived in the Second century.

§. 3. As the origin of all worship arose in fear, and the sun and moon were considered by the early untutored mind to be gods, and especially the sun to be a god of fire, the fire having at first caused pain, it therefore could not well be otherwise than that any unusual occurrence connected with the sun and moon should be looked upon with dread. Hence, an eclipse was a thing of superstitious fear. This, above all things, would be noted and remembered.

We find at Babylon, nearly four hundred years B. C., the Chaldeans had tables of eclipses. And the story is perhaps true, that at the time of Alexander's conquest, the Chaldeans possessed a series of observations which went back nineteen hundred years, and which Aristotle commanded Callisthenes to bring to him in Greece. It was the analytic and generalizing head of Aristotle that reasoned so well and soundly on these tables. Two hundred years after this, Hypparchus took these tables and reduced the motion of the moon to rule; and so accurate was his deduction, we find Cleomedes, in the time of Augustus, saying that "we never see an eclipse happen which has not been predicted by those who made use of the tables."

So much for the Grecian thought, and what it accomplished in astronomical science. We have left unsaid anything about Euclid and Archimedes, the mere mention of whose names will suggest to the student large fields traversed in mathematics and mechanics, by hundreds of deductive heads unknown to history, which these two men only represent. We will now pass to consider the effect of monotheism upon physical science.

§. 4. From Ptolemy to Copernicus there was no advance in astronomy. This is called the *stationary period*, and occupies thirteen hundred and fifty years.

But that there is any such thing as a stationary period we may well doubt. The human mind seems to have an historic ebb and flow, like the ocean, but a stationary period is something not known to history. Mankind may not progress in some one or many branches of thought, but they compensate it in some one or many other directions.

We are also led to seriously doubt that mankind retrograded in the Middle Ages. There was only a warfare against Physical sciences, and more especially Astronomy. But this warfare certainly strengthened the reasoning faculty of man. If Astronomy suffered, Logic gained thereby. Never before was the mind so sharp and subtle, as we see exhibited in these metaphysical discussions of the Neoplatonic School, when even the *Virtues* were arranged in physical, moral, purificatory, theoretic, and theurgic orders. Socrates or Plato could not boast of greater analytic or synthetic powers than this school exhibited in her Proclus and Plotinus. Not even Aristotle could boast of a more logical head than we find among Scholastic philosophers of after times, when the monastery formed the cradle of modern philosophy.

We find, also, that there were many discoveries to be accredited to the so-called stationary period; glass, gunpowder, type, the compass, and many more, of which gunpowder alone did more to immediately advance civilization than all the discoveries of the ancients; and the mariner's compass not only opened up the highways of the ocean, and proved the Grecian theory of the earth to be true, but it unsealed the lips of thought, which Christianity had closed.

It is impossible that there should have been a stationary period. A Dark Age in regard to Astronomy there undoubtedly was, but this was only the night in which Physical Science slept. When it awoke it was refreshed, and arose to gird on the armor of experimental battle. As there is unconscious cerebration while we sleep, so also that force which was to evolve Physical Science was active, all unconscious though it slept.

§. 5. What was the cause of the Dark Ages? We affirm, it was the theologic spirit of the age, which made a central tyranny of the Church. The god-thought was not allowed to branch out from the Christian Catholic trunk. In fact, the Polytheism of the world was called pagan, and so lopped off from the religious tree of Christendom. All there was of it was a great hollow trunk, trifurcated at the top. The hollow trunk was the church in which alone the pope presided; the branches were Jesus and Mary and Jehovah. It never bore a leaf or a flower, much less the fruit of science, save *Logic*, which is the primary necessity of Theology. Around the barren trunk the world revolved. All minds were stricken down with fear. People were compelled to go up to pay tribute to the church; were compelled to acknowledge the Pope as authority, and were made to swear by tradition under penalty of eternal death, which was torment without end, that outside of this there was no god.

There was a three-fold tyranny connected with this: the Jewish conception of Jehovah, with his command: "Thou shalt have no other gods before me,"—the Bible as the only and infallible word of God,—and the Pope as its only holy and infallible interpreter. The carnal Reason of man had therefore to bow to this theologic tyranny. All that could possibly be evolved in science from this tyranny, was that which comes directly from metaphysical speculation.

The first notion, therefore, was, as soon as Christianity became a fixed religion, that physical and spiritual things conflicted; that the light and transitory things of time must be banished from the mind. And so says Eusebius, the great light and authority of the church: "It is not through ignorance of these things admired by them, (the natural philosophers,) but through contempt of their useless labor that we think little of these matters, turning our souls to the exercise of better things." And Lactantius, of the same century, the Third, pronounces the investigation of physical causes "empty and false." He also administered a withering rebuke to the cultivators of astronomy, as follows: "To search for the causes of natural things; to enquire whether the sun be as large as he seems; whether the moon is convex or concave; whether the stars are fixed in the sky or float freely in the air; of what size and of what material are the heavens; whether they be at rest or in motion; what is the magnitude of the earth; on what foundations it is suspended and balanced,—to dispute and conjecture on such matters, is just as if we chose to discuss what we think of a city in a remote country, of which we never heard but the name." This was surely a withering rebuke to the man who thought about the ground on which he trod, or about the sunbeam which gladdened his eye; and when it came as a sort of God's command, it was necessarily connected with fear, and must intimidate.

This Christian divine tries to destroy the Grecian hypothesis of the sphericity of the earth by exclaiming: "Is it possible that man can be so absurd as to believe that the crops and trees on the other side of the earth hang downwards, and that men there have their feet higher than their heads." Saint Augustin, however, admits the sphericity of the earth, and shows how absurd and contemptible the notion is of inhabitants on the opposite side, "because no such race is recorded by *Scripture* among the descendants of Adam."

It was in this manner that all astronomical speculation was squelched by the early defenders of the church. These speculations were considered absurd, trifling, impious and detestable, and all those bold and true theories which had come from the unfettered Grecian mind were studiously thrust out as of pagan origin and contrary to Scripture. This conquest of the church led to the adoption of a more biblical notion, known as the geography of Cosmas, who wrote in the Sixth century: "He describes the earth as an oblong floor, surrounded by upright walls and covered by a vault, below which the heavenly bodies perform their revolutions, going round a certain high mountain, which occupies the northern parts of the earth, and makes night by intercepting the light of the sun." This geography being deemed Scriptural, was ever after used as a mighty engine to demolish the true theories which the Grecian mind had wrought out, till the great breaking up of this central tyranny of the Catholic god-thought by the Protestant Reformation.

As late as the Eighth century, the heathen theory of antipodes was not wholly overturned, for we find one Virgil, Bishop of Salzburg, not assenting to the Christian notion that the earth is flat. "And it is said when he was reported to Boniface, Archbishop of Ments, as holding the existence of antipodes, the prelate was shocked at the assumption, as it seemed to him, of a world of human beings out of the reach of the conditions of salvation." Kepler asserts that he was reported to Pope Zachery, and deposed from his bishopric. So you see how this notion of the rotundity of the earth came at last to be a very unsafe doctrine, as Tostatus declared it to be about the time Columbus sailed.

Now all this is consonant with the steady onward progress of thought. The theologic thunderbolt was only leveled against the Physical sciences, and especially Astronomy, as this was said to be opposed to Scriptures; but Thought, in other channels, was working out its own salvation. Theologic fear suppressed it in one direction, but it only became intensified in another. What Astronomy lost, the *Reason* gained. This old Catholic Church had in her womb, unconscious to herself, the Luthers and Galileos and Newtons, who *must be born.* Theologic fear could intimidate for a while, but it could not curb the Almighty and divine *mental force.* The old Catholic Church, with its hollow trunk, in which a Pope dwelt and clasped his infallible book, and with its trifurcated top, without a leaf or flower, standing there lonely, and black, and grim, the central god-thought of Christendom was by no means to be forever barren and fruitless. Though dead at the top, it was alive at the root. From these roots shot up the Luthers, and Melanchthons, and Brunos of the Reformation. The religious scepter was not wrested from the hand of the pope, but *new* scepters were multiplied by breaking the power of the Church. The bible was not destroyed, but its *tyranny* was destroyed by placing it in the hands of the people, who interpreted it according to Reason, and while assenting to its authority, unconsciously made it bow to their own judgments. Neither was the Christian god-thought destroyed, but the attributes of the Trinity became multiple and conflicting. The "Thus saith the Lord" spoken by Moses, which once made all Jewish heads bow to Jehovah, and afterwards all Christian heads, when spoken by the infallible pope, came now not as the real word directly from a central God, but as an emenation thereof reflected through the reason of man. This broke the god-thought into as many fragments as there were minds to contemplate Force. This is a freedom from theological tyranny more perfect than Greece could boast. Science is now not only possible, it is necessitated. The head is ripe and the tyranny of Theological Fear is broken, because opinion is divided. Theology must now become antagonistic to itself. Having served its purpose, which is to evolve Science, it has preserved the seeds of death within it, and must die in combating itself.

§. 6. Now, if the foregoing reasoning be true, the Protestant Reformation must precede the establishment of modern astronomical science. The causes of the reformation had been long at work before Luther, and only culminated with him, in 1517. At this point of time the Catholic Church was shattered—the tyranny of the central god-thought was broken. Let us now see how and when modern astronomy was born.

After Astronomy had slept for thirteen hundred and fifty years, Copernicus took it up, just as it had been left by the Grecian mind. It had been preserved in Grecian beauty by the wandering Arabs. This science had come on the wings of Speech, in her rythmical flight, from the Grecian poet. This Grecian song had been translated by the Arab, and taken with him in his wanderings. It had thus been preserved from contempt and neglect by a people unlike those who held the science to be "vain and transitory," "contrary to Scripture," and "unsafe." Copernicus took it up to see how "*foolish*" a thing the Grecian thought had wrought out. But this foolish thing begot its own like in his head, and as a basis of thousands of years of thought in experiments, and records, and investigations, and hypotheses, which the barbarians had given him, he solved the problem of the motion of the stars. The truth staggered him. He bent in fear before the yet prevailing creed of Christendom, and for thirty-seven years did not dare to publish his discovery. Nor did he dare to open his lips upon this discovery for seventeen years, and until Magellan's boat, Victoria, had gone round the world. The day he died he received a copy of his work, which was to make known his discovery, but never opened it. This was twenty-six years after Luther shattered the Catholic god-thought.

Till now the Christian world had defaced the beauty of the Grecian thought, little dreaming that the noblest thought of the Christian New Testament had been borrowed therefrom. They tore down the Grecian tower of strength, and in the high places of scientific truth, where Pythagoras, and Aristotle, and Hipparchus had sat, they set up the terrible image of Hell and its devils, to frighten all who said there were other gods beside Jehovah, and that the Pope was not his only infallible priest. Fear smote the land with a theologic curse, and the dens of idolatry multiplied, as the images of Mary and her Son were struck out by the chisel of the artist, who imitated the Grecian thought in sculpture, but failed to copy the Grecian spirit of Truth.

This, then, is the order in which Science is evolved: First, it must spring from the primary conception of Force. This Force is affirmed to be the god, and the "why" is involved therein. But the question "why?" is the basis of all Science. In this first conception of a god it is unitary, and all phenomena are attributed to the active god. Worship is born of Fear and Pain, and Theology of *Wonder*. But Wonder is the incipient "Why?" Of this comes *Logic*, or true mental ratiocination. But Logic is born of Number and Equality, which is Diversity in Unity. Force is here divided up, and the god-thought becomes multiple. This destroys the tyranny of Fear, and thus Science is permitted to grow.

§. 7. That it is necessary to have the god-thought precede Science is quite manifest from the fact that the animal loves rest rather than labor and activity. He must be driven to toil and to study. Mankind are averse to thinking in logical order; and while induction is a necessity of sensation, deduction is only produced by the most active incentives. The love of knowledge in the early race was not sufficiently strong to *compel* any great exertion.

Evil, myriad shaped—Pain, Hunger, Suffering, Death—produced Despair and Hope, for Despair and Hope are only the two poles of one force. The one implies the other, and the one will always produce the other. But the Evils of the world which tortured the body must produce their counterparts in Hope; that looking forward to realize earthly happiness, which painted boundless wealth, perfect health and perennial youth on the background of the Future. It may be said these are vain and illusory, and produce nothing in science, but serve only as theological food to make madmen in the world. But will some one tell us how Chemistry could have come in any other way? By those vain and illusory hopes, the Alchemist labored night and day, suffering all the ills of poverty during life, to wring from Nature the secrets of her hidden *lore.* Nature held up to the vision of man no heavenly and angelic lie when she showed him a piece of dull lead, in which he found some silver and a trace of gold, but he interpreted the vision falsely. "Ah!" he said, "I now have it; I will transmute the lead into gold. But what will drive out the evil spirit and retain the good in the baser metal? Something, surely; let us call it the *philosopher's stone.*" And thus the Alchemist was driven madly on in search of this phantom of the brain. But if the philosopher's stone could transmute the baser metals into gold, it might transmute pain and disease into pleasure and health; nay, turn old age into youth, and thus become the elixir of life. But it is plain to be seen that this doctrine and belief of the Alchemist had parentage in the god-thought of earlier times, that men were changed into gods, and that the gods had power to expel evil spirits, to change water into wine, rods into serpents; nay, even people into beasts and trees. In further proof of this we cite the decree of Henry the VI., of England, who declared "that the clergy should engage in the search for the philosopher's stone, for since they could change bread and wine into the body and blood of Christ, they must also, by the help of God, succeed in transmuting the baser metals into gold." From the god-thought we have Astrology and Magic, which gave birth to Alchemy; and in the wild rambles of Alchemy we have the first discoveries which laid the foundations of Chemistry. And the word *gas*, so often on the lips of the chemist, is only the ghost of some ancient god-thought.

In all this theological speculation, in all this rambling after the philosopher's stone, the "*Why?*" has been forever involved; and in no other way is it possible for us to imagine that the question could have been asked. And in no other way can we imagine that such boundless zeal could have been produced save by these theological phantoms of the brain. *The phantom destroyed Rest, and made search compulsory.*

§. 8. But as Theology is the mother of Science,

it is not at all strange that she should scourge her wayward child. It has ever been the disposition of Theology to assume the highest authority. She has ever tried to make all things bow to her. She dictates the method of worship as to time, place and object. She dispenses temporal and spiritual blessings, and makes the necks of king and subject to bow at her feet. She rules with a rod of iron, and punishes without mercy. She proclaims no law without a penalty, and has never been known to reprieve an offender. She punishes so long as disobedience lasts, and holds the culprit with a vice-like grip. But in all this Science is begotten in her very image, for it is the sole attribute of Force to beget its own like. Force personified in the god is only Force made real in Science.

But why, we ask, must Science be scourged? That it may gain strength through antagonism. Who is it that scourges Science? *Theology;* nobody else. Nobody else has the right. This she does in anger, forever driving Science from her embrace. He goes from the house where he has been cradled, and learns to live without her. She pursues him in vengeance, persecutes and curses him, till large enough to master her; and after the first encounter, when she is conquered, true motherlike, she immediately embraces, caresses and blesses him; and seeing her child full grown and conqueror of the world, she dies and he buries her. This is, perhaps, a true allegory of this Mother and Son.

Any one who has studied the history of the Inductive Sciences must have noticed with what precision, care and accuracy its devotees have aimed to labor. The Deductive Sciences are in themselves accurate and true, but it is not so with those which have come from observation and experiment. It is therefore necessary to have true observers and nice experimenters to establish an inductive truth; or, rather, to arrive at truth inductively. Chemistry must have no careless and stupid experimenter in her laboratory; Geology, no hear-say, caged-up bookworm of a cave or monastery; Astronomy, no blind poet to sit and chant to the stars, but practical, careful, studious, unwearying men work there; men who, when they have discovered a truth, know it, and can prove it. Else Theology, who stands by scolding for "this trifling waste of time" in the philosopher's "contemptible pursuit" after these physical things, should he fail, strikes away his head, or his freedom, for his impiety, and the world has gained nothing. But should he be successful and reach the truth, he can well afford to suffer or die for it. Thus Bruno was burned at the stake, and Galileo imprisoned. This tyranny of Theology makes men most cautious in the investigation of physical causes. No knowing how many truths have been discovered, and have been buried with their authors, because of this Theologic tyranny which compelled man to be *accurate*. And thus, when Science comes, it is radiant with the glory of

Truth; and girt about with its own invincible strength, it comes to conquor.

§. 9. Life and truth only come through a holy warfare. Force in the universe has a record of a great warfare. It wages a continual battle in the world. Let us take one illustration: There is a simple element in nature called oxygen gas. Its action upon organic matter is highly destructive. It attacks, in fact, all substances with which it is not already combined, with greater or less energy, to destroy them; that is, to change them, or to literally burn them up. The oil in a lighted lamp is no more consumed in a few hours by oxygen combining with the carbon and leaving carbonic acid gas, which escapes in the atmosphere, than is the fence nail consumed in the same number of years by oxygen combining with iron and leaving rust. Both are processes of burning up; that is, the force of oxygen overpowering carbon and iron. This is the cause, also, of animal and vegetable decay. When a tree rots and withers away, it is burnt up by oxygen. When a person starves to death, he is burnt up by oxygen. Thus, also, every organ of the head, and every tissue of the body, is being daily and hourly consumed by oxygen; and were there no physician in nature, no holy oil distilled to supply the loss, the lamp of life would soon go out. But we do find a holy antagonist in the light of the sun. This wages an almost even-handed warfare against this silent and invisible demon of death and Evil. And in this warfare of Oxygen and Sunlight a divine compensation is produced, leaving food, life, health, beauty and knowledge on earth. Says Youmans, in speaking of the Chemistry of the Sunbeam: "We have seen that oxygen gas is the foe of organization and life, its affinity for the other organic elements being such that it perpetually rends them from their combinations, thus inducing constant decay and dissolution. We now perceive that the solar rays are the great antagonists of oxygen. Under their influence the mineral elements are changed to living forms. Under the influence of oxygen they are returned again to the inorganic world. If oxygen dilapidates, *they* renovate; if *that* decomposes and breaks down, they construct and build up; if *that* is seen in the falling leaf of autumn, they are proclaimed in the exuberant foliage and blossoms of spring. If oxygen is the mainspring of destruction upon the globe, wasting, burning, consuming and hastening the dissolution of all things, the solar rays constitute the mighty force of counteraction. They reunite the dissevered elements, substitute development for decay, call forth a glory from desolation, and life and beauty from the very bosom of death."

But the record of this conflict is the exact record also of Theology with Science. *Knowledge* has a record of many facts in the world, and it has only come through a holy warfare. If we call Force the gods, we have, in the above warfare of Oxygen and

Sunlight, a scientific review of all the theologic fables of the world. The early mind could easily perceive a mighty warfare going on between the different forces of earth. These forces were called gods, spirits, angels of light and darkness, controlled by the *Powers* of heaven and hell. Here we have Michael and his angels battling against Satan and his angels, which story the Jew borrowed from the Persian theology. In this the Persian poet was not mistaken as to the great fact of the warfare, but only as to its cause, and meaning, and result.

Homer's Iliad and Milton's Paradise Lost are grand epics written to commemorate this Theologic warfare. They were both written in honor of Evil; of war in heaven and trouble on earth. They were also both written when the tyranny of the god-thought was broken; the one when Grecian theology had emerged from the unitary and central god, perhaps of Fire; the other when the Catholic Church was shattered. The former was written at the dawn of Grecian science; the latter at the dawn of modern science. The one was both the requiem of Theology and the natal song of Science in Greece, the other in Europe. It is thus the causes which lie back of and herald great movements and revolutions in either theology or science ever produce like results, because the forces which evolve them are ever the same. The causes which gave Greece her Homer, and Europe her Milton, were identical and the same. The scientific spirit became more intensified in Europe, because the mind became more liberated from the tyranny and fear of the god-thought.

§. 10. The above is only an illustration in one department of nature. But the truth is, Force can not act without an exhibition of this antagonism. And why? Because Force ever acts in equal and opposite directions. In all its expressions, physically, mentally and materially, it exhibits polarity. If you raise twenty pounds from the earth, the impression of your foot in the soil will be twenty pounds more perceptible. If you are opposed, resistance becomes a necessity of that opposition; *else the opposition will extinguish you.* The worm dies beneath your tread but the serpent rises up and strikes you. If you give, you must have received. If weeds grow in your corn, to save the corn you must root out the weeds. If disease wars against your body, to save your life you must kill the disease. If tyranny sits enthroned over a nation, to save the people the head of Tyranny must be stricken off. If slavery gets rooted into the soil of a nation, it will spread till a stronger force destroys it. Vice-like ignorance has to be pulled up by the roots; this is accompanied by pain and bleeding. It is a war of forces, and the stronger will always prevail. War is the watchword of Nature. People may cry peace! peace! but there will be no peace; for peace is satisfaction and death.

§. 11. But strength only comes from these opposing forces. Mental and physical strength are born of antagonism.

A celebrated exploit of Hercules, the god of strength, so goes the Grecian fable, was his victory over Antæus, the son of the Earth. "Antæus was a mighty giant and wrestler, whose strength was invincible so long as he remained in contact with his mother Earth. He compelled all strangers who came to his country to wrestle with him, on condition if conquered, as they all had hitherto been, to be put to death. Hercules encountered him, and finding that it was of no avail to throw him, for he always arose with renewed strength with every fall, he lifted him up from the earth and strangled him in mid-air." This fable has more beauties than one. It shows what accurate observers the ancients were. Physical strength, which is *force*, was personified in the god Hercules, who was not able by physical strength alone to subdue the giant who had the miraculous gift of increasing strength. But mental force came into play in Hercules, who discovered the *science* of Antæus' strength. With this discovery the victory was easy.

It is thus man learns through experiments which fail. He is also like Antæus a great babe yet, drawing nourishment and strength from mother Earth. He is just learning to walk, and falling often, cries out "evil!" Yet the fall gives him renewed strength. It is the *falling* which the world records as evil, yet it is in this very way and no other, that he gains sufficient strength to walk or stand erect. Two or three more falls of Antæus and it would have been all over with the mighty powers of Hercules. Now let Hercules represent the god-thought and Antæus Science, and in this case we would have had Science prevail; but as it was, Theology was yet conqueror. It is in this way also all the theological stories of the "Fall of Man" have come about. These have been by no means false stories; they have been true allegorical representations of Evil in the world. Man called the *perfection* from which he fell only child-like weakness and innocence, and the *fall* those accidents which overtook him when he went out in quest of food and knowledge. With the food of experience must come the knowledge of Good and Evil; the Moral and Science of life; the ever-repeated how and why.

See how naturally this comes. It requires an active life to learn. How man is urged on by the necessities of life! He could not be moved in any other way. Hunger is continually gnawing at his vitals. Want is continually knocking at his door. Hungry children cry for food—if not actually, prospectively—if parents remain idle. So they work with body and mind to provide for the morrow. There stands Want, lean and gaunt, the terrible ghost of Hunger on the threshold, who says to father and mother: "Hie thee out and bring in food and raiment; labor and watch, or I will snatch away thy little ones." And sometimes parents wish they could not love so tenderly, lest they be compelled to sorrow too bitterly.

What appears to us the evils of hunger, are at last all that would save our lives. Without hunger we would not work; and without work, death. Without Evil, no labor; no active mind; no dissatisfaction; no progress. So it is only a question with us: which will we take, the evils of the world, or nonentity? And herein there can be no difference between what is called physical and moral evil. The force which evolves the one also evolves the other. As there is no growth of the body without the pains of the nerves to compel us to protect it against the blind forces which are ever ready to destroy it, so there is no moral growth without remorse of conscience, without shame and disgust, to protect us against those blind forces which are ever ready to turn man into a thief, a murderer, a child of lust, an idiot, or a devil. To say we can progress without Evil is just the same as saying we can progress when perfect.

Evil may, then, be considered to be the *means* by which the Infinite Force of the Universe evolves conscious finite intelligence. The same means keeps it going, reproduces it, and drives it on to the better. This is *progressive intelligence.* The Infinite Force is the Power; Evil is the lever which moves the Intellectual and Moral World. It begets knowledge by driving the animal away from ignorance.

This *driving away* is a process of *scourging*. With knowledge the blessing comes; yet only partially, because knowledge is only acquired in part. Evil drives to activity, and Science crowns this Activity. Science is the fruit of conscious thought. This is rooted in the soil of Ignorance, and is nourished by the forces of Evil. We are now prepared to more fully illustrate this in our next chapter, on *Special Evils*.

CHAPTER VII.

SPECIAL EVILS.

§. 1. Your good neighbor is stricken down in cold blood by the hand of an assassin; a burglar, grateful for cold cash, breaks into a store and takes away the contents of a safe; Lust lays his polluted hand on some fair daughter, and despoils her in your midst: these are notorious individual crimes and outrages. We thus become so enraged at some creatures in the shape of man that we wonder what they were ever made for. But there is a god's-fact speaking out of these men, which will one day ripen into *Moral Science.* We look upon snakes, toads, flies, mosquitos, lice, curculio, chinch-bugs, and grasshoppers, and wonder what this countless swarm of torment and trouble was ever made for. We plant our corn, and wonder why God could not have made it to grow without weeds and briars, which make us toil and sweat: and if we were disposed, we could, in our ignorance, write a theologic fable about it, saying "that God cursed the ground for man's sake;" which fable, when knowledge had crowned the head of man with *science*, would read: "and God blessed the ground with briars and weeds for man's sake."

Then, in our domestication and civilization, we try to handle fire, and this fire-god of the untutored mind often burns us up. We make us instruments to work with, so that we may live better; and these tools of the inventive genius, forged by this god-Vulcan of the head, cut, bruise, maim and kill us. We capture and subdue steam, and it destroys millions of lives on land and sea. We make gunpowder to equalize the rights of man through the muscles, and we tread on the magazines of our own wrath and destruction, and are blown up by the million. We look abroad in civilized society, and find a land studded with jails and penitentiaries, with iron grated cells and massive walls, to confine those who would unlawfully take the people's life or property. We find asylums for the poor and insane, the halt, the dumb, and blind. We find nearly every well-constructed house with as many locks as doors, to lock out the burglar and thief. We often find a nation of soldiers, with all the munitions of war on a large scale, keeping guard over a race of slaves; and thus Evil is placed in great black letters before our eyes. And we are now compelled to exclaim: Whence all this mental and physical deformity? in whose laboratory of vice and wickedness was all this Ruin created? by whose hand was it created? And there swells in our breasts the feeling of opposition to all this; we rise up in indignation against this monster Evil; we would war against and overthrow it; the slave we would liberate, and punish the master; we would make war against war; we would rob the robber and murder the murderer; we would open the prison doors, if our own safety did not compel us to keep them shut, from a sympathy for our fellow-man. This sympathy makes us care for the insane, the halt, the blind; makes us educate the dumb through the fingers, and school the villain to industry who is imprisoned for a crime. Nay, we would preach a salvation from death beyond the grave.

Here we have the conflict of Good and Evil lettered in Holy books; lettered in the history of nations; lettered in the flesh of man. What a world of science is contained in the question of Burns!

"If I'm designed yon lordling's slave,
By Nature's law designed;
Why was an independent wish
E'er planted in my mind?"

Or we may ask: If we are designed the slaves of our own passions, appetites, lusts, by Nature's law designed, why do we oppose in the flesh these appetites, passions and lusts? Why do we strive to better, not only our own condition, but the condition of our fellow? We do strive after the better, the higher, the nobler, in man. We each of us have an ideal manhood or womanhood for ourself and the race, grander and better than it now exhibits; an ideal life better than it now lives. And following on after this ideal, we pass on to the better, so that

> "Each to-morrow
> Finds us better than to-day."

The answer to the above may all be summed up in one sentence. Man is driven out to search after knowledge, and stumbles over the precipice of his own ignorance. There is a silent monitor within, which says: "*Let the actor beware!*"

§. 2. How shall I act? say Morals. This can only be answered by Experience. The precipice, the thorns, the hard unmellowed earth, the floods, the winds, the sleet and ice, the scorching heat—in short, *Pain*—has wrung out of the flesh the only answer that has ever come. Man cannot reason from actions outside of himself, and deduce a correct theory of morals. Were this so we might say: Look at the ant, oh! man, and be a slaveholder, a kidnapper, a sluggard. We might say: Look at the eagle, and be a robber; the fox, and be a thief; the rattlesnake, and be a murderer; the alligator, and be a cannibal. We might say: Look at the beast of the field, and abolish marriage; or lay not up for yourselves food and raiment, and thus advise you to live vagabonds and beggars; asserting, also, that this is the normal condition of man. But this would be false reasoning; for while this might be the normal condition of some men, it is by no means the ideal conception; nor is it the true condition of those who have already risen far beyond the beast. The time was when kidnapping was thought no evil by the majority of men in America. No one would be justified in now arguing in its favor, and adducing proofs from natural history and past human conduct. The reason is, the inferior are no guide or example to the superior. The Carib or Osage indian would be no moral criterion for a Parker or a Frothingham. It is false to suppose that morals are fixed and external, like a scientific truth. They must change with the changing conditions of man; must grow with his growth; must be a law contingent and necessary to the individual in growth, but not absolute and eternal. They must apply to the individual, not the race. They are special, not general. The moral law which would apply to the individual, Beecher, and fulfill all the conditions of his life, would not apply to any other individual living or dead, or who may live. Those conditions which evolve action, and which give Henry Ward Beecher happiness, and do not injure any other man, will never be produced again in any other person, and have never existed before. This is why a perfect moral law never has been given, and could never be obeyed if given.

§. 3. If one is blindfolded and put into a strange house, he can only learn imperfectly what it contains, by stumbling around in ignorance, and then only conjecturing from the touch. Well, just so it is with the child; it is taught wisdom from experience; and the world of Mankind is taught wisdom by stumbling over Blind Conjecture in the night of its ignorance. Knowledge is the lamp which shines with increasing brightness as man diligently plods onward. It is the oil of the head which keeps this lamp burning. As the child falls in learning to walk, so mankind falls in learning to live; and the fall is called Moral Evil. Without the fall there would be no knowledge from which to construct the moral of life. The "how?" could never be answered. The most vital and self-evident truth of the whole Bible is the story of Man's Fall. In fact, the fables of the world are all moral axioms. They are the first truths of experience; they guide, and cheer, and shine like stars in the night. Man is compelled to go forth in action; it is no choice of his. He is created and set in motion on this globe by forces far anterior to his life, and without his knowledge or consent; but the road he is to travel, be it crooked or straight, is, in a measure, one of his own choosing. He may shun obstacles, or stumble over them; step on thorns, or provide against them; labor, or go hungry. If he acts in harmony with the law of his own being and the material world about him, the result will be good to him; if not, the result will be bad. He thus exemplifies a freedom hedged in by necessity.

It is the law of common prudence which always commands: "Let the actor beware!" This supposes a conscious will-power in the actor, however high or low the intelligence. It is this which says to the animal: "There is danger around you." This is a conscious and intelligent force, which is to protect the creature against the unconscious and blind forces around it. Gravity would hurl you to earth from the top of a tower, did you not consciously, and by force of will through common prudence, make your footing sure. The law of gravity relates to the material world, and is blind; the law of common prudence relates entirely to the mind. The one is a material, the other is a mental force. This mental force is one of knowledge. Now, there is no force so potent in the world as this force of the head, called knowledge. What is knowledge for? Only to enable us to harmonize the material and mental forces; or to harmonize the mental, and control or shun the material forces, would, perhaps, more nearly express it. For example: if a man builds his house near the bank of a river, below the high-water mark, to be observed on the trees and by the drift-wood along its course, then he must expect to be drowned out, or his house swept off sometime, perhaps by the next spring's freshet. And if he marry a woman with neither good sense nor a healthy body, he must expect to have senseless or unhealthy children; or if a woman marry a man who is a drunkard, and she not very vigorous in mind, as she must necessarily be to do so, then she must expect, if she have children, that the chances will be in favor of idiots. In the first instance, the state of things was not in harmony with the law of the freshet, for the man's good; and in the second place, the state of things was not in harmony with the laws of reproduction, for the child's good. Now, this is the very manner in which Moral law is evolved, which only comes through the failures of life, or the evils of experience. The sweeping away of the man's house gives him this moral command: "You ought not to build your house there again." And the idiot children proclaim to the parents, in no unmistakable speech, that they ought not to build children out of such materials again.

§. 4. But it is evident man himself may produce evil in two ways: by acting in ignorance, which may be termed negative evil or error, and also by acting with the full knowledge that evil is to be the result, which may be termed positive evil, or sin. Thus you tell your child to bring you a piece of iron from the ground, not knowing it is hot. It picks it up and gets burnt. Now, should you tell the child with the full knowledge that the iron is hot, it would be your sin, while in the other case it would be your error. But this is by no means all of this case. *The child is burnt; not you.* Yet you have committed the error, or sin, while the child only suffers the evil. The evil is the effect of fire on the child's hand. True, you may suffer secondarily through sympathy; but the child it is that suffers the evil primarily through physical pain. Now the moral law is violated by you, through willful knowledge or prudential neglect, and is evolved through the experience of the child. But this is not all. The child finds that you are *primarily* the cause of the evil, and an antagonism is hereby necessitated. If it can distinguish between knowledge and ignorance, and thinks you knew the result beforehand, the antagonism produces hatred towards you from injured self, which is only self-love evolving hatred; or, in the second place, if it thinks you did not mean it, which conclusion it could only gather from a belief in your ignorance, the antagonism takes the form of a lack of confidence in you. In either case the child is taught *self-reliance.* But this is the very soul of *Morals.* This evolves the science of individual action. But again: The cause of the evil, directly, was the fire which burnt the hand. This was *unconscious*, and no blame can be attached to it. It would be foolish, then, to say: "Fire is a great evil, do not touch it;" for while it is a great evil, it is also a great good, and proves good or evil to man just as he uses it. In fact, this may be said of all the material forces of the world.

§. 5. Now Man is a compound of mental and material forces. The unconscious mental and material forces largely predominate. Man cannot be blamed for being acted upon. He is the percipient of external and internal truths, which manifest themselves to him by their own inherent force. How man acquires knowledge is utterly inscrutable; or how he feels pain. He is made to act, and then moved by being acted upon.

But what is it that guides him when he asks: "How shall I act?" To evolve the Science of Morals we must answer the question: "*Why* does he act as he does?" It may be an indefinite answer to reply: Because of *Conditions*. Yet this is the answer, and the only answer possible, which makes morals undefinable. These conditions, which control the direction in which man acts, are multiple, varying and conflicting. These necessitate choice, which is the result of judgment, the product of number and equality. When one acts thus it may be called rational action,—an act according to Reason. This is different from those actions which spring directly from feeling, or intensified sensation; as when the child picked up the hot iron, the feeling would compel it to instantly drop it; or when a child falls from a second-story window, the mother rushes to pick it up; or when one assaults you with a deadly weapon, you instinctively assume the defensive. In these cases there is no choice of actions.

Now, the emotional faculties of man are all great batteries of feeling. They are the forces which move him, and are in and of themselves as blind and irrational as the steam which drives an engine. Thus his love and hatred he cannot prevent. That is, the *feeling* called love and hatred. In fact, a feeling cannot be prevented; it must precede all prevention. These may not be always expressed, outwardly; but it is *Reason* which is there, controlling the *course of action.*

Thus, also, of a belief. It is as irresistable as a feeling, and to be removed you have, as with the feeling, to remove the cause. It is thus Religion, Love, and all those feelings which move the man, to be brought within morality, have to be controlled by Reason; for there is an immoral religion and love, as well as an immoral hatred and revenge, when expressed in action.

Now, when man acts blindly, he has nothing to assure him of the good effects of his action; that is, if he lets the emotions drive him on without the control of Reason. In this case he is in the exact condition of a ship at sea without a rudder. It may happen that it can be brought safely to land by the blind forces which move it; but the chances are largely in favor of its sailing perpendicularly downward to land. It is control, the guidance of Reason, that man has always lacked. The forces which make him, and drive him, have but seldom been controlled. Thus many of the evils to man arise from the stomach. Too little or too much food,—that which is poor or improperly eaten. A hungry or deranged stomach makes an ill temper; an ill temper brings hasty words; these bring on strife; and strife has set over against it a long list of evils,—murder, robbery, war, and those human deeds of revenge so often witnessed in the inferior races, who are at best very poorly fed. It is thus, also, evil is not always connected with its immediate cause; as when a son is born and educated to live a life of theft and dissipation, or a daughter is born and educated to live a life of prostitution, or is driven to it from hunger. One is not to blame for his grandfather having had hungry and bad neighbors; yet the thunder-bolt of wrath which he forged in revenge, it may be the grandchild's misfortune to be compelled to pick up, through the command of inherited defects. Some people feel bad, and "blue," and melancholy. They do not know what ails them, and are in doubt often whether to go to the doctor or the minister for relief. If to the latter, he is sure to tell them it is a change of heart they need; whereas, in ninety-nine cases out of a hundred, it is a change of diet they need. Instead of a new heart, it is often a new liver they need. Instead of minister's prayers and tears, they absolutely need soap and warm water. Some earnest enquirers, anxious about their souls, are only suffering the penalties of inherited disease. Thus some poor weeping woman, nervous and troubled about her soul, feeling as though she had lost the kingdom of heaven and must find it; feeling as though she were an eternal bankrupt, is only a bundle of nerves whose uneasy, twitching threads run many generations back to the nervous battery of her disease. She is mistaken in thinking that her soul needs salvation; it is her body, which was lost in her mother's womb. It must be expected, for force ever begets its own like when not counteracted; that, if a father drinks whisky, the child, that is conceived after the draught, will smell of the bottle, and the sour grapes of dissipation will set the children's teeth on edge.

Now, all this is only to make people *think*, and is the means of compelling people to study the established laws of pro-creation. It is Evil, with fiery tongue and scorpion sting, whose touch is palsy and whose breath is mental blight, which can, and only can, and must, some day, evolve the *Science* of Pro-creation. For it is a fact of this world, that man can only be tortured into logical thought and moral action. It thus becomes necessary that Evil must result from the ignorant, innocent, and unintentional error of man, just as certainly and alike appalling as though from willful and premediated sin. Were this not so, Evil would be an incomprehensible tragedy to man. It would be a world with a Devil and hell, but no God; it would be a world of feeling, but without science; a world of wild, erratic action, without a logical thought to govern. But all these special evils we witness about us, make up page after page of the *Record*,—the story of the bruises, the sores, the pains, the losses, the wailing and anguish, the diseases of head and body,—all incident to weakness and ignorance, which man is to generalize into the Science of Living. The "How?" can come in no other way. It may seem strange to some that *wisdom* can come in no other way; but what is stranger still, the head will not retain wisdom without the touch of Evil occasionally. After Evil has evolved the Science of Living, no man would follow it without a little severe jogging of the understanding. So that Evil must be a modified yet constant companion of man. Never let a child walk for fear of falling, which you can prevent by your own strength, and the child would not walk when grown. It is the falling, incident to walking, which will make it a *prudent* walker, not subject to falling, after strength has been acquired by exercise. It is the tired body that enjoys repose, also. Without the aches of toil we would have no joy of rest; without the gnawing of hunger, no pleasure of the palate. Ague and mosquitos will drive people from swamps and miasmatic localities to higher and healthier ground; and the penalties of vice and licentiousness will drive the poor sin-sick prodigal, who has been filling himself with husks among human swine, home to his father's mansion. What the world has called a devil's malice, is only God's medicine. It is this which brings its cure some time, and ignorant man is compelled to drink the cup, though mingled with gall and wormwood, or though like liquid fire.

§. 6. Moral Evil, then, means wisdom. It continually cries: "Get knowledge!" and "Let the actor beware!" It was once thought, in the theologic sense, that God talked audibly to man, in good Greek and Hebrew, and that he wrote on parchment and stone his commands to men; but science reveals no such God. The God of Science speaks to man with a million tongues. He speaks in a million ways, silently, audibly, omnipotently, unmistakably, in the body and mind of man, in the body and mind of the race. His prophet and priest is Evil. God did not, in personal shape, speak to the American people, and say, in good English: "American slavery is the sum of all villainies." Yet he spoke it through the mouth of Wesley, who had learned the science of action. And he spoke scientifically through those mighty evils which always accompany slavery. He degraded the slave, and doubly degraded the master. He made the latter weak, overbearing, and aristocratic. He wrought foolishness in his brain, put a lie on his tongue, and made him believe it, that slavery might be damned. He made him insolent and ill-behaved towards Freedom. He puffed him up with pride, and sowed the seeds of malice and spite in his head, which drove him on to assault Freedom in her own temple. Driven out thence, he wove a net to ensnare her. But the war-god drew over him the meshes of his own net, and extinguished him by making him go through the wine-press of outraged Freedom. It is thus the God of Science talks, and gives his revelations to man. Oppression gave to the English people *Habeas Corpus*, and every Bill of Rights so proudly esteemed by this people. It was the Iniquity of England, under an idiotic king, towards her colonies, which gave to the United States the Declaration of Independence. It is thus Freedom and Wisdom are evolved from Tyranny and Idiocy. God did not say to Moses audibly, nor write it on parchment in good Hebrew: "If the children of Israel go four days without food in a strange land, they will get hungry and steal;" but he wrote it in the pit of the stomach of mankind, and so made a law for both Jew and Gentile.

§. 7. The Evil called Theft is one of God's ministers. It is prophet, priest, and law-giver. Wisdom is some day to be enacted out of Theft; for it holds a part of the great Book of the Law of God. When a man steals your breadcorn, remember there is a cause somewhere independent of the theft to account for it. May be, he got hungry and had to steal. May be, his grandfather's averice blossomed into theft, and thus transmitted theft and wealth to him as a legacy. Thus vice may be of slow growth. It may take several generations, through a train of circumstances very slight, and apparently not sinful or wrong, to perfect one natural-born thief. Here is a case in point:

A little girl of very wealthy and Christian parents, living in a western city, was found to have an uncontrolable desire to steal, and often did steal. She began when quite young to steal her playmate's pieces of silver coin. She at last stole from a store in the city, was found out, talked to and punished, but to no effect. At last, in stealing from a certain merchant, she was observed, followed to her father's house, the money seized and the facts brought directly under the father's eye. He was wealthy, a strict Christian, and a member of the church. He had before talked to her, scolded, expostulated, whipped, and for hours prayed with his little thievish daughter. She, in tears, would acknowledge how naughty she was; how wicked it was to steal; how sure she was of going to hell when she died; and would, all lacerated and bruised, promise to never do so again. Yet, for all this, she would steal with fear and trembling, even when her father gave her all the money she wanted. Once the father, for two weeks, made a prison of his garret for her, locked her in, fed her only on bread and water, prayed and wept with her three times a day. At last womanhood, pride of position, affluence and care, suppressed the outward exhibition of this abnormal craving for money within her.

A train of circumstances altogether human made

her a natural-born thief. Here they are: Her mother, before marrying this child's father, was a widow. By her former husband she had a son, whom she gave away before marrying again. Her two first children from the second marriage were fine girls. But at this period in life her only son from her former marriage unfortunately came to see his mother. He was then almost a young man. The lad was poor and his mother living in affluence, the wife of a millionaire. The wife and mother asked her husband for some money for her boy. She was refused even a dollar. She then went to work secretly, and under false pretenses, to obtain it of her husband. She would often go to the store and steal small sums at a time. Several months elapsed in this manner, and having obtained quite a sum, gave it to her boy and sent him back to his adopted home. Not long after this the third daughter was born, and she grew up to be the troublesome little girl who had to be imprisoned in her father's own house,. unmercifully whipped, who had the picture of hell presented to her young imagination, and for years mingled her sobs with her father's prayers.

The above is one of hundreds of similar cases. The wisdom which is to be enacted out of Theft will come some day; and the thief is only a sort of devilish book which we are compelled to study, for it is continually kept before our very eyes. The thief is the product of forces as natural as the earth we tread. There is established in Nature a general and immutable law: "*That like begets like.*" This is the sole characteristic of Force. This moves the atom, and compels like atoms to assume like motions. In regard to the pro-creation of animals and plants, under like circumstances, like begets like; theft begets theft, murder begets murder, lust begets lust, and goodness, piety, love, these beget their own like. And the parent mother of the young child unborn, induced within it, or impressed upon it, then and there, her own strongest feelings and desires; and when the child was born, the forces of theft came coiled up within it; and when it grew up morally distorted, and the mother beheld the moral ruin and appaling disposition of her child, she was only looking at her former self, under the tyranny of her husband. It is thus the God of Science talks, and holds up the mirror to every parent. It is thus he opens the eyes and ears, and drives away the stupidity of man. It is thus he shows man wherein he has made the failure, and wherein he can better the abortive work.

Very much of the stealing in the world comes from poverty, and the tyranny of the rich over the poor. Society is so organized that the rich man grows richer and the poor man poorer, which ever must produce crime. How to remedy this we do not know; but one thing is evident: Crime will be kept festering in the flesh of Society till wisdom is enacted out of it, and the thief becomes unnecessary. At present the thief is a necessity, as much so as is law and religion. When we can get along without crime, we can get along without law and religion, for crime is the parent of both these. It would not cure the evil of theft to hang the thief up by the neck till dead; nay, you may kill off all the thieves in the world to-day, and the next generation, in proportion to its greatly diminished numbers, would doubtless be as rife with theft as this. The reason is, the seeds of crime are lying dormant in society, and the very institutions which are trying to destroy crime are producing it. Theft is not an isolated and independent thing. It is not alone begotten of theft. But other transactions, which take the dignified titles of *law* and *religion*, often beget it. It is only the ripened fruit of that *cunning* which we see in the trades of life, in "sharp dealing," whether in driving a bargain or in getting souls into a church.

We would refer the reader to a further consideration of this subject in a discourse, in this volume, entitled "Salvation and Damnation Before Birth," and we will pass to other considerations of the subject.

§. 8. Without sorrow the feeling we call happiness would never have had a name. We know nothing, in fact, of happiness, only as we contrast it with sorrow. There is, perhaps, no unalloyed happiness. The old adage, no rose without a thorn, seems to hold good always. This fact let that deep thinker and close reasoner, Jonathan Edwards, to affirm: "The miseries of hell would augment the pleasures of heaven." The only fallacy in this is in localizing hell and heaven. It is perhaps more nearly the truth to say heaven and hell are within and around us always. They are necessary feelings produced by the conditions of life, and the one implies and necessitates the other. They are the two poles of one force; and if man is immortal, heaven and hell are eternal. How vain it would be to talk to a person of happiness who had never felt sorrow. It would be, we imagine, like expatiating upon the beauties of the rainbow to a person born blind. There would be the colors and the happiness, but no *knowledge* of either. Little would we sympathize with the afflicted, had we not suffered ourselves. Seldom would we feed the hungry, had we not hungered ourselves. How seldom would we strive to bind up the broken-hearted, had we ourselves never had the cords of affection broken. As there is no night without its day, so there is also no sorrow without its joy; and as the tree is prepared by the frosts and storms of winter for the budding springtime and the gorgeous summer, so the cradle of affliction prepares us for our happiest hours. All must go through hell to get into heaven. Materially man is a plant, rooted to earth; he draws his nourishment therefrom, taking deep root in the soil out of which he grows. When a tree is well planted in good soil, it takes deeper root and a firmer stand by being rocked in the storms of winter. It is thus we are rocked in the storms of trouble. We are cradled in affliction and schooled in sorrow. Experience is our stern and severe teacher, who often drives us into thought by cruel torture. In this school we often suffer and despair; but without it we would never taste the delights of pleasure, nor behold with an appreciative eye the blending beauties of the rainbow of hope. It is the blending of light and shade which makes the picture, either on canvas or in character. Without shade there can be no picture; without Evil no character. It is the scientific skill of the artist which brings out the picture through the antagonism of light and darkness; and the scientific skill of the man or woman which is to bring out the beautiful moral character through the antagonism of good and evil.

It is thus we find a meaning in all the evils of the world. Evil brings its revelation of Good, come from whence it may; and to secure the good, Evil must come. And so it drives us over our own ignorance, stumbling down to error, in all the relations of life, in family, church, and state. Evil also comes to us which we have had no hand in, given to us from our ancestors, many generations back; handed down from sire to son. These evils blind us in mental darkness, draw us into errors by phantom follies, or drive us madly on in paths of lust.

Now, were there no meaning in Evil, no good to

be evolved therefrom, but that Evil is only Evil, then indeed would the condition of the world be sad and deplorable. But we find Evil established and governed by fixed and general laws. We find herein effect following cause with unerring precision. Law and penalty are linked together, and the law manifests itself only through the penalty. "Step on this thorn and suffer, or provide against it;" this is the admonition of Evil. But that the thorn is an evil we have no reason to conclude. It is often considered so by the unthinking, because pain arises from it. It is not the thorn, nor rattlesnake, nor mosquito, nor grasshopper, nor miasm, which is the evil; the evil primarily is in us, in the shape of Ignorance. We do not know of the thorn or the snake, or we would provide against it. It is not the Alcohol which a man takes into his stomach that is the evil; it is the drinking of it improperly. The evil is in the *act;* not in the thing. Strychnine is a great good; it does not change its nature at all if taken into the stomach; it is not rendered any less good by eating it. The evil is in the use of it. The bad act, the wrong act, the evil act, always brings its penalty and its wisdom therewith. It is thus this whole world is perfectly good in and of itself; and the law of each thing proclaims itself, *and is true to itself.* This is the everlasting law of beauty, and harmony, and good in the universe. Each string of a musical instrument is true to itself. If it be made double, as in the piano, and the tension is not alike on each, it proclaims the discord. The strings talk of their discord and harmony audibly, as though they had tongues; and they talk with such precision as no tongue can imitate. Now, the life of man is just like a performance on a piano. It may be a tune, or jumble of sounds; the tune may run smoothly without discord; it may be one of many variations; it may roll in crescendo and diminuendo like the waves of the ocean, or it may be a monotonous jingle of a few notes; it may ascend to the complex and scientific overture of a Beethoven, or desend to the monotonous drawl and humdrum of a Chippewa indian; and yet each one will be true to itself. What would delight the Indian would kill Beethoven, either in life or music. *Every force of the universe is true to itself.*

Now, every wrong act has its penalty. The penalty proclaims that it is wrong. Were there no evil effects to follow the drinking of whisky, it would not be wrong to drink it at any time. Nor is it the drinking of it that produces evil, for it may be sometimes taken without injury; but it is the *unwise* use of it. No one can justly command as a law: "Never drink whisky; it is a monstrous evil," any more than one would be warranted in saying: "Never eat any food; it is a monstrous evil;" for whisky may save life in the counteraction of a poison, and food may be taken to gluttony and thus destroy life. All that can be said is: Eat and drink temperately; that is, according to Reason:

this is the moral of eating and drinking. But sin or error can never go unpunished. The person who commits the sin or error, however, may not feel the penalty; it may be reserved for his offspring to suffer it, who are innocent of guilt. Yet because persons do not suffer for their error or sin, does not therefore prove they are forgiven for it. It is perhaps in this way the notion of forgiveness of sins has come into the world. It would be quite natural to suppose so, seeing that the penalties of the iniquities of the fathers are visited upon the children, not only to the fourth generation, but to the fortieth. In the light of conscious existence hereafter, however, the original evil-doer might be made to suffer secondarily through sympathy. According to the old notion of a local heaven and hell, this sympathy of the righteous would itself turn heaven into a secondary hell.

It is thus no sin can be forgiven, either in a theological or scientific sense. In the Christian theology, Christ is said to suffer for the sins of the world; and the righteous are saved, not because they can sin with impunity, but because Christ bears their iniquity through sympathy and actual suffering. The Christian theology does not hang by such a rope of sand as to have a scheme of salvation which admits sin, even in those who are saved, without some one suffering therefor; for sin without suffering is a contradiction in terms. The grand mistake in the Christian scheme of salvation is to suppose heaven to be a state or condition of absolute bliss, and that a certain belief is necessary to produce it. Now, absolute bliss is impossible, and belief no more depends on the will of man than does sunlight or the earth's motion. Belief is as necessitated in man as is spring-time in the year, and obeys laws as fixed as those which move the heavenly orbs. There is no such thing as free belief, any more than free love or free hatred. These are all necessitated, and depend on causes anterior to and superseding the will. No one can gird himself up and say: "Now I will believe so and so, and secure this or that blessing;" for whether he will or no, the belief is independent of it. Now let us take a case in point. We will define a sin to be a willful violation of a known law of God. You get drunk knowing that it will injure your offspring; you fall into the gutter of licentiousness, transmit the lust of your heart and the smell of the bottle to your child; he has a mania for liquor all his life, proves a curse to you, to the mother who bore him, and to the world. Now, can you believe, by willing it, in such a manner, that God shall forgive you for your drunkenness, and prevent the effect on your child? How can God forgive you? No one can imagine. It is beyond the power of man to conceive or guess. Nothing would be so calamitous to man, were it possible for one such sin to be forgiven. The forgiveness of one sin might turn the world into a hell more literal than the ancients ever pic tured the abode of devils. The forgiveness of one sin is just as impossible, as the annihilation of one atom of matter. Then, again, it is a contradiction in terms. It is just like saying a force may act without any effect. It is like affirming an effect *is*, which may be so obliterated that it never *was*. The truth is, if an effect is produced, it is an eternal fact of the universe. Now, *a sin is an effect* which has been produced. As such it *is*, and always will be, an eternal fact of the universe. And if it could be forgiven, it would be so obliterated that it never was.

§. 9. The faculties of man are all necessary and good. But we have just seen that the improper use of a thing creates evil, which is true to itself by bringing its penalty and wisdom. It is thus, also, a faculty may be perverted in the excessive, abnormal, or improper action thereof. The love of food may be perverted into the love of alcohol and tobacco, and thus produce great evils. The love of property may push itself forward into theft. Hatred may go beyond a righteous indignation into savage revenge. And thus evils come by the legion, with their pains and penalties; and poor fallen and constantly falling man, keeping a record of his falls each day, at evening looks over the list, and constructs therefrom a chart for future guidance.

In this regard let us look at man in his Religious and Sexual emotions. He presents in these two phases the most prominent acts of his life. They move him, next to hunger, with the greatest violence and energy. They are two of the mighty forces of his nature. And first of the Religious faculty. We have elsewhere defined this to be that which prompts man to worship. This brings men and women together in the greatest numbers. It has dotted the world over with churches, cathedrals, temples, pyramids, monuments. It has its sacred groves, and caves, and mountains. It has made holy the ground on which prophets and priests have trod, and the lands in which peoples have dwelt. But as it is one of the most powerful, when perverted it has been one of the most abused; and by pervertion we only mean its *normal* action, without the guidance of Reason. The religious faculty is ever true to itself, however erratic or intensely it may act. It is in itself blind and irrational, and Reason is all that makes it pure, and beautiful, and moral. It has specially incarnated God in bits of wood; in cats and dogs; in crocodiles and serpents; in golden calves and living bulls; in statues of ideal men, and in the living bodies of strong men. It has driven men mad in honor of a holy name or thing. It has whetted the two-eged sword of Revenge sharper than the Damascus blade, to hew in pieces the princes of the earth, the people they ruled, and the children they begat. The holy fanatic has eaten the flesh and drank the blood of the man who would not worship his god. The lands of whole nations have been devasted, devoured by fire and cut down by sword; all that stood or breathed have perished, to appease the wrath of a hidden god. In this lust after God the greatest armies have been marshaled, the longest wars have been waged, the mightiest battles fought. The earth has drank up rivers of human blood, shed in the name of Religion. The genius of men has been called forth to invent instruments of death, and machines of horrid torture, to rend, rack, behead, crucify, and mangle the flesh of those who would deny the creed or doubt the popular religious dogma. Men and women have been made to confess themselves guilty of crimes of which they were entirely innocent; so that Marquis Beccarria was compelled to submit this problem to the religious world: "The force of the muscles and the sensibility of the nerves of an innocent person being given, it is required to find the degree of pain necessary to make him confess himself guilty of a given crime." Young princes, as a daily pastime, have learned to hurl the lance at the hearts of men, as targets, who were imprisoned for the religion they professed. Men of generous culture or of great learning, and women of eminent piety and virtue, from the humble cottage to the throne, have been led out for matters of conscience and butchered before a mad rabble lusting after God. The limbs of men and women have been torn from their bodies, their eyes gouged out, their flesh mangled and slowly roasted, their children barbarously tortured before their eyes, because of religious opinion. Woman has been taken from her dungeon while giving birth to her babe, to augment the pangs of child-birth by fire at the stake. Armed men in the priest's employ, with all the horrid machinery of the Inquisition behind them, have been organized under a spiritual head, and called the "Militia of Jesus Christ," to kill heretics. All this and much more, which even to name would be barbarous, has been done for the sake of Religion. A blind infatuation has possessed the mind of man like a demon, and fanaticism has driven him on to the most barbarous and savage acts, in the holy name of Religion. Religion, in thy name what barbarities have been committed, what hellish deeds have been done!

But is there no meaning in all this? Was the Sphinx to propound her riddle always, that she might sacrifice the innocent on the altar of Ignorance? Is there no Edipus to solve this riddle? Surely, it can be solved. The meaning is two-fold. The incentives to scientific pursuits and investigations come from the god-thought. Science must be born of Theology; must literally come in pain and agony. Theology matures when the god-thought is divided and complex; when theological speculation is diverse. And when Science is given to the world, Theology expends all her forces in combatting her own self. Thus we have had the holy wars of the world, which only mean: as Science shall live and grow, and proclaim her own power, henceforth Theology becomes unnecessary, and must destroy herself. The bloody wars between the Catholics and Protestants are perhaps ended; and they will now pass away in intellectual combat, because the Protestant wing, in being so much divided up, is the true representative of Science. Should the Protestant Church, however, ever unite under one banner, with a central god-thought, as the Catholic Church now is, then there must a bloody and exterminating war ensue. If the scientific world has anything to be thankful for, it is the division in the Protestant Church; and that zeal which keeps them divided is a continual showering down of God's blessing upon Science. While the church is divided and distracted, Science is permitted to invoke the god of fire in the laboratory; the god of the stars through the telescope; the god of the flesh in the dissecting room; and the student is permitted to boldly generalize all the phenomena of Force into a Science of Evil, which, as it investigates the causes of all Science, must be itself the Science of all sciences.

§. 10. But let us now pursue the Sexual emotion. As with the Religious faculty, so also with the Love of the opposite sex. There is nothing in this wrong. It is true to itself. But its course is erratic when Reason does not guide. This faculty is also blind. And how truly the ancients reasoned when they painted the god of Love blind. This is, perhaps, to-day the blindest of all man's faculties, if there can be degrees in blindness. What we mean is, it is the least controlled by Reason; that is, it is yet the most shrouded in ignorance, because the family relations are the most sacred, and the god of the hearth-stone drives out every scientific intruder.

Without Reason, Love is lust. This, also, like the religious faculty, has had its sacred groves, and caves, and mountains. It has its gods and goddesses, before whom mankind bow down in worship. Its idols have been made and broken in every land, and in every city of the world. Long wars have been waged, mighty battles have been fought, in behalf of this god of the heart. The blind old poet of "Scio's rocky isle" has left to the world, in Grecian song, the sad story of the Trojan war; the story of fair Hellen lost and won. Rome numbers among her greatest battles those fought for love. Nothing is so sad in all history as the story of Virginia, after Appius Claudius had looked upon her with lustful eyes. Tears are wont to come when we read how the father, to preserve his daughter from being a prey to this vulture of womanly purity, killed her with his own hand. And those words of his, as he raised the knife to strike the death blow, come down to us from the old Roman Forum, breathing the spirit of wild, sweet tragedy:

> "Farewell, sweet child, farewell. Oh! how I love my darling.
> Now clasp me round the neck once more, and give me one more kiss.
> And now, my own dear little girl, there is no way but this."

How sad the story of Hagar and her little son Ishmael, turned out by husband and father, Israel's great patriarch and progenitor, to famish in the wilderness. How the blood quickens in rage at the conduct of King David, after he beheld with lustful eyes Bathsheba, the wife of Uriah, fairest daughter in all Israel, commanding Joab, the great captain of his armies, to place Uriah in the forefront of the hottest battle, that he may be slain and his wife thus made an easy prey. What foul pollution; what blackness of life; what chief sin of all sins, must follow the life and blast the memory of that man who can murder for the sake of adultery. And so it was with David. What a physical and moral blight rested on the children he begat. Father and children were cursed of God in their own generation; cursed with miseries of mind, with loathsome disease, with premature decay, and death. The words were lettered in every muscle and every faculty of David's children: "It had been better never to have been born." The first child from this lustful murder died young; but another lived to inherit his father's double crime. Beginning his reign with three horrid murders, he afterwards eked out a miserable life of satiety and disgust, with a seraglio of a thousand wives and concubines. Never so plainly has the law of inherited-like been written in the history of man, as in the life of Solomon. The son of Lust and Murder, his after life was enacted long before he was born.

The meaning of all these evils is not only plain to be seen, but it is fearfully depicted in the life of man. Such things show how the holiest emotions may be turned into damning passions; and that which would produce the most bliss, may be made to produce indescribable woe. But from the woe there must come the science of human reproduction.

Not only does blind love destroy the life of man, but from it comes domestic scenes of discord and anger. There is no hate in the world but has a love basis of some kind. Love precedes all hate, and hate grows therefrom. Love brings jealousies, and tears of bitter anguish. It brings demons of madness in many a horrid shape and business. Sweet Revenge unsheaths the secret dagger; Incontinence riots in many a foul deed under cover of night. It has set over against its name a long list of crimes, the blackest in all the dark deeds of the race,—murder, suicide, infanticide, fœticide, incest, rape, prostitution. Half the drunkenness of man springs from it. Its pathway is that trod by the blind: eyes they have, but see not; ears, but hear not; heads, but think not. They grope in darkness at noonday, and themselves dig pits and spread snares which entrap them. All this means *Science,—Moral science; the rational act; the enthronement of Reason.* These evils are, and ever have been, crying aloud to man: "*Give Love eyes.*" The scientific Cupid must have eyes. As religion without reason is Superstition, so love without reason is Lust.

CHAPTER VIII.

THE SOCIAL EVIL.

§. 1. We are now prepared to ask: What does prostitution mean? What is its cause? How shall it be remedied? Can it be cured?

Prostitution comes to mankind as naturally as sunlight. It is no more unnatural than eating and drinking. It obeys the great law of Demand and Supply. Life and death, vice and virtue, are at either pole. It by no means arises always from lust in man, or lust in woman. The demand is with man however, which must precede the supply.

In searching for the cause of prostitution, we are logically compelled to assert it is two-fold in woman, arising from her religious nature and physical necessity; that is, the supply to man's demand is granted through this two-fold *condition* of woman. It may appear at first difficult to prove this; but we will lay down the following propositions, and then adduce such arguments as the facts of the world will warrant.

1. The cause of Prostitution principally arises in man's lust, desire, or necessity, which demands prostitution of woman.

2. Woman submits to his authority through her religious nature and physical necessity.

Of the first proposition we may state, we cannot conceive of a supply, as such, without some demand to precede it. Now, the question is one of fact: Does woman demand prostitution of man, or man of woman? This can only be determined by finding the strict meaning of prostitution. We will take the popular meaning, the soul of which is, that a valuable consideration shall pass between the parties. In which direction does the consideration pass? and who submits, the man or woman? Now, prostitution involves either or both of these causes: a sale or compulsory submission; and the distinction between the two is: when it is a sale, the one who receives the consideration is considered the guilty party; but when submission is compulsory, the guilt would rest on the aggressive party. But who is it that sells, the woman or the man? Surely, it is the man who purchases, and the consideration passes to the woman. Scarcely ever do we find a woman buying the virtue of man. In compulsory submission, when mental or physical force is used, it is man who is the aggressor. Scarcely ever do we find a seduction or a rape of man by woman, or of money given to man by woman for the purpose of satisfying sexual desire. It may be laid down, then, as a conclusion of sound reasoning, that the demand is with man and the supply with woman. Now, as it takes the two parties to complete any act of prostitution, and the demand arises with man, we may logically conclude the cause which precedes is in man, who demands prostitution of woman. Our first proposition is, therefore, proven.

2. Woman submits to man through her religious nature, and physical necessity.

Sexual love seems to be different in mankind from that in the lower animals, which precludes any analogy being drawn therefrom. But the roots, as it were, of all human faculties, we may trace far down into the animal world. Of all man's mental faculties, the religious faculty is perhaps the feeblest in all animals below man; yet we sometimes see it exhibited in the dog and allied species. The females, also, are not dependent on the males for food, and there is but little tyranny of the males over the females, and but little lust among them, till we come to those animals most resembling man. Now, in most of the lower animals, what is called love is only sexual desire, and is a physical necessity, a purely reproductive force. But that which makes one woman love one man, whether exhibited in polygamy or monogomy, is entirely different from sexual desire, yet perhaps is nearly or quite always connected therewith. Sexual desire makes love between the lower animals; but often therein we see an incipient cause of a higher and more lasting love, such as the female lion exhibits, who seems to choose the strongest lion for the father of her offspring. This is only the incipient worship of Force in the animal, and primarily arises in fear. It is Force which conquers and creates fear, which at last ripens into worship.

It is perhaps a universal characteristic of woman to worship a great man. It is at least a very noticeable one. It seems to be quite inherent in woman to zealously admire a man of power, either of head or body. Woman has to have something to admire of a manly and commanding nature in her husband, which compels her to respect him independent of any love she may feel for him. Love is thus intensified through her religious faculty; and worship is only expressed in admiration and love. The wonders of Force in any form compel worship in the reflective creature. This also creates the feeling of conferred superiority. It is a worship of Force. The ancient wife who looked up to, and did the bidding of her husband, only exhibited the action of her religious faculty. This compelled her to be faithful; to lie at his feet; to acknowledge him as her lord and master; to submit to him as his slave. Hence have come the sayings: "Thy desire shall be unto him, and he shall rule over thee;" "The husband is the head wife;" "The wife of Cæsar must be above suspicion;" and also the more modern saying: "Husband and wife are one; and the husband is that one." Take away this feeling in woman which confers superiority on man, and the institution of marriage becomes one only sustained by physical necessity. In other words, had the wife nothing to worship in her husband, the marriage relation would only depend on *tyranny and want.* No sexual love could hold them together. Love is of such a nature that it can be destroyed by a word. The castles of bliss which Love builds may all be shattered by one blow. Love can be produced, intensified, and destroyed, by the actions of men and women. A person may first hate and then love another, or first love and then hate. This is of daily and hourly occurrence. But what is more lasting than sexual love, is the religious sentiment, the worshipful feeling, which the world's history shows to be more intense in woman than in man. It is this which makes matrimony a success. It is devotion, and nothing else, which makes it lasting. It was this feeling of religious submission to the husband that made divorce almost unknown until within the last hundred years; and then it was the husband who always put away his wife for his lust after other women, or for her faithlessness to him, caused by the worship for some other man. If a woman loves a man and nothing more, then any abuse will destroy that love; but if she can worship him, no abuse from him will destroy that worship. Yes, even a woman can hate, but at the same time admire a man. Love in itself is fickle; it comes and goes like the winds; but what remains and is permanent and substantial, comes from the religious faculty; the admiration of worth; the worth-shipful devotion. This is what produces that confiding nature in woman; keeping secret all home troubles, faithful to a fault, and suffering in silence rather than expose the faults of her husband. This disposition in the wife begets also in her husband that sympathy and gallantry which is far more powerful and lasting than any sexual love. This is the cause of marriage; what produces and perpetuates it. Produce an exact equality between the sexes in all things; in feelings, desires, and physical powers; constitute woman so that she will have as much to admire and worship in woman as in man; establish in law and society this equality; give her an equal chance to subsist, hold and acquire property with man, and you would at once destroy prostitution, but at the same time might destroy marriage. Men and women would then become like the beasts of the field, without either prostitution, marriage, or worship. Marriage and prostitution are the two poles of a double force— *Want and Worship*—which, in their action, obey the law of Demand and Supply. It must follow, then, as a logical necessity, the greater the increase of prostitution, the less marital fidelity; or, in other words, the more prostitution the more tyranny of man over woman, which the history of the world proves.

It is from this worshipful nature of woman that men who have the insignia of honor upon them;

who represent any *uncommon power*,—talented speakers, and especially preachers, princes, and kings,—can so easily seduce woman, and what makes "fallen" women so anxious to boast of the embraces of many eminent men. It is thus a talented preacher, of strong sexual instincts, the man who administers to the religious nature of woman, is of all men the most dangerous to connubial fidelity. This is the reason, also, why kings are worshiped and courted by their subjects, and why, of all mankind, they are the most licentious. So long as woman worships a man, that man can control her; he becomes, in the strictest sense, her lord and master; "her divinely constituted head and authority;" and her marriage with him is *lasting*, if not happy.

The worship of Jesus is far more general among women than among men. Perhaps in the Protestant church there are twice as many women as men. The reason is plain. Jesus is woman's *ideal man*, whom she must worship. Woman will always find some Jesus to worship. The same fact is witnessed in the Catholic church, as the cause of nunnery. What awful lessons come from the convents of Catholic Europe during the Middle Ages. There was woman incarcerated voluntarily for life, under vows the most terrible and binding, eking out a life set apart to the worship of Jesus in idleness and prayer. The devout thought herself possessed of Jesus, who came into her cell at night. Wedded to Jesus in her phantom love and real worship, the virgin nun thought marriage with man but carnal lust. To think on man, was horrid; to look on him, madness; and to wed him, would secure the eternal frown of Jesus, her ideal man, her lord, and her husband.

A large class of facts could be generalized under this head; but the above will suffice. Excessive sexual love soon begets satiety and disgust; but there is no reaction in the feeling of admiration. Worship expends its force in an ideal and infinite direction; and worship is the secret of a holy and lasting marriage.

In the inferior races this superiority of man, acknowledged by woman in want and worship, is displayed in her abject submission as the slave and property of man. Woman is bought and beaten by her husband, and taken to his home to be his faithful slave and wife. An Indian will trade his wife for a pony, or swap an old squaw for a young one, and give a pony into the bargain. But it is the religious faculty which perpetuates slavery, of whatever sort. Did not the slave worship his master, there would never be a slave. The worshiper always submits to the tyranny of the master, whether man or god. Deductively we are led to this conclusion, from the nature of Force. *It compels its own worship.* But history also affirms. This basis of slavery is noticed in two remarkable facts in American history. The American indian has never been successfully enslaved, though often tried. He has also but little feeling of *devotion*. In the Negro it is intense. The Negro is confiding and faithful; the Indian suspicious, and of all treacherous beings, the most treacherous. The Negro worships with a zeal which no white man can equal.

It seems thus that all forms of slavery arise out of, and are perpetuated by, the selfish demand, on the one hand; and, the supply being given, through Want and Worship on the other. There must be the actor, and that to be acted upon; the one who demands, and the one who gives the supply; the authority, and the submission. Prostitution is the result of the same force, and obeys the same immutable laws.

In regard to want driving woman to a sale of her body, this is but too truly proven by constantly recurring facts, and needs only to be stated to be admitted by the intelligent reader. Wherever, in fact, there is an inferior or dependent class, there is always more want attending it than in a superior class. The more enslaved, the more degraded will a class be; and, with degredation, Want runs riot. Want drives woman not only into dens of vice, but builds marble halls garnished with licentiousness. All this comes, then, from two things: the demand in man, creating slavery and want; and the supply in woman, in strict accordance therewith.

The foregoing are some of the many facts which present themselves in support of the second proposition, viz: that woman submits to man's authority through her religious nature and physical want. As Force compels its own worship, and makes religion a necessity of man, so Want ever begets dependence and submission. Riches and poverty are the two poles of the cumulative force. An excess of one necessitates an excess of the other. The force which produces a millionaire at one of its poles, must have twenty people of want at the other. Every prince of fortune is complimented by a squad of beggars whom he represents. Then Hunger will drive man into theft; woman into a sale of her virtue. There is in this no law of Nature violated; nay, the prince of fortune and the beggar, the thief and the prostitute, are the result of a law as natural and eternal as that which keeps the earth in its orbit.

§. 2. How, then, shall we remedy the evil of Prostitution, and save the institution of marriage? Surely, not by waging a warfare against the prostitute. She is the result of a cause over which she had no more control than over her birth, or the wealth of her neighbor. She could not help being a prostitute, any more than the negro could help being made a slave. To strike at the prostitute, would be by no means striking at the cause of Prostitution. This is just like slavery. There is on the one hand the master, on the other hand the slave; the demand and the supply, the prostitutor and the prostitute. How did we abolish slavery in the late war? by striking at the slave, or the master? How long, think you, would it have taken us to have ended slavery, by leveling all our guns and expending all our forces against the negro, instead of the master? The negros themselves would have risen up against us, and defended southern slavery, as a divine institution. What kind of morals would it have exhibited, if an exterminating warfare had been begun against the negro for being a slave? Well, the prostitute occupies in Nature the same position of the southern slave. She is produced by the same forces; is governed by the same laws. To destroy Prostitution, the same course must be pursued as against slavery. The cause must be removed, *the demand destroyed*, or in some manner counteracted. But in the popular method of warfare against Prostitution, the slave, and not the master, is the victim; and true to nature and the eternal laws of God, the prostitute is compelled to defend Prostitution, when in very truth she despises it. If in trying to remove a living and growing effect, the cause be not removed, nothing is effected. All agitation, cutting and clipping, only aggravates and intensifies it. If you wished to kill a tree, you would be called insane to begin by cutting off here and there a small limb; for many more would spring out where you had cut off the one. But this is the very manner in which Church and State are pruning away at this evil. We must strike at the root of the tree; at man more, and woman not at all. It would be infinitely better to let Prostitution entirely alone.

It is the man who invests money in Prostitution, because he demands Prostitution of woman. Without man's demand and money, there would be no such thing as Prostitution in the world. But the Church and State cry out: "Abomination! unclean! the harlot must be put down! whoredom must be squelched!" leveling the shaft at the harlot, but not at the men who make, and the institutions which support her.

As a class, prostitutes have much business tact. They are by no means devoid of sense. As a class, they are the most business women of the world. They know how to defend and advertise their profession. It is notoriety they seek; and while they know they must advertise, they are willing to pay for the advertisement. Now, as no proprietor of a newspaper would be justified in publishing their cards, giving name and location, and as no minister would be guilty of announcing them from the pulpit, they contrive to get published in both paper and pulpit. The harlot, therefore, manages to get into a police or recorder's court; and there, before a crowd of men who have congregated to gain knowledge, gives her name and the number of her house, unveils her face, answers such questions as are put to her in such a manner as she thinks will win the admiration of the men around her, pays her fine and goes back to her house or rooms, well satisfied.

The morning paper comes to her hand, and there she sees her name and location shining out in a local, as a part of the consideration which the public return, for what the law had but yesterday taken from her. If there be anything startling or appalling connected with this, the local contains it, and the minister takes his text therefrom, and publishes her loudly and long in the pulpit. If he mentions no name, his congregation have read the local, and know whom he means.

It is thus the Law says: "Put down Prostitution!" then seizes hold of the harlot, who is demanded and made by man's lust and money, holds her up to the gaze of hundreds of lustful eyes, and charges her a small pittance for the advertisement. In this way the State largely increases prostitution; not only by increasing the demand, by awakening the passions of men, but by advertising so thoroughly the harlot. Now, the church is as dumb as a sepulchre as to the cause of Prostitution. No word is uttered against the man who demands the degredation of woman. No word against the institutions, the Church and the State, which support, publish, and produce Prostitution. *Man* is the cause; but he rules Church and State, and selfishness blinds his eyes. He does not see that it is his tyranny and lust, and only these, which produce the evil he so boldly denounces. He looks abroad in society, and waxes wroth; he would tear down the evil, and trample it under his heel. He gathers hold of the prostitute and rends her in pieces, and buries her in dishonor. But from her dead body arise many to fill her place. From the teeth of the dragon he thought he had killed and buried, arise an army to war against him. Society must strike right, or not strike at all. Prostitution is true to itself. It has the seeds of death within it. But if a warfare be waged against it, the battle-ax must be leveled at the full front of man. No woman must be touched, it matters not how vile. Hew down the man who is patronizing, in any form, the sale of woman's virtue. Bray him in the mortar of public condemnation; make him lift the heel of tyranny from the neck of woman, no matter how high or how low he may stand in society. The prostitute is not to blame for being made a prostitute by man; she is born of society, and may be the product of either sin or error. The fool is not to blame for being born a fool; neither is the fool nor the prostitute lost in the economy of God's method of teaching the race. God has need of the fool to teach parents how to make a wise child, without running risks of idiocy or disease. He has need of the slave and the prostitute to teach the world's statesmen wisdom. He has need of the thief for a hundred lessons in regard to property. He has need of the murderer, and every other abnormal phase of man, to lead the world on to wisdom and up to virtue.

Go into our cities, and look at the brothels which

stare both Church and State full in the face. Well may they veil their faces in shame before the bald front of this polluted monster, bred in the great black sea of despotism. Society has in it great rivers of vice, down which often float the noblest and fairest flowers of our mountains and hillsides, plucked from their homes by destroying hands. They are set afloat on the stream, and their course must be ever downward, till they are swallowed up in the mighty maelstrom of our Social Evil. The State looks on and laughs; the Church scowls and looks black at it; folds up its sacerdotal robes, and often, on tip-toe, passes by on the other side. The statesman loses his daughter on the dark tide; the minister another daughter flower, sent down on the dark river. Fear and pride strike these fair daughters dumb; shame hides them away from the world, and they go down, in a few short years, to the silent halls of death, the victims of Church and State. God has need of the statesman's and minister's daughters, going thus down to death, joining their fellow-sisters in the world's great carnival of Lust, from which they never return, to teach the State and the Church that woman has the same right to life, liberty and occupation that man has; and it seems that it is only Prostitution, in the councils of Almighty God, that will abolish the tyranny of man over woman. No; it is not the slave who must be killed to abolish slavery, nor the prostitute who must be harmed to destroy Prostitution. The world is full of lessons already taught on this subject. Many times has both Church and State been sunk in the great black sea of Prostitution, blotting them out forever.

§. 3. But it matters not how the Law seizes hold of the slave and victim; whether in ire to crush or in sympathy to save; the result must ever be failure, because it aims at the effect, not the cause of the evil. We submit the following from the New York *Tribune:*

"FALLEN WOMEN IN BOSTON.

"BOSTON, *June* 21, 1870.—The arrest of a large number of fallen women in Boston created a decided sensation throughout the country about six weeks ago. When these women were brought before the court, many of them were placed upon probation, through the efforts of Chief Savage. At noon to-day Chief Savage appeared in the municipal court, before Chief Justice Bacon, to render an account of his stewardship. In opening the case, Chief Savage made the following address:

"'May it please your Honor: Some six weeks ago we had the unpleasant duty to present to this court a large number of complaints of a peculiar character, which we believe requires peculiar treatment. There are those who seem to think there is no hope for fallen woman. The police do not believe it. While we have little sympathy with the willful, plotting, hardened criminal, we believe that in many cases these women are victims rather than principals in crime; and that wholesome restraint, useful employment, kind treatment and encouragement will save some of them. Acting upon this belief, we came here to ask your Honor to pursue an unusual course. We asked you to impose the restraint by placing before them the gates of a prison, yet giving them one more chance of escape, while we would have the opportunity to try the experiment of kind treatment and encouragement. And please allow me here the opportunity to thank you and all good people for the wise, humane course pursued on that occasion. In entering upon 'the experiment' on that day, we promised you that such as had homes we would send them there, and such as had none we would provide them with homes; and we told you that kind hearts and open hands would furnish the means. In this last, I assure you, we have not been disappointed; and we are here to-day, your Honor, to render the first account of our stewardship. Of the number arrested on that occasion, Fathers Cook, Cullen and the police took special charge of one hundred and thirteen. Twenty-five were put on probation before the opening of court, and eighty-eight, pleading guilty, were also bailed for future appearance, giving them all one more opportunity for reformation.

"'Up to this time we have sent home to parents and friends living out of the city..	49
Sent home to parents and friends in the city	7
To places of respectable employment out of city	5
In places of respectable employment in city	10
Sent to charity home temporarily	5
Sent to insane asylum	1
Sick at her old abode	1
Surrender by bail	5
Whereabouts unknown	22
To be accounted for	8
Total	113

"'Your Honor, we have spared no pains in this work, and good people have come forward with their aid and encouragement. It is not all that we could wish, yet I trust something has been done to justify 'the experiment.' If we save but one, were she my daughter or yours, we would think it worth all the labor.'

"Chief Justice Bacon replied to these remarks

by saying: 'that the course taken by the court, in reference to these cases, appeared to be the best that could be taken, and gave the best promise of suppressing this social evil, which is so flagrant. It was taken with the understanding that each individual case should be looked after, and he should now inquire if the process of law had been duly respected.' The individual cases were then called, as assigned, and reports as to the condition and prospects of each were given. Some of the women were present to answer, and others were responded for by Chief Savage, or some member of the police force. The several cases were then continued or defaulted, according to the merits of the cases. The report of the Chief shows very gratifying success in this noble reformatory work, and all good citizens will rejoice at the result of the experiment."

The above effort to save through sympathy is surely commendable in spirit, but it can only be calamitous in result. Nature has never been known to heal a great evil in this way. An individual may be saved, but the evil itself not only remains, but is intensified.

It is said the above method is one of experiment; yet it is an experiment as old as the tyranny of man over woman. A fretful and cross parent has been known to beat and lacerate a child, and then, in tears and sympathy, hug and kiss the child, and ask its forgiveness. Man himself will ruin woman, pollute and curse, and make woman join him in the curse he has wrought upon her. He will cast her into the ruin of bodily pollution, and then, in tears of sympathy, try to save her from the death of the pit. And he will call this an experiment, which haply may lead him to wisdom. But no wisdom will be enacted till he learns that man, and not woman, is the cause of her ruin. It is pure Reason, and not emotion, which has led the world on to wisdom and virtue. It is the emotional nature of man which has brought prostitution, and keeps it and propagates it in society. It is sense, not sympathy, man must exhibit in his dealing with woman. In the above experiment, the Golden Rule is set up as the law which is to lead to good. But what is the meaning of the experiment? What is proclaimed by this course of action? Why, simply this: "Let us save *one*, if by saving her we slay a thousand who are yet innocent." It would be far better for the world to take each "fallen" daughter who is to be thus saved, and substitute in the place of this sympathetic treatment a public scaffold and guillotine, and before the assembled male prostitutors of Boston, strike off head after head of these victim-daughters, and, having stuck their heads upon pikes, place them at each street crossing, and write thereunder:

☞ THE PROSTITUTE! ☜

THIS IS THE PRICE OF MAN'S LUST!

THIS IS WHAT MAN DEMANDS OF WOMAN!

Although this would by no means cure the evil, it might make men think. There is a deadly dearth of thought on this subject of Prostitution, and until men begin to think, there is no hope for woman. They are doomed to the blind action of Emotion. Sympathy, fidelity, religion, are powerless to save. It is the god of the head, Science, which can only save. The Emotions are the blind forces which drive men to action. They are the steam in the engine. Reason must evolve from acquired knowledge the science of action, mark out the way, and guide therein. It is not Emotion; it is rational, logical thought the world lacks. The evil of Prostitution will be kept standing, forever pointing with finger of Death down to hell; and army after army of "fallen" women will march thitherward, deaf to the entreaties and lamentations of fathers, mothers, husbands, lovers, till mankind *think*. Some terrible event connected with this evil must occur which will react against the cause; which will grind man, not woman, beneath the car of Prostitution.

There is a sublime virtue and manly duty standing out in the act of that old Roman, Virginius, killing his "own dear little girl" rather than see her made a prey to the lust of Appius Claudius. This made Romans think. Appius Claudius went down. The thought, however, took the direction of politics; not of the Social Evil. The civilized world must be made to think in this direction. The police of Boston may have been actuated by the highest and purest motives; but for every "fallen" woman they thus remove from Boston Lust, that insatiable Lust will have its new victim, its fresh fallen virgin guilt. A hundred other daughter flowers must be plucked from the New England hillsides, for each hundred that are withdrawn from the greedy lust of Boston men. As long as the mill is grinding, it must be fed. If what comes out from the bolt is spoilt and damaged,—unfit for the bread of life, though originally good as it went into the hopper,—it had better be turned back into the hopper again and again, rather than have an endless supply of pure grain spoiled, and then continually thrown out as useless. This mill of Prostitution will grind up ten thousand as readily as ten, and ten will supply it as easily as ten hundred.

Man must be made to feel the terrible necessity of self-control; and when Prostitution strikes away a virgin daughter, the anguish which prostrates him to earth is only to drive him into thought, and wring out of the flesh in agony the Science of Life. He must know that the cause is in man, not woman. The *disease*, the *lust*, or *necessity*, is coursing in the veins of man. The fire of this hell is in his blood. Here is the *sexual waste*. Here is the demand. This demand is a force which compels its own worship, and Tyranny riots with his slaves. *Want* and *Worship* are the paths which lead to his embrace.

As selfishness forever blinds, perhaps nothing will be accomplished in the right direction till woman, who is the slave and victim, is taught to see her true condition. *Want* is now educating her very fast. She still wants more *torture* to strengthen the frontal lobes. It is through torture she can only become wise in all the affairs of Church and State. She must be made to realize the force of an *idea;* to fear a cause and profit by an effect. She must be made to *think* science. The science of life grows from within; no process of filling up from without will answer. Till one becomes scientific from within, no experience of others will do him any good. Not until woman becomes truly scientific, will she apply the Science of Life to the reproduction of the race. Not until her front head controls the emotions, will any permanent good be done towards her redemption. When woman has learned her own responsibility as mother, before she is a mother, then, and not till then, will she be fully prepared to grapple with Prostitution and put it under her foot.

That Prostitution is now on the increase, we do not doubt. It must continue to grow and fester in the flesh of society till the Science of Life has been evolved from it. When this science shall crown the life of woman, then will Prostitution gradually diminish, and in the course of ages finally disappear. It requires time to improve a generation of men, because the improvement is to be made only in the application of the principles of breeding. The disease is to be bred out, not cut out, nor healed by soft ointments applied to the living organism. The world wants wise mothers, as the true doctors of the race. But in the mean time let the prostitute alone.

Touch her not as a prostitute, it matters not how vile. If Prostitution must be struck, strike the man who patronizes, in any manner, the sale of woman's virtue.

THREE LECTURES.

LECTURE.

SALVATION AND DAMNATION BEFORE BIRTH.

People are not made better in a moment of time. They are not changed in the twinkling of an eye fróm corruption to the incorruptible, as declared the sage of Tarsus. There is no maneuvering of an unseen hand that can, by magic, turn hatred, lying, lust and disease of man, into love, truth, purity and health. According to the world's theology, after thousands of years, God has not succeeded in reclaiming the Devil. In this is couched a greater defect than the creeds of Christendom will admit; for behold! millions of devils might be turned into millions of saints, by changing the heart of the Devil.

There is no convertion that can transform a human-born devil into an angel of purity. You may put upon him the livery of heaven, but he will be devil still. You may put the lamb's fleece upon the wolf's back; nay, you may nurse him from infancy on sheep's milk, but this will not give him the lamb's disposition. The lamb's flesh will only taste the sweeter to him after having been deprived of it so long. How useless for us to profess other than we are; our actions will only throw back the lie into our teeth, and everybody will cry: "You wear a garment other than your own."

It is, perhaps, because men and women are not made better in a moment of time, after professing some doctrine,—Atheism, Spiritualism or Christianity,—that people who disbelieve in Atheism, Spiritualism or Christianity, are apt to cry out: "What good!" not so much against the people themselves, as against the doctrine they profess.

Now the mere fact of professing anything, never makes the person any better. I do not see that a Methodist is any better than a Campbellite, or Baptist; or Congregationalist, Spiritualist, Atheist, or Infidel. Honesty and dishonesty are found in and outside of all church organizations; among believers of creeds, and scoffers at creeds. Arrogance, pride, meanness, are found wherever great bodies of men and women congregate; and meekness, nobility, and goodness, are also found everywhere among men and women. Even a life-long profession of any particular faith, creed or dogma, never makes the person any better; with or without it, the vile are vile; the pure are pure. The Devil has been a Christian now these two thousand years, and still he is prone to the same old tricks of envy, fraud, deception, war and lust. The Church makes woman no better as wife and mother; man no better as husband and father; yet, in the relations of husband and wife, and parent and child, the world must be redeemed.

How superficial are the religious dogmas of the world. The creed commands a belief, not the righteous act; a doctrine, not a fact of the soul. The Christian asserts that the children of God are created by Christ Jesus in the church, not by parents in holy wedlock; that salvation is by grace alone, not through God's unalterable laws of pro-creation; and that instantaneous and miraculous regeneration is to be forever needed on earth, long after the person is born; not that a person generated right in the first place is all sufficient. The fact is, a belief that an instantaneous conversion will save and regenerate the race, is now what is literally damning it, past the redemption of forty generations of the wisest and noblest effort.

Great changes in religion and politics are brought about slowly. Age after age the rights of man have been taught as expressed by Jefferson; and, yet, age after age they have been trampled upon by rulers and people. The Golden Rule has been taught by the wisest and greatest men since the earliest recora; yet, it is not practiced to-day in Church and State. How long it took America to abolish slavery, and how bloody the work. It was an institution deeply rooted in our soil, and fostered there by Church and State, recognized in the Constitution of the nation, and supported by nearly every Christian denomination. It was founded in, and defended upon Ancient Authority—Holy Writ. Polygamy flourishes in American soil to-day; not extensively among an ignorant and debased people; not among African importations, nor Asiatic migrations; but among the highest type of man, of Caucasian blood, of Saxon head, of civilized birth and modern culture, claiming, too, the peculiar and fascinating title of Christian. So you see the world has not yet got past the example of the patriarch, and Jewish greatest and wisest rulers. Yet, polygamy is gradually dying out, not through wars of opposition and force, but silently, through Nature. Polygamy shows there is something rotten in the marriage relation, and itself contains some truth, else it would not be. So of Prostitution, which vexes and scourges the land. To this foul goddess are sacrificed, often, the first, the brightest and fairest sons and daughters of the world's civilization. This only shows what horrid crimes against Nature and God's laws are committed under sanction of man's laws and hoary-headed custom.

Much has been done to better the condition of man in the world. Revolutions have righted old and time-honored wrongs. Liberty has been baptized often anew, invoking therein the name of some new and unpopular god. The genius of man has brought ease to muscles of toil, through countless labor saving machines. Thought brooding over the world of matter and force, has produced science, which now comes with promised healing in its wings; but it is extremely slow and waits on Evil. The world now, as of old, is sick and needs a physician. Alas! Jesus has been preached now these eighteen hundred years, and yet the world is dying of soul sickness and many a loathsome malady, and to-day needs a Savior greater than a Jesus. Mankind are daily stumbling into the fiery hells of pollution, and no where to be found is the Christ's blood that can wash them pure. They are victims through ignorance, of the "Flesh and the Devil therein."

To the scientific the reason is quite obvious. The evils which affect the world are radical. They are rooted in the flesh of mankind. They cannot be pulled out in a moment of time like a decayed tooth. They are so rooted there, that the best breeding of forty generations would not remove them from the world. The diseases of the world are only healed in the slow processes of Nature, age after age improving but slightly on the past.

Now there is but one way to convert the sinner; there is but one way to reach the greatest possible good of the race, and save the world, or make of it what God designs; and that is to improve the child. This can be done in but one way; understanding how to produce it. This knowledge will raise marriage to the dignity of a science. It will paint Cupid with eyes, and not, as now and with the ancients, blind. That is, our love must look through reason prospectively to the child long before marriage. In this the sciences of Physiology and Biology, and a proper knowledge of human temperaments, will work wonders; for upon these a proper and harmonious marriage must be based. Then, after marriage, the child must be planned long before it is born. Till this wisdom comes and this care is observed, Nature will torture mankind with crime and idiocy born into the flesh, which nothing but Death can eradicate. After birth the child's education is but a secondary consideration; it is an after thought, it may be a help if applied rightly, but can never change the fundamental work which has been done for the child before birth. From poor materials the mechanic can only construct a poor work, however good the design. The parents are the architects and mechanics of their own children, constructing them out of their own bodily forces. And the teacher only develops what is in the child; he produces nothing. The illy-begotten child can never afterwards be fashioned to act a good life; the well-begotten child can be guided aright. No one ever cursed father or mother without just cause, and thousands there are who have done it, and will continue to do it.

To lastingly benefit the world, then, we must go back of the disease to the cause, and not attempt to accomplish everything immediately, nor in the first thousand years. We must act for coming generations in scientific breeding. We must do in this regard what Jefferson did for politics, what Jesus did for ethics,—enact a principle into the life of people. I sometimes think these two men must have been born far superior to most men of their respective ages; made well before birth in body and mind. These two men will be better understood a thousand years hence, unless an intellectual and moral blight seizes upon the race. Doubtless Jesus whispered into the ear of Jefferson the American idea. It is God's gospel applied to politics. And Thomas Paine was certainly our political "John the Baptist," who came preaching in the American wilderness, saying: "Repent, for the Republic is at hand, and the Kingdom in the world's politics will soon pass away; for kings and noblemen of only inherited wealth and position have heard the crack of doom." But one kind of nobleman there is in the world of true sterling worth, and that is God's nobleman, born sound in mind and body; born into harmony with the best conditions of life.

But there are degrees of harmony and soundness. These measure the man. Man's nobility can never be measured in bodily strength and mental calibre. This is evident when we consider the great and general laws which govern the race. But one political law has God enacted in the constitution of the race: "The equal right to use normally the unequal powers of mind and body;" and one moral law has he enacted, which is virtually the same as the other: "Do unto others as you would have them do to you;" and one physical and mental fact forever comes with stunning effect upon us: "As a man is made before birth, so is he." A bible writer expressed the same thought when he said: "As he thinketh in his heart, so is he." As the thief thinketh, so is he; as the profligate thinketh, so is he; as the idiot thinketh, so is he. Yet, who made the fool and the villain? This is a question which ought to make every mother's son and daughter think many a serious hour. It ought to trouble them many an hour of many a day.

To understand this question aright, we must look about us a little, and draw such just conclusions as the facts of Nature will warrant.

If we look abroad, we see imperfection everywhere. Even an oak tree cannot grow a perfect and ideal oak. When yet a little bush it is trod on by man or animal, and made to grow crooked. The soil is not deep, and the rocks prevent the roots from going down deep for nourishment, and it is dwarfed during life. The winds blow off many a limb; the prairie fires scorch it often; the freshets uncover its roots; or the drouth withholds the nourishment of the skies, and it stands a crooked, gnarled, and dwarfed tree. The acorn from which it came might have been of an inferior and dwarfed kind, and so inferiority of stock added to meanness of culture. But if the acorn had fallen in richer soil, in a more congenial spot, where the circumstances were the most favorable to the growth of the oak, and it had been of the best variety of seed, then another and far better tree would have been the result. Here we say the *blind forces* of Nature were favorable to its growth, whereas, in the first instance, they were unfavorable. Here is only a play of blind forces, with no special design behind them, for the good of the coming oak. But man is a curious force; he is a tabernacle of design, wherein dwells a god. Now let him take the acorn from its forest home, where it had fallen, perhaps, into the crevice of a rock; bear it away to a deep, rich alluvial soil; plant it therein; fence it away from the tread of animals; dig about it; guard it from fire; water it during drouth, and it grows rapidly in beauty and grace. Now the winds only strengthen its body and make it take deeper root, and all Nature seems to add to its growth, as it goes on from day to day, 'mid sunshine and storm, prophesying of good materials to some coming generation of man.

What is the legitimate conclusion from these facts? Why, surely, that God designs the best to the oak only through the conscious thought of man. The oak tree can be perfected only through man. As the acorn fell in the forest by the force of gravity, so will it lie. It may be removed by the rains, or carried off by the squirrel, but with no *design* to make of it a perfect oak, in accordance with the informing law of the acorn. Man picks it up with such a design, and God operating in man, by and through this mental force, reaches the perfect end in design. Here man can overcome gravity through the force of will, in conscious design. Knowledge and design are the ideal forces of the universe, which mould, form and construct in the material world material things and objects; and must, eventually, make all material laws, or the blind forces of the world, subservient to them. It is in man's conscious thought that the oak tree is perfected. The perfect oak must take root in the brain before it does in the earth. It must be transplanted from the head to be depended upon. This is the highest act of *creation;* the creative act. What is creating? Moving matter into new forms. This may be done blindly in accordance with Natural law, or through design, foretelling the result. In this, the highest sense, man is a creator.

Would you create an oak tree? You pick up an acorn which only contains the *antecedents of growth;* the pent-up forces of ancestral oaks. You have within your hand the law, but within your mind the ideal oak and the conditions of perfect growth. You may speak life or death to the ideal fact which the material acorn represents. You may control the fact of the oak's future existence or non-existence by planting the acorn in good soil, or by casting it into the fire and roasting it. Now, if you roast it, God Almighty could not make an oak tree from that acorn. And, why? Because the force of fire drove away the living principle of the acorn, destroying the temple in which it dwelt. The angel of Death drove out the angel of Life. In other words, the material conditions of the incarnate oak were destroyed, and conditions always govern growth. If God could make something from nothing, then man could make oak trees from roasted acorns, or potatoes out of mud balls. There is a God's law governing growth, or all change. This law is unchangeable. Which means that God never works contrary to his established laws. If he did he would be inconsistent; and we could count on nothing as certain in the universe. There would be no Science, no such thing as Truth. But man often works contrary to God's laws, and in his ignorance, often asks God to counteract his own commands. But this may be depended upon; if the whole world of mankind should all get down on bended knee, at one moment, and ask God to sprout the roasted acorn, he would continue about his business, regardless of the united prayers of the world. So much more value is the law by which he sprouts one little acorn than all the prayers of earth. Nor would he change the law, that the oak when grown will produce after its kind with a generic likeness, but an individual variation. No prayer could produce any change therein. Figs from thorns, and grapes from thistles, we frequently find expressed in man's laws and prayers, never in God's laws or actions. In the roasted acorn the law, by which the oak tree is produced from the acorn, had been annulled and it could never be prayed back to operate in that acorn. The conditions of the future oak had been destroyed; no other conditions in the universe would answer.

But suppose, instead of roasting the acorn, you plant it; it sprouts and grows thriftily for two years, when you throw upon its tender and frail body a rail, leaving it bent half-way to earth for two years more. You then remove the rail and endeavor to straighten it. All endeavor, all fervor of prayer is in vain. It was inconsistent with God to grow a straight tree with a rail on the slender and frail twig. And because inconsistent, impossible for him to do otherwise. The law of perfect growth in the oak had been violated and it was compelled to grow crooked. Thus many a person's after life has been made crooked before birth, and God's laws vindicated therein. Hence, we say; that which is not consistent with the perfect and infinite Force of the universe, has not arisen through any design therein. We say the idiot is not inconsistent with God's laws of producing mankind, only inconsistent with the law of producing sound men and women. The idiot is the slender sprout with a rail on it, bending its head to earth. Nor does God fail in producing the idiot; for, from this defect of the head, people are driven to study God's laws of producing sound heads, and mankind are benefitted through the science of Reproduction.

But to return to the chief function of man in the

world. We have said: it is in man's conscious thought that the oak tree is perfected. In fact, there can be nothing perfected or made to improve with a perceptible growth, without man. Take the fruits of the world. It was in the mind of man that the Early Harvest, and Golden Pippin, and Russet, and Belle-flower and Wine-sap, were made. Without man it was only possible for God to grow, in the long ages, the wild crab-apple and hawthorn. Man took the wild apple, administered to its growth and schooled it in the way it should grow, year after year, and age after age, till he made himself an article of food, as God designed. How many ages passed in which God only grew crab-apples, because no dust quickened by scientific knowledge to perfect what he had begun, is known only to infinite intelligence. So it is with the berries of the wood or prairie, they are only perfected by man in the gardens of culture. A few hundred years of culture by man has raised the potato from an almost unpalatable esculent up to one of the chief supports of human life. Man took it while yet imperfect, just where God had left it in the wilds of Peru and the Carolinas, and went on with what he had begun to perfect it. Without man on earth, God could not make a perfect potato. Neither can God grow perfect corn nor wheat, nor aught that grows for man's support or pleasure, without man's implements of sharpened steel, baptized in the sweat of holy toil. Even the flowers of the field bloom fresher, with more lively tints, and yield a richer perfume, within a few generations, under the perfecting hand of man.

So it is with the animal world. God could not make a perfect cow or horse, without the result oı man's knowledge, applied with the conscious design to perfect or improve them through the principles of good breeding. The Arab is choice of his steed, given him from the hand of Allah; but he himselt has added a third to its speed, over that which God had conferred, by bringing together favorable qualities in mother and sire; bettering the foal in man's head, through care and thought, and often in experiments which failed. This is only taking hold of Nature, and making her obedient to the will of man. And now, so perfect has become the Science of Breeding, that man takes the powers of creation in his own hands, and makes a horse to suit his purpose, whether of strength or speed. So, too, of the ox kind, he makes an animal to produce the most beef or milk, or best for the yoke, to suit his purpose. Without man it is possible for God to make of the ox kind only the Buffalo,—in all parts of the world the same in color and disposition, and almost the same in size and shape. John Sebright said, with respect to the color and shape of pigeons: he could produce any given feather in three years, but it would take him six years to obtain head and beak. Here man moulds and paints the animal, in accordance with a pattern prescribed. The animal world is plastic in his hands; it is the clay in the hands of the potter.

The principle upon which man creates and manipulates the world is this: The force which moves the variable atom is a unit, and ever tends to perpetuate itself, but always varies under new conditions. Like produces like, under like conditions. Man can control the conditions, and vary the coming animal, physically and mentally. He thus improves the animal or plant in design. First it is made better in the Ideal; then the Ideal is incarnated in flesh. This is the highest form of the creative act.

So you see that in the organic world God could not perfect it without man. To state it in another form, which is perhaps more scientific: It was impossible for God to perfect the work in animal or plant without incarnating himself in man as *Science*, which is the Christ of the world. So he came into man, not suddenly, but slowly and insensibly, in long ages of development, in many a faculty, to think, to know, to reflect, to plan, to construct, to improve, to beautify, to love, to hope, and to aspire after the Ideal. The Ideal is the crowning thought. It is the image of God in man: the power which moves matter into human expressions. And there is now in each reflective mind, held up in the Ideal a better man or woman than God has yet produced on earth. It is said God made man in the "beginning," and that he made him perfect. It is, perhaps, nearer the truth to say: God has not yet finished making man; the job is not complete. Man is a growth, not a miraculous and instantaneous creation. He is not yet born into the Ideal manhood and womanhood. He is still developing; still growing day after day, age after age. We see man himself by and through the laws which govern life and procreation, improving the man, into whom God breathed the breath of life, and left grossly imperfect. Man surely is his own creator in the highest and noblest sense of the term. He is made by an eternal covenant co-partner with God for the finishing and perfecting of earth, plant and animal.

But *how* shall man act for his own good? The more knowledge, the higher the life; the better the action, the greater the good. There never was an evil or calamity which overtook man but pointed to wisdom. The pearl of truth is taken from the heart of Evil. Experience is the school in which the world learns wisdom. We are herein taught the science of living; the science of doing. A few generalizations may not be here amiss.

There are certain principles, the result of subtle forces in the universe, which we call material laws; such as gravity, the laws of chemistry, light, heat and electricity, of birth, growth and decay. These laws are constant and fixed. They are the result of a blind force, and as effects of such, are irrevocable. There is no repeal of, nor appeal from them. These forces, for the good of plant and animal, have to be overcome or their effects prevented, for they often conflict or run counter to each other. The man who picked up the acorn in the forest to plant it in his field overcame, not the material and fixed law, of gravity, which made it fall to earth and would keep it there, but the conditions into which gravity had forced it. Here a higher force, one of Intelligence with a future good in design, overcame the effect of those natural conditions which would dwarf, cripple or destroy it; these conditions being the result of blind forces. Man's intelligence must control the conditions of his birth and growth, or he becomes the result of conflicting blind forces.

It thus becomes apparent that Harmony is the word which expresses the law of all good. To live, to grow, to produce good, we must place ourselves in harmony with the established laws of the mental and material world, and control the conditions of life. This is a conflict of mind with matter. It is the mental world subduing the material; it is finding out the relation of things and adapting them to each other. It is conscious design controlling blind force. Gravity has no conscious will-power behind it, for any special good to man. Gravity would hurl us to earth from the top of a tower, did we not, consciously, by force of will, through common prudence, make our footing sure. The former relates to the material world, the latter to the mind. To produce harmony, is purely the result of mental force controlling the conditions of life.

In Dr. Howe's report on idiocy, to the Legislature of Massachusetts, in 1848, it is stated that out of 359 idiots, only about a quarter of them were found to have had temperate parents. Seventeen of these were also found to be the children of parents closely related by blood. "On examining into the history of the seventeen families to which these individuals belonged, it was found they had consisted in all of ninety-five children; that of these no fewer than forty-four were idiots. Twelve others were scrofulous and puny. In one family of eight children, five were idiots."

When an idiot comes into a mother's lap, it ought to be mourned over as an act of divine providence. Yet no one ought to be foolish enough to say God created it, and failed. So far as God is concerned, the idiot is no more a failure than a Newton. The parents failed, not God. Put a pint of whisky into almost any man's stomach, and he is for hours a senseless, blubbering idiot, or a raving, staggering maniac. A child produced in such a mental state, ten to one will be a physical or mental wreck; and almost sure to be, when there is added the close relationship by blood. Were this not the case, then surely would God fail. For the drunken parents, when Reason is dethroned, and Passion hot as the fires of hell, must set on fire their children, of their own lusts, or fail to light the lamp of intelligence, because of their own mental darkness, is as certain as that God has written the law on tablets of flesh and mind, that *Like produces Like.*

This is a law of the mental world. Hate begets hate. Anger begets anger. Love begets love. Jealousy makes the food it feeds on. This is a law which is irrevocable. You cannot annul it in the legislatures of State, in the councils of Church, nor at the family hearthstone. You might as well try to vote the icy Labrador into eternal summer, or abolish in the councils of Church the sweet influences of sun and moon, as to try to produce bright and healthy babes from whisky and folly.

No, God does not make the idiot, nor thief, nor murderer, nor son of lust, any more than he makes a reaper, or threshing machine, or steam saw-mill, or any other work of man. It is only an expression of the established and eternal laws of mind and body, and of the material world, which govern the production and operation of steam mill, threshing machine, reaper, child of lust, drunkard, murderer, thief, idiot. It is upon an eternal principle that the steam saw-mill acts; and it matters not to God, whether a log or a man is placed in front of the saw; it would saw both with a full head of steam on. And if the best man on earth was sitting on the log, and about to be drawn up to the saw, God would not miraculously shut off the steam to save him. In all these things, God works only through man. He teaches him "How" thorough his failures, and points out wisdom in the evils which afflict him.

A mother sitting at her chamber window playing with her child, a year old, accidentally lets it fall out on the stone pavement, twenty feet beneath, and it is killed by the fall. Who killed this babe, God or the mother? Let us see. Suppose the mother asks a philosopher: "What made my babe fall and get killed?" He wisely answers: "Gravity, madam, which draws all loose substances to earth. There is a certain law, madam, governing the falling of bodies." "Well, but who made Gravity?" enquires the mother. "Nobody;" responds the philosopher; "it is co-eternal with God. Ask as well who made God. This for general purposes is a blind material force. It acts on all objects. It is as instrumental in giving life as producing death. It is a blind material force. But mentally you may know; and you have maternal love to prompt you to common prudence, for the care and safety of your child. Had you obeyed the law of your own being, you could have saved your child. So you see, madam, you are punished for your ignorance or lack of prudence, just the same as though it were willful, so far as God is concerned in it. Many a similar sad catastrophe happens to many a mother's child before it is born, madam." "How so?" inquires the mother. "You remember," says the philosopher, "the little foolish child that was such an annoyance to its mother, your neighbor, who long watched it with care, to keep it from falling into the fire, or death of all kinds which surrounds us; and that at last it fell from the door-sill, which was the death of it. There was an accident, madam, at both ends of its life. It was made by accident, and wept over; it was born an unwelcome thing, and wept over; and accidentally went out of life, and wept over. It was nothing but tears to its mother. It was a failure from beginning to end, madam, entirely an accidental thing. God made that child, madam, just as much and no more than he kills the man who accidentally blows his own brains out with powder and ball. It is in accordance with the laws of the material world, but in violation of the higher law governing human life and action."

Upon this very principle men and women produce the bodies and form the characters of their children. The forces are constant which produce the child, whether healthy or diseased, in body or mind, just as gravity is constant which killed the child in falling from the window. And the laws which are the result of these forces may be studied in the failures of pro-creation, no less than in falling towers or moving tempests. By contemplating the fool and the villain, and by having them thrust upon parents and society, people may, at last, be tortured into an investigation of the causes of idiocy and crime; and this will eventually compel them to study the laws of pro-creation so as to learn how to make a sound child.

It is said man is made in the image of God,

This is "begging the question," and putting effect for cause. It is, perhaps, true, and the world's history seems to prove it, that God is made in the exact image of each person who has power of mind enough to conceive of a God. Should we place before you a man who is all diseased without and within, covered all over with foul, scrofulous sores, cross-eyed, hair-lipped, loose-jointed, knock-kneed, hunch-backed; a physical dwarf, whose head comes almost out of his stomach; who has added to this physical imperfection that mental blight called idiocy; soul-scarred and sin-stained from his mother's womb, and say to you: Ladies and gentlemen, this is man, the greatest work of God, made in his own image. What kind of a conception would you have of God? What would you think of the wisdom of God in creating this imbecile and slobbering idiot? No doubt the egotism of mankind would be wounded were we to say: a monkey is made in the exact image of God. Yet there are apes in the world far superior to some abortions who take the dignified title of man. Viewed morally, the case is just as bad. Was Nero, or Vitellius, or Constantine, or Jeffreys, or Joshua of old, made in the exact image of God? How, then, about the image of the Devil? It is to us blasphemy to say that God made the idiot as an omnipotent work of skill, designing him to be perfect, and that therein God failed; or, that the idiot is a "freak of Nature," a curse to parents, a perfect blot on the human page, produced by causes over which parents had no control, and that thus they are innocent of the child's idiocy, or that God intentionally, specially and miraculously made the murderer, or thief, or child of lust. These are all made by men and women; all failures in the pro-creation of the race. But after they are made by men and women, God enacts wisdom therefrom by showing parents wherein they have failed, and wherein they can better the abortive work. God designs always to teach wisdom from the failures of man. The idiot gawks at his mother, while she weeps over the intellectual darkness or mental ruin of her child; and God designs that the idiot shall gawk, writhing the mother in mental anguish, that women, before marriage, may study the child's good long before it is born.

It is an infamous slander on God to say he has anything to do directly, in special creative acts, with all this army of murderous, thievish, lying, lustful, idiotic men and women, whose life germs have been perhaps mingled with the drunkard's cup; started for earth in currents red with the crimes of lust, and spawned into existence in dens of vice, or in embellished houses of legalized Prostitution. Do not be mistaken! God has nothing to do with these births of the world. They are accidental products of creative ignorance. They are specimens of man's fall. They are the curse of his disobedience. They are brought forth in violation of God's laws, which he has writ on tablets of flesh, not in harmony with them. And it is the Word of God, proclaimed in all Nature, that he intends to have the murderer cut at the throat of his mother; the thief to steal the trappings from his father's coffin; the idiot to blubber and talk gibberish, slavering in the very face of his mother; and the child of lust to corrupt the currents of human blood, till mankind shall learn wisdom, and create the child of good materials, after the ideal pattern. This is the cause of the fool and the villain, and God's design therein.

The general principle upon which God works, is to suspend no law of Nature for the accommodation of his choicest child. Man has given him the power to make and improve himself, with the means of knowledge at his very door. It is for us to do, to perfect, to complete what, without our own design, could not have been done. The materials God furnishes; man fashions them either into a house or a child. He makes the rude hut or the princely palace, the intellectual giant or the idiot. As the animal and vegetable world could not be perfected without man, so neither can he himself be perfected without his own care and culture.

The child illy born is the result of man's ignorance, but from the failure he is to learn wisdom. This is the order of Nature in all departments of life. Man is a growth in knowledge as well as structure. We think the Osage indian holds the analogous relation to the most civilized man that the crab-apple does to the standard apple of our orchards, or that the buffalo does to the Devon or Durham of our herds. And as God could only grow wild crab-apples and wild buffalo without man's care and culture, so also he could only grow wild men without their own care and culture in their own pro-creation. Nature brings the animal and vegetable up to a certain point by the law of natural selection, without any special design. This is the blind law of the survival of the strongest in the struggle for life. But there is a point at which Nature stops, and there rests, till man, with *design* for the good of himself, controls the conditions of life, and brings the animal and plant to the crowning perfection of domestication. Here it is the survival of the fittest, not always the strongest. The former is in accordance with the *blind* law of force—the survival of the strongest; the latter is in accordance with the law of design—the survival of the fittest.

We think this fact will be admitted before long by the religious teachers of the world. Certain we are, no permanent good can be done towards man's salvation, till it is admitted, and the old theological twaddle about binding Satan be stopped. When a good race of children is produced, then will Satan be bound; then will be the millennium; then will the Christ appear. This need not be a thousand years hence with the most advanced race; but with the whole world it may be many thousands. But some families may have the millennium already—

doubtless do. A young woman, sound in mind and body, finding a suitable matrimonial partner, being joined and living in marriage as God designs, may bring the millennium within one generation, and she herself see the infant Jesus, in her own lap. Verily, this generation would not pass away before this were fulfilled in that family established under God's laws of marriage. It is more possible for heaven and earth to pass away, than for God to deceive the man and woman of sound mind and body, scientifically married, who understand the laws of pro-creation, and will live up to them.

Would you know then the prime cause of the fool and the villain? It is because the child is not planned before birth. There is no design to make of it a perfect child antecedent to the creative act, and without this design in the mind of father and mother, the blind forces of Nature are ever ready to turn the child into a physical or mental wreck. I look upon the perfectly organized child, which is yet to come, as a work of art; as much so as the thorough-bred animal which adorns the farmer's field or stable. The time will come when thorough-bred men and women will be the envied God's nobility of earth. The adorning with social "manners" amounts to but little. This outward culture is but the "tinsel and ruffling" which hides all that is real.

The breeder of thorough-bred cattle or horses, has a model in the head which he tries to produce in flesh. So, also, there is in man, the ideal man and woman, better than earth has yet seen, which, some day the world will produce, through the conscious thought of man. It is only here in the Ideal world that God has created the better man; yet, by no means perfect. The Christian world project this ideal conception back to the time of Jesus, and worship him as very man, and very God. But they are mistaken when they make him a finality of human perfection. The world is continually producing her Jesuses after the ideal Jesus of the human soul.

Look at the work of an unknown hand in the Apollo Belvidere. That master work of art, preserved from the destroying hand of the barbarian, unable to appreciate its beauty and grandeur, has come down to us the crowning glory of the Grecian thought. And yet it must have fallen far short of the ideal perfection which, alone, the artist built in his own mind; for there must be added to this, that mental beauty, power and loveliness, which chisel cannot carve, and which mind alone can see. When we add the greatest moral beauty to the best physical form, which mind can fashion in the Ideal, then we conceive of man, as God is commanding us to create him; as God is now creating him in us.

Nor can man be bettered save in design; first creating a better man in the head before he is put into flesh. Suppose you had a hundred thousand dollars to invest in the erection for yourself of a business house in some city. You make an estimate that it will cost one half of this sum for the materials. So you purchase fifty thousand dollars worth of materials: so many perches of stone; so many thousand brick; so much lumber, iron, glass, nails, lime and sand, and pile them all down on the ground together, and then set your men to work, to lay stone on stone, and brick on brick, without a plan and specifications. You have ignored an architect, and have no design of your own. Do you think you can construct in this way a house with any assurance of success? A million to one it will be a failure. Well, it is just the same with the human race. A million to one we are failures. But suppose, on the other hand, you go to an architect and state your case to him, the object of your house and the amount you have to invest in it. There is the architect in his little room ten by twelve, or less, inside of four bare walls. He closes his eyes and looks within. He seems dreamy and hates to be disturbed. He locks himself in and dwells in silence alone in abstract thought. He is building a house without an atom of matter. It assumes definite proportions: so many stories high, so many feet for each story, so many feet at base, so much depth, so many feet for cornice, frieze and entablature,—the proportions to please the eye, so as to make a house of beauty, nay, even imposing and grand. Then he runs through its different apartments and arranges and economizes space, to make it commodious and convenient, airy and light; when lo! he has it constructed there in his own head,—an edifice far more perfect than you can employ workmen, the most skilled and experienced, to put into material form; as it is always impossible to put into material form that surpassing real of the Ideal creation. The architect draws off, as best he can on paper, the edifice with plan and specifications. With this your house is no failure, and when finished is a model of beauty and convenience. The unthinking rabble praise you; for there is your name carved in large letters on its front; but you alone know how to appreciate the quiet and obscure architect, who deserves all the praise which the unthinking millions are bestowing on you.

Well, fathers and mothers should be the architects of their own children. The blind forces of Nature are only the mechanics; the hewers of wood and drawers of water, to be guided by an architect's hand. They know nothing of the design; care nothing about the beauty, the worth, the life of the child. We think the facts of the world will bear us out in the assertion, that among the vast millions of earth's population the child is neither designed, nor scarcely a thought bestowed upon its construction. All is left to the blind forces of Nature. No wonder, then, that the word "failure" is set over against the life of so many people of the world.

Let us look at the office of the mother. Let us begin with her before marriage, when she has not yet loved the partner of her life's joys and sorrows,

Within her mind should be the Ideal of the man she is to wed. This Ideal should be based upon the scientific fact that like temperaments should never marry. There is much, however, to be learned upon the physical and mental adaptation of proper marital relations. A law must some day be established, inductively from the evils of marriage. Facts are now beginning to accumulate which promise great ultimate good. Marriage now stands where Astronomy stood in the time of Hipparchus, where Geography stood in the time of Cosmas. As the Christian god in the time of Copernicus, guarded with flaming sword the entrance to the starry world, and frightened away all who were disposed to investigate, so the god of the hearth-stone drives away every scientific intruder. But the bonds of marriage are now becoming like flaxen threads in the fire. The green withes of early love, dry and rot with age, and often fall off the yoked pair unconsciously and without a struggle of discord. There is much to be learned about proper selections, and much about preserving the union after the alliance. But when Marriage is raised to the dignity of a science, there must be the Ideal of the more perfect pair. This Ideal will sift, sort, exclude, reject, till the ideal fact is fully satisfied. Then Love will bow at the feet of Reason. Woman must know that Love without reason is Lust, and is the world's curse from of old. Love is like the religious faculty; blind and strong as fabled Samson, and stands in society between the two pillars of Church and State; and when not guided by Reason, would tear down the social fabric on its head, destroying thousands in the fall. This these two faculties have often done, are still continuing to do.

Oh! young woman, tremble at the first emotion of Love. Go into your soul's closet, and pray that Reason, and Knowledge, and firmness, and right, shall guard you, and guide you into the light which Science shall shed on your way. Pray with the head that divinest of all prayers, that Knowledge may come in there and bless you; pray with the prospective thought that *wife* may bring to you joy or pain untold, and that *mother* shall be to you heaven or hell on earth. Be aware of the fact that in your body shall circulate the materials, sound or unsound, of your child's mechanism; that your bodily health and strength shall be imparted to it; that disease and bodily imperfection may also pass from your veins into its own structure; that overwork, toil and drudgery will descend in weakness, also; that the impress of your own soul may be stamped on the mind of the child; that goodness, purity, peace and love, may bring an angel of your own into your lap; or Murder, which is in your thought, may wait to strike through the hand of the child you shall bear; that your dissipation may riot in debauch long after you are dead, in your own offspring; or the villainy of the man you wed may image back his secret social crimes, in the child you long may have to weep over. Oh! mother, thy office is always the holiest, yet may be the vilest on earth. Mothers of the world, from thy womb ascend the angels of heaven or descend the devils of Hell. Thou art the Savior or the Destroyer of the children of Time. No power hast thou, like fabled Chronos, to devour thy own unruly children. They come back to curse, to fight, to torture you, and from them you can never flee away; or they come like a fairy band, wreathing the blessings of heaven on thy head, and playing sweet melodies on harps strung with the cords of thy affections.

Man, do you think you understand the duties of husband and father? Is your wife a slave crouching at your feet? Do you hold that she shall come and go at your bidding; that she was made to minister to you, and that this is the sole purpose for which she was designed? Do you believe that there was any special curse pronounced upon her, as that, her desire shall be unto you, and you shall rule over her? Do you believe that she is only a necessary appendage to man, a thing by which he is to people the earth, and which is to satisfy his lusts? Then woe to the world because of you. From your loins come Polygamy, Rape, Prostitution. These image back your own domestic life, and reflect the darkness of your soul. Under your rule the black artist of hell finds life pictures to paint. Under your rule Disease, Murder, Lust, leap from your own heart into your children's veins, and lurk there like robbers of the highway, under cover of wood or night, to again strike down their victim.

We look upon woman as the equivalent of man, who as wife has the right to her own body, and as mother has the right to dictate terms to the father of her children, and to resist the unhallowed abuse which she always receives when a slave to him. In short, we look upon woman truly enlightened, and raised to the dignity of a free human being, as the Savior of the race. We worship at the shrine of *Mother;* one who understands the functions of her office; one who understands the relation she sustains to her child, and the child to the race; one who fully comprehends the awful consequences of ignorance, sin or error, when an immortal soul is charged up to her account. We honor the Emersons, the Parkers, the Davises, the Jesuses of the race. We admire their genius, their learning, their inspiration, their bold and pregnant speech, their pure religious life and manly character, but we worship at the feet of one such *Mother*. In her household you will not see a husband, like the oak-tree of unfavorable birth and circumstances, torn and gnarled by the blind forces of the world, dwarfed and rotten at the heart. No child of hers will you find scorched by the fires of Lust, or crouching in spirit, trod on before birth by the heel of a tyrant. No child blighted or withering for the want of physical or mental food; *but one of design, made for a purpose*, a glory to her, and a blessing to the race.

How useless it is to talk then of regeneration, saving grace, the blood of Christ, forgiveness of sins, sanctification, justification, in view of the appalling fact, that our mothers bore us. In view of this fact nobody can understand any of these terms. One word will express them all—*mistification.*

It is proper generation not regeneration that the world so much stands in need of. What process of regeneration will right a physical imperfection, scrofula or hare-lip? What kind of regeneration will give a front-head to the idiot, or a top-head to the malevolent? It is fast being found out that the fool and the villain cannot be regenerated. They have been spoilt in the making. They are broken vessels of flesh and mind, and can never be mended on earth.

Saving Grace.—What is it? We would call it the wisdom of woman as wife and mother.

Forgiveness of Sin.—What is a sin? A willful violation of a known law of God. You get drunk, knowing that it injures you, and you fall into the gutter of licentiousness. You transmit the lust of your heart and the smell of the bottle to your child, and he has a mania for liquor all his life, proves a curse to you, to the mother who bore him, and to the world; and God can forgive you for your drunkenness, can he? *How?* The forgiveness of sin is a contradiction in terms. I place my foot willfully in your path; you tread on my toe, for which I suffer, and I cry out, pardon me for your stepping on my toe; and you say: granted through the suffering of some one of your relatives. This is the whole story of all the praying to God to forgive sin, which has ever been prayed in Christendom. There is no forgiveness, no justification in Nature for sin. There is no santification for the sinner.

The Blood of Christ.—Will the blood of Christ wash out the body's pollution and prevent the transmission of disease? Will the true and devout Christian be exempt from the effects of violated laws of pro-creation, and his children be born pure and heirs of heaven? No vicarious atonement can prevent the effects of our sins or errors on the coming generations of man! no blood of Christ will wash away the diseases of the flesh transmitted to our children! no holy light of the immaculate Son of God can illume the dark chambers of the idiot or the insane! no Holy Ghost will overshadow the son of man, begotten in drunkenness and lust! The popular scheme of salvation falls dead at the feet of Science. People can only be saved at the inner courts of family, before they are born; designed in wisdom and begotten in love.

A Change of Heart.—Ministers talk learnedly about a change of heart; about the Holy Spirit striving to convert some hardened sinner, not of evil deeds and thoughts, but of unchristian belief. But the minister himself is floundering in the abyss of Ignorance. A pure skin and healthy stomach is of far more consequence, than a profession of religion. The Kingdom of Heaven is often lost from the want of soap and warm water. Inherited disease often casts people into a hell, from whose fiery flame no profession of religion and no change of heart can save. Instead of sinning against God, man is sinning against himself. Men and women are often thrown out into life, complete failures of creation. Conceived in sin and brought forth in iniquity, how can a change of heart or the prayers of ministers save them? No prayer of priest can penetrate back to the cause of the failure. No prayer can cure the disease, no profession of religion can purify the fountains of adulterated blood, no rite of church can give relief.

Ministers urge men and women to prepare for the next world. Would to God they would spend all their talent and earnest breath in teaching them to prepare for *this* world. It is not an imaginary hell beyond the grave, that mankind must be saved from; it is the hell of this world, its fires and its devils. It is not the soul of man that must be saved so much after death, it must be saved before birth. It is not death, it is life which is a fearful thing. It is the life which the prospective child is to live on earth, when conceived in sin and brought forth in iniquity, which is most calamitous and fearful. It is a mistake to suppose God can save men and women from the effects of error or sin. They can only save themselves. As well say that God can save the child from bodily death, that fell out of the window, twenty feet down, on the stone pavement, its brains dashing out with the fall.

But wisdom rises out of the follies of life, and the path to success is pointed out in its failures. Truth, or the fixed purpose of God, sets over against the errors and sins of men and women as living rebukes of shame and disgust, the monsters of the flesh and the idiocy of the mind, to teach virtue and wisdom. And the villain of the state, the street, the brothel, or the pulpit, reflects the wisdom of God on the failures of man in the night of his ignorance, as the moon reflects the glory of the sun upon the night of earth.

LECTURE.

SUNDAY,—ITS HISTORY, USES, AND ABUSES.

In the land of Jefferson and the Declaration of Independence, a man was fined for working. He paid his fine, and his county and state ought to have been the richer for it; but that they were, you may well doubt.

A man worked, and was fined therefor? Yes; but it was unlawful labor.

Was it for selling liquor in a dram-shop? No; that is not work.

Was it for taking corn away from his neighbor's barn without lawful right? No; that would be stealing.

Was it for reaping where he had not sown, or gathering where he had not strewn? No; not at all; you misunderstand. He was not even tilling his own soil, for which he had a fee-simple and a God's patent; but working with implements of wood and steel, neither stolen, borrowed, nor unpaid for.

What! In brewing corn and rye to make whisky, to make men drunk; to bring ruin to head and heart? It were better to raise the bread-corn for himself and family, and for the stranger that may come within his gate.

No; you still misunderstand. This man was an honest man; not a gambler, nor thief; no liquor dealer or brewer; no city wag, with ill-behaved mouth or stomach; no profligate country clown; but a *man*,—that being who has centered within him the attributes of the Universe. Such a man, in such a country, and for such labor, as you will see in the sequel, was fined. The result of it was: an honest man was made poorer, and the State no better off. But this opens the discussion, in which grave practical and theological questions arise.

The evil, sin, or misdemeanor, is not in the character of the man, nor in the kind of labor he does, nor how he does it; nor in the object of such labor, but in the *time* in which it is done. That is, there is time recognized by Church and State called "holy time," as distinguished from secular or unholy time. This holy time is considered to be one of the seven days of the week, and varies with the religious views and beliefs of widely separated nations. There is, then, a holy day; for the Grecian, Monday; for the Persian, Tuesday; the Assyrian, Wednesday; the Turk, Thursday; the Jew, Saturday, and the Christian, Sunday. But with this last we have only to do in Kansas.

This holy day, called Sunday, is the only one which is to be entirely dedicated to God. Once, people in this Christian land were commanded, by statute, what to do, and what only to do on this day. Then meeting houses were filled with worshipers, according to "law and gospel." Those palmy, Puritan days of New England are, perhaps, passed away forever. Now, the command: "Go thou to church," is only heard from very few parental lips. There is no fear of statute, or terror of hell hanging over it. The statute does not command what shall be done on Sunday, it only prohibits certain acts from being done. Happy is that man who sleeps all day Sunday, rather than use contrary to statute this day. After the statute had ceased commanding what to do on Sunday, it was only left for the Christian minister and priest to command, and so long as these were feared they were obeyed. I have known little boys and girls to run and hide from the minister when he came to their father's own house. Such little boys and girls feared the minister, and would think it very sinful not to go to meeting on Sunday, if he commanded them to do so. The world has many such full-grown boys and girls; full-grown in body, not in Reason, who call Sunday-worship religion, and this religion a duty everybody in the world owes to God.

If this holy day means a solar day, then, geographically and astronomically, it is false to teach a Sunday observance to the world. For no one can travel around the world from East to West, without gaining a solar day. The sun will rise upon that man's life one time less for each time he circumnavigates this globe from East to West. Who is to correct that man's calendar? Were it possible for a person to travel around the world in six days of twenty-four hours each, starting westward on Monday morning at sunrise, he would travel but five solar days, and would get back to worship on the sixth, instead of on the seventh. The good missionary, who goes from Oberlin or Andover to convert the heathen of China, may be offering up his Sunday-morning's prayer, while his good Christian brother at home is doing his Saturday evening's work. Thus the sphericity and rotation of the earth, abolish the notion of a particular day which is distinguishable the world over, from any other day. One can even sail away from all solar days of twenty-four hours' duration, and find one day and night a twelve-month long. Sunday was never meant for Dr. Kane and his party of Arctic explorers, in their winter quarters, far this side of the Polar Sea, where a night of one hundred and forty days enveloped that latitude; and where, for many a Sunday, its noonday was the black image of its midnight.

It is not, then, a certain solar day that can be considered holier than the other six solar days; and it must, therefore, be asserted that one-seventh of the time is to be kept holy, in accordance with the minister's prescription, and the statute's prohibition.

What particular seventh part of time? and how shall this particular seventh part of time be kept? These are questions which have never been fully answered. There is a chaos of theological thinking and legislative action thereon, all arising out of vague notions of time; false theories in regard to the earth, as to its origin, shape, position and motion; false conceptions of God, with all the limitations of human weakness, working hard, getting tired, and resting; together with the debased views held in regard to man.

A moment's thought must set one right in regard to this notion of holy, or unholy time. Time is the measure of motion, and is as purely abstract as number, size and distance. As well say that seven is holier than five, as that some time is holier than some other time. Time is relative and applies only to the finite. We may mark time upon the dial of a clock or watch. The second, or part of a second, is struck off by a perceptible movement. We can see the second hand move directly under the eye; it takes the closest observation to see the minute hand move; and look as intently as we may we cannot see the hour hand move; yet it is in motion, or time would not be indicated. And thus we only indicate time relatively, as compared with motion or change, and call it cycle, year, month, week, day, hour, minute, second; whereas absolutely there is no division of time. There is the infinite Abyss, in which time is swallowed up. To the absolute and infinite God there is no such thing as time, nor any such thing as space. God's life is the infinite *Now*, and his being the infinite *Here*. To the Infinite it must be all *Now* and *Here*.

Strictly then the word holy, can only be applied to action, for there can be no such thing as holy or unholy time. The action may in this way name the hour, or day, or place; as that was a holy day, or that is a holy place; because just deeds were done then and there. And also, that was an unholy day, or that is an unholy place, because unjust deeds were done then and there. And thus it has come about, that worship paid to the gods on a certain day, and in a particular place, has rendered both the day and the place holy, because to worship the gods was deemed the best and holiest deed of men. But it would be very silly in this age to assert, that the best deeds of the world are done in a meeting house on Sunday, and that no worship could be as good elsewhere, and at other times. We can by no means say, that Sunday is a holy day because all the good deeds of Christendom are done on that day, and that the other six days are unholy time, because that is the time in which all the unholy deeds of Christendom are done. This would be ignoring facts.

But why was the man fined for working on Sunday in the Free State of Kansas? Was it because the Christian bible had it so recorded from the pen of inspired lawgiver or prophet? No; not a word to this effect in the Old Testament,

Was it because Jesus of Nazareth, or his apostles so commanded? No; not a word in the New Testament upon the subject of Sunday, or Sunday-worship. No word about a fine, about attending church, or what is lawful, or unlawful to do upon the Sunday. The Bible commands nothing; says nothing upon the subject, and every Christian says: "I take the Scriptures of the Old and New Testament to be the only infallible rule of faith and practice."

Then the man was not fined because he violated any biblical command, nor because he was not a Christian? No.

Nor because he violated any physical or mental law? No.

Why then? How foolish your question? It was because he violated a statute of Kansas, which says in plain English without obscurity or ambiguity: "Every person who shall labor or perform any work other than the household offices of daily necessity, or other works of necessity or charity, on the first day of the week commonly called Sunday, shall be deemed guilty of a misdemeanor and fined not exceeding twenty-five dollars." This is why. No need of Bible or Christianity to explain that. This too is the common law of the land, and was imported in the Mayflower, and in many a ship besides, from England and still other lands of Europe. It was not imported from Africa in Christian ships of slave traffic, but was found ready waiting and in religious use for those dusky sons of toil as soon as they landed in Georgetown or Puritanic Boston. In the inscrutable providence of God, it was a jubilee of rest to the black barbarian, driven to toil early and late, under the lash of Christian task-masters. And if man neglected to mention it in his Bible, God did not forget to write it in the Constitution of Man, so that it might be read for the good of toiling men and women. Sunday is founded upon the same demand of human nature, which establishes, and has established all days of rest among different peoples of the world. The sufferings of man, have long preceded every law which has been enacted for his good. The over-worked or hard-worked man needs rest, whether driven by a master, his necessities, or his own greed for worldly gains. Then Tired Nature cries out: "Give me rest!" This is how it came in the statute of Kansas, and English statutes and the Common law. So England said in her fundamental law in the time of Charles II., (1678,) for Puritanic comfort: "No tradesman, artificer, workman, laborer, or other person whatsoever, shall do or exercise any worldly labor, business, or work of their ordinary callings upon the Lord's Day, or any part thereof, works of charity and necessity only excepted." This is the parent of our statute; and at that time the Sunday rigor culminated in England among the Puritans. This consummation had been long in coming. But it was as irresistible as the ocean at its flood. Those things which acted as causes had been done; they could not be undone, and the effect was inevitable. It was in vain that James I., sixty years before, (1618,) proclaimed against the Judaical observance of Sunday, and encouraged after divine services, all kinds of lawful games and exercises. For this he must be branded as impious and profane, and seven years later, under his successor, a law must be passed to strictly forbid this ungodly license, and to annul this ungodly proclamation. How futile were the efforts of James I. He had grappled with the Inevitable. It was all in vain to try to annul by proclamation, the long face, and the long prayer, and the long sad Sunday of the stern Puritan. Why, surely! Was not Shepherd expelled from the House of Commons in the Eighteenth of the king's reign, and disgraced before a whole nation for his biblical argument in favor of less rigor on Sunday, and for saying: "David danced before the Ark of the Covenant, which seems to justify sports on that day."

Seventeen years before this, things were running quite loosely. Sunday was not tied up by statute. Then sports and recreations were not only justifiable, but recommended on this day. An occasional stray shot from Parliament is felt by some tradesman, as for example: "Shoemakers are prohibited from exposing for sale shoes on Sunday." Yet, labor was partially prohibited in the time of Elizabeth. In time of harvest, however, England was free to labor in the field, and this strictly in accordance with Christianity, under the Most Protestant Queen. It was then thought, this was not at variance with the Bible, nor Nature herself; for what God had sent, it was not wicked, but wise, on any day to save. In fact, England had no statutory respect for Sunday, more than other days, till the time of Henry VI., (1449,) and then the preference, it seems, was shown for Easter Sunday. Fairs and certain feast days were then prohibited on Easter Sunday, and certain other Sundays. Upon this famous Easter Sunday, the little English boys and girls would run through the streets crying, or singing:

> "Christ is risen, Christ is risen,
> All the Jews must go to prison."

It is said that Easter Sunday was kept peculiarly sacred, because it is the day in the year on which Jesus of Nazareth rose from the dead. This we know is not true; for Easter Sunday may come on any day between the 21st of March and the 26th of April. Constantine had it established at the Council of Nice, and it depends on the Moon and the Vernal equinox, instead of on the resurrection of Jesus. The word Easter is perhaps derived from Ostera, the Teutonic goddess of Spring. This goddess was worshiped by our forefathers, the ancient Saxons, and a festival was held in honor of her, each returning spring. Here is perhaps the history of Easter Sunday: The Sun, in passing from the

Winter solstice, may be said to have risen when he reaches the Vernal equinox. The earth has passed from her death of winter to her life of spring. This came through the direct influence of the Sun-god. But the month which immediately followed the sun-god's resurrection, was named *Oster-monat*, or Easter-month, by our Saxon ancestors, in honor of Ostera the goddess of spring. And the festival of that month, in honor of this goddess, was perhaps the origin of our Easter Sunday, which would be indicated by the first full moon, which followed the Vernal equinox. It may safely be affirmed, from all the evidence which the world now has, that Easter Sunday originated more from the worship paid to the Sun and Moon, by pagan Saxons, than from Jesus of Nazareth, or Jewish Passover.

The respect paid to Easter Sunday, by statutory enactment, was the beginning of all English and American legislative enactments which have since followed. And we see from this there is a god-idea connected with it, as well as a demand in human nature, when one man is made the slave of another. From man's necessity came the day of rest, and from the god-thought it became holy and reverenced. Slavery in some form has always been connected with the day of rest. Slaves were imported into Europe from the western coast of Africa in 1443. Six years after this England paid her respects to Easter Sunday through Parliament. The slave trade grew in importance and became respectable in

Christian Europe. The Pope patronized it, and paid his respects in a series of bulls. The Most Protestant Queen Elizabeth protects John Hawkins in the Negro slave traffic, and herself shares the profits. The Sunday, also, grows more respected, and perhaps reached its highest point of severe and rigid observance at the time the slave-trade was the most patronized and respected. Even a member of the church in Boston, who might be guilty of

> "Hanging of his cat on Monday
> For killing of a mouse on Sunday,"

was one of the first two men in the Colonies to sail "for Guinea to trade for Negroes."

The Negroes doubtless thought the Sunday observance the best part of Christianity.

From Henry VI., of England, back to Constantine, a period of over eleven hundred years, we find no Sunday superstition coming in the shape of legislative enactment. One ecclesiastical decree did come from the Council of Orleans against field labor, but the stomach of man did not heed it. Sunday, during all this time was the Christian holiday, and was, perhaps, not kept as sacred and holy as those days of the week which were not holidays; as days of festivity are generally days of debauch.

When Constantine gave the Roman religion the name of Christianity, he adopted the Christian Lord's day, as then known and observed among Christians, and thus placed it among the Roman holidays. These holidays were quite numerous with the Romans, and were kept as days of pleasure and recreation. They were days of religious or patriotic expression; days of intellectual or physical feats. They were considered about as sacred as our Fourth of July. But as the old Roman religion was at last baptised in the name of the Triune God, and christened in honór of Christ; so by adopting the Christian holiday, this must have special honor, and become the chief of holidays. After this it came gradually into reverence, as in the slow course of years the name of Jesus the martyr, who had been preached to the world as the Christ, became more and more reverenced. And although Constantine gave the Christian holiday a place in the Roman calendar, it was by no means kept sacred from labor by even the most zealous of Christians; for in the year A. D. 321, he ordered the suspension of all business in courts of law, and all other business, except the manumission of slaves and *agricultural labor*. Thus the Christian farmer, in the time of Constantine the Great, and long centuries after, thought it no sin to work on Lord's day, and did work in the most secular manner; and perhaps never dreamed of a holy day, or a holy time. Not even Luther or Calvin thought Sunday a holy day.

This legislative enactment under Constantine was the first in regard to Sunday; it was by no means the last. Sunday through statutory enactment has now become a part of the *worship of Jesus.*

As the Hebrew Jehovah was a jealous god, and would allow the worship of no other; so the Christian Sunday soon became a jealous day, and would allow the celebration of no other among all the festal days of those early times. And it comes down to us a growth, as a tree grows from the seed by insensible gradations; it is a growth like the worship of Jesus. When we go out the Code of Justinian, and beyond the time of Constantine, we go into outer darkness to find any authority "sacred or profane" for the worship of the Christian Sunday. We search "Holy Writ" in vain for the name of that day. What does the name, itself, denote? Why, surely! the day of the Sun. The day dedicated to the worship of that shining orb; and it is of very ancient and heathen origin. It was worshiped long before Elegabalis brought it into the Roman Empire from Emesa on the banks of the Orontes, which had been honored there in his own name, in the worship paid to a Stone fallen from heaven. This, also, was the peculiar object of the devotion of Constantine the Great. The Christian Lord's Day, took the name of the Pagan Sunday. The two are identical. And Sunday means not the worship paid to Jesus of Nazareth, but to the Sun.

The Jewish Sabbath has a history fully as interesting and quicker told. It belongs to the astronomic history of the week. Quite an advance was made in astronomical discovery before the week was established, and to explain the origin of the week, not only gives us clear conceptions of the causes of holy days, but also beautifully shows the origin and course of thought, and how closely the mind hugs material forms. The rudest form of the god-thought is Fetichism, the worship of God in a thing; fire, sun, moon, or the like. This god is the "Hidden," the "Wonder worker." To give to each department of Nature a presiding god or goddess, with human attributes, is Polytheism. When the conception of God is purely human with extraordinary power, it is Hero-worship, or Anthropomorphism; the worship of a man as God. These gods, it was once thought, lived upon the earth, but at last departed, taking up their abode in the heavens among the stars; so, also, stars were called after their names. And thus came the notion that the stars influenced the character and destiny of men. This has given the world that renowned and complex system of Astrology so prevalent before Copernicus. A group or constellation of stars would represent one god and his labors; another group would be set off to another god or goddess. The Sun himself was a god, the Moon a goddess. But by long observation it was found certain five stars changed their positions with regard to certain other stars which did not change their position. The five were called wandering stars, or planets; the others fixed stars. These five stars the Grecians named Mercury, Venus, Mars, Jupiter, Saturn; and arranged them in this order from the marked difference in the rapidity of their motions. This is the true order which they sustain to each other and to the sun, in regard to position. The Egyptians arranged them in the same order and gave them god-names, also. These wanderers were known beyond the historic age by Grecian, Egyptian and Indian astronomers, and arranged in their true order. Peculiar characteristics were attributed to these planet gods. Saturn, whose movement was extremely slow, was rightly supposed to be farthest away, and was considered cold and gelid in nature. Jupiter, whose motion was a little more rapid, was at a less distance and temperate. Mars was fiery and warlike, as his color indicated. Venus, the bright beauty of morning and evening, was the goddess of Love. And Mercury, the nearest to the Sun, whose motion is so rapid, was the swift-winged messenger of heaven. These five wanderers, with the Sun and Moon, became the seven luminaries of earth and were made to preside in their heavenly spheres, and to rule over successive days on earth; and these constitute the seven days of the week. This is the oldest testimony of man's astronomical knowledge, which has come down to us. And it comes from all nations of the East. The Jewish account of creation makes it date back to the beginning of man's existence. The Brahmins, of India, whose history dates back of Buddhism, and back of Egyptian, Assyrian, Jewish and Grecian history, had, also, the week of seven days, and these days presided over by the heavenly bodies. And says Whewel, in his able history of the Inductive Sciences: "It has been ascertained that the same day has, in that country, the name corresponding with its designation in other countries."

Now let us take the names of these seven luminaries, and we have for the names of the seven days of the week, Saturn's day, or Saturday; Sun's day, or Sunday; Moon's day, or Monday. But at this point we find the wedding of Eastern and Western mythologies. We have discarded the old names of Mars, Mercury, Jupiter and Venus, which ought to follow, and have adopted the names of the Teutonic deities. We have, therefore, Tuesday, from the Latin Tuisco, the name of the Saxon god of battle, instead of the Grecian Mars. This is the Tig or Tyr of Northern Mythology. Hence, with our ancestor's Tuesday, was court-day. And why court-day? Simply because our ancestors appealed to the god of Battle to settle their disputes, instead of to lawyers, as now. The battle was fought on Tuesday, and one day ended it. Then we have Odin's day, or Wednesday. Thor's day, or Thursday. Frigga's day, or Friday. It will be here noticed that, in the Teutonic version, there is but one goddess to figure in the week. She names the unlucky day, Friday. There is a superstitious notion to-day, running throughout Christendom, that it is best not to begin any new undertaking on Friday; and in Law it is the custom to execute the sentence of death upon a felon on Friday. No man under judicial sentence, in all Christendom, can hang by the neck till dead, on any day except Friday. The reason is, in all early mythologies, woman was considered the cause of all Evil in the world; and, hence, her day of the week is the only unlucky one. Thus Custom and Law honor her curse. It is said no nation in the world deems this a holy day.

Now let it be noted that these last deities, of Teutonic mythology, corresponded in character exactly with the Grecian deities, whose names were given to the wandering stars; save, perhaps, Odin, whose history is quite limited, confused and conflicting. It thus becomes apparent that we have a week whose very history is a record of vast eras in thought, wherein the story of the stars has come down to us with their god-names and god-histories.

This will explain many historic allusions, many mythologic conclusions, not otherwise understood. Thus the Jewish Sabbath is our Saturday. This is Saturn's day. Saturn was a Roman deity. The name is synonymous with the Chronos of the Greeks. His chief characteristic is *retributive justice*, who is said to have devoured his own unruly offspring for the evil they had done; as time may be said to devour all things. In Egypt we find the goddess Nemesis, whose characteristic is *retributive justice*, presiding over the day, and naming the wandering star. But the history of Jehovah, the God of Israel, in bringing his people out from the land of bondage, is simply the story of the great and god-like work of *retributive justice.* This Egyptian and Grecian characteristic is confirmed and proven in the fact, that Jehovah had the same day made holy, upon which he would neither work nor suffer his chosen people to work. Hence, Saturday has a history which penetrates Saxon, Roman, Grecian, Egyptian and Jewish times; and like Sunday, when considered more sacred than other days, must be referred back to the mythology of the world's ignorance.

It is well to trace the history of these two days, that we may see by what authority they are pronounced holy; by what authority they shall be held as holy; and by whom they ought to be reverenced as holy. We can now understand why the Bible says nothing about Sunday. The Bible writers doubtless knew nothing about it. And why the Sabbath is considered holy by the Old Testament writers, and considered of but little consequence by the New Testament writers.

But says the Christian: "The bible commands a Sabbath observance, which has been changed to Sunday." Let us see! By whose authority was it changed? Not by Jewish prophet, nor Christian apostle. Not by the authority of Jesus or Paul. Not by any word of the "Holy text." The Sabbath was never changed into Sunday, for the Sabbath and Sunday both exist. The Sunday is not founded upon biblical ground; it has not even the

Rock of Saint Peter on which to rest. The Jewish Sabbath was meant only for the Jews, as the Bible fully proves. It has no identity with the Christian Sunday. It is the peculiar day upon which to pay worship to the god Jehovah. Speaking through Ezekiel, he says: "I gave them my Sabbaths to be a sign between me and them." And through Moses, he is recorded as saying: "Wherefore the children of Israel shall keep the Sabbath, to observe the Sabbath throughout their generations for a perpetual covenant. It is a *sign* between me and the children of Israel forever." The Bible writers never said it is a sign between any other god and his children, nor between Jehovah and any other of God's children outside of the Jewish nation.

The Sabbath is declared in Deuteronomy to have been ordained because of slavery: "That thy man-servant and thy maid-servant may rest as well as thou." "And remember that thou wast a servant in the land of Egypt; and that the Lord thy God brought thee out thence through a mighty hand and by a stretched out arm. Therefore, the Lord thy God commanded thee to keep the Sabbath." This is the work of *retributive justice*, and goes far to strengthen the history of Saturday, as being the day of the cold and gelid Saturn, whose movement is so slow in the heavens.

But that the Jewish Sabbath was not meant for the Christian Sunday is quite obvious in the popular observance of Sunday. The strictness of the

Sabbatical law is nowhere enforced, and has never been enforced among Christians. Even the rigid Puritan came far short of it. And though the Puritan, when we look at his mental characteristics, gives us the clearest conception of the ancient Jewish god, we by no means can give the Puritan credit for living up to the biblical commands. But as he was of all Christians on earth, both before and since his day, the nearest like the Jewish Jehovah, so also he came the nearest of all Christians, to living up to the commands of Jehovah. But if the biblical command in regard to the Sabbath must be taken as applicable to Sunday, then: "Ye shall kindle no fire throughout your habitations upon Sunday," and death must be the penalty if you do: "For whosoever doeth any work therein shall be put to death." Suppose that to-day, "an holy day," a Sunday of rest unto the Lord, while walking just outside the limits of town, your attention is attracted by much noise, as of many talking, and the cries and groans of a man, as in dying agonies. You look up and behold a great crowd of men, and in front of that crowd a man tied to a tree. You stop in amazement to see this defenceless man pelted with stones. If you have a heart of granite you may stay and witness the closing scene. The victim is pelted till he has not a whole bone in his body; till his eyes burst out of their sockets, and his brains are dropping down to the ground. The crowd cease; the man is dead, and you approach with a timid step of distrust. Of a man who seems to be a commander of men, venerable and bearded to the girdle, you inquire what this is all about, who he is, and what the authority for so dreadful an occurrence. He tells you, he is a high priest, a minister of the true God; that this vain fellow who had just been killed had gathered sticks yesterday, on Saturday; and furthermore, that this is just the manner in which God has commanded us to deal with these Sabbath-breakers. You, though believing in the Bible as the only infallible rule of faith and practice, had never before seen a practical illustration of its teaching, and being unable to master the situation, shake your head thoughtfully and rather instinctively.

"Don't you believe it?" asks the priest. "What says our law? We have not only Moses as authority, but an example."

"But I never read Bible that way before!" say you, pointing to the murdered man.

"Listen," says the high priest of God, "and I will read what you hold to be infallible, and the word of God." And he reads from the fifteenth chapter of Numbers, as follows:

"And while the children of Israel were in the wilderness, they found a man that gathered sticks on the Sabbath day; and they that found him gathing sticks, brought him unto Moses and Aaron, and unto all the congregation. And they put him in ward, because it was not declared what should be done with him. *And the Lord said unto Moses:* The man shall be surely put to death: all the congregation shall stone him with stones without the camp. And all the congregation brought him without the camp, and stoned him with stones, and he died, *as the Lord commanded Moses.*"

"There, Mr. Caviler," says the priest, "what do you think of that? There is your infallible Scripture for you. '*And the Lord said unto Moses.*' Do you believe the Lord said that unto Moses? 'And he died as the Lord commanded Moses.' Do you believe this?"

You, though a Christian, shake your head instinctively, and stammer out: "Yes, but those ancient times are not these times; our humane Sunday takes the place of that barbarous Sabbath."

"Barbarous! Hypocrite!" says the priest. "You claim a Sunday observance founded on our Sabbath, yet no where and at no time do you follow the teachings of the Bible thereon. You ought to follow the Law in regard to the Sabbath, and take the Bible as your guide, or else acknowledge yourself an infidel. When you condemn this act of mine, you condemn Moses and the Prophets; you deny the Word of the Most High God, and to escape from the word *Infidel* you cover yourself with hypocrisy."

The priest argues well. Now let us test the matter and see whether or not the Christian really believes the Jewish Sabbath is pushed one day ahead into his Sunday. This can be decided by asking: Will the Christian take the Bible as authority, and apply its Sabbath injunctions to his Sunday? To make it true, this must be done. Then, gather no sticks, and kindle no fires on Sunday, and kill everybody who takes the name of Christian, who does so. There is no civilized Christian to-day on the face of this earth, who believes that any body of men would be justifiable in putting a man to death for picking up sticks on Sunday. There is no civilized Christian, surely, who would do such wickedness. Christian, do you believe God commanded that a man should be killed by slow and cruel, nay, savage torture, simply for gathering sticks on Saturday? Surely, there is no one so debased as to believe it; many may be weak enough to assert it, never having witnessed such barbarity enforced. If it be Christianity to believe it, you insult God and defame mankind, by calling any one a Christian. How much less, then, is it religion to believe it? Truth, when wilt thou unveil Falsehood? Hypocrisy, when wilt thou begone?

Well, we can sympathize now with Jesus when he said to those old orthodox Jews in regard to the strict observance of the letter of the Law: "Hypocrites! ye have omitted the weightier matters of the Law; Judgment, Mercy and Faith." We can also sympathize with Paul when he says: "The letter killeth, but the spirit giveth life." I think the great religious heart outside of the Christian church, in Europe, and especially in America, think too little of Jesus; but little appreciate his work, and understand but poorly, the terrible times of his age. What severe trials that bold heart passed through to give example to the precepts he taught. When he said: "The Sabbath was made for man, not man for the Sabbath," it was in defense of having violated it. Jesus was a Sabbath-breaker; not because he thought thus to annoy the Jews, but because not consistent with any moral Law that it should be deemed sacred. Such a precept by the great Teacher, could only be enforced by example. He, therefore, commands the person he has healed to carry his bed on the Sabbath day; an act strictly forbidden in the Old Testament. The devout Jews thought, therefore, his doctrine was not sound, that it could have no force of truth or divinity in it; and they exclaimed: "This man is not of God because he keepeth not the Sabbath." But Jesus argued: If the Sabbath was made for man then it is lawful to do well on the Sabbath days, and man is lord, also, of the Sabbath. Jesus thought that day was like any other day. Work may be done if work is needed; man may rest if he is tired. This is the undisguised doctrine of Jesus. The author of the Fourth gospel even makes Jesus deny the authority on which the Sabbath, as a day of rest, is founded. John makes Jesus deny the Fourth commandment. "My Father worketh hitherto, and I work." That is: God at no time ever ceased working. Surely this is the doctrine of Reason, and it would be strictly in accordance with a brave religious reformer to say so. And the argument was: If God had never ceased working, then Jesus, himself, would not. The time of labor and rest for man is established in each revolving day.

The special day is added for the slave. But God rests not. We see no rest in Nature. The Sun rises each Sunday and Sabbath morn; at eve the stars, in their silent courses, look down and "have us to bed." On those holy days the corn will grow, and the wheat ripen, bidding man save what God hath sent. Truly, God worketh hitherto, and still works.

It was Paul who took up the doctrine of Jesus, and preached it to Jew and Gentile in downright earnestness. He even did more than this: he preached Jesus and the Holy Ghost to "Disciples" who had no knowledge of either. To a Christianity without either, he gave both. He preached, not so much Jesus Christ, as that Jesus *was*, or is the Christ; and baptized, not in the name of John the Baptist, as those Christians who knew not Jesus were in the habit of doing, but in the name of the Holy Ghost. (See Acts, xviii: 5, 25–28; also, xix: 1–3.) Surely, then, the doctrine of the great Teacher in regard to the Sabbath he also must teach; and he accordingly says: "Let no man judge you in meat or in drink, *or in respect of a holy day, or of the Sabbath days*, which are a *shadow* of things to come; but the body is of Christ."

That is, coming events cast their shadows before. The Sabbath with Paul was merely the intangible shadow of the Christ, whose body was Jesus of Nazareth. He thus blotted out the hand-writing of ordinances, which was against mankind, and nailed it to the cross of Jesus. In strict accordance with this, he says to the Romans: "One man esteemeth one day above another; another esteemeth every day alike; let every man be fully persuaded in his own mind." This was entire freedom; "the glorious liberty of the children of God;" positive, natural, and true to the spirit of Jesus. The old ordinances are no longer binding; they were made for a past and dead age, and must pass away. Those "beggarly elements" of day and time-worship must be buried. The Christian must no longer be in bondage to these; and he cries out to those Gallatians who are about to backslide: "Ye observe days, and months, and times, and years; I am afraid of you, lest I have bestowed upon you labor in vain." If Paul could look now upon the Christianity he gave to the world, he might be tempted to cry out: "I never preached that Jesus was the Christ, that it should come to this Sunday worship; this shadow of Sun, and Moon, and Star worship. Verily, ye are reposing in ignorance and illiterate preaching, and would reject me and Jesus also. I am afraid lest I have bestowed upon you labor in vain." All this is sorry comfort to the worshipers of Sunday or Saturday, who are compelled to acknowledge, they are no more sacred than other days of the week, or else reject all these weighty matters of history which are here adduced.

Let us now look at its philosophy and meaning, and point out some of the best uses to which the Sunday can be put.

Sunday is one of the effects of man's development. It came primarily through the god-thought, and was one of the results of Superstition, which may be defined to be religion without science; and secondarily through man's necessity. These are the two causes which have given us the holy day as a day of rest. It became needed as Oppression warred against the body. Tyranny, slavery, greed of gain, driving the human beast of burden to inhuman toil, made "Tired Nature" cry out for rest. And the holy day of the god-thought came as a jubilee to master and servant. To the slave under the Hebrew hand it was a jubilee of rest. And the Sabbath of seven weeks of years was a high day to the slave of Hebrew blood. With the black slave of Europe and America, the Sunday must have been a joyful day. Nothing could make him believe it was not writ in the ordinances of God. And so it was, though not found in the Christian master's Bible. To the tired laborer who toils from ten to fourteen hours each day, crowded by an employer's avarice, it must be a welcome day. To the New England farmer who toils late and early, year after year, in a rocky soil, it is a day most devoutly welcomed by the tired flesh of man and beast. And may it in mercy be continued in use, so long as the sewing girls of Boston and other cities of the Christian world, are ground beneath the heel of avarice. Here is a picture of slavery to-day which the Sunday of our Christian superstition cannot cure, and which it can but slightly alleviate. In one of the best clothing establishments in Boston over one hundred girls are employed to sew. The work they do soon kills them. Sitting week after week at a sewing machine, their backs give out, and work to them is gone forever. Thus testifies Dr. Dio Lewis, of Boston: "One hundred American girls, such as our sisters, cousins and daughters, if we have them, are taken into that great establishment, one of the very best in Boston, and in a year or two are spoiled forever; unfit to do anything more but to illustrate how much a woman may suffer, without complaining and without dying; ground up in such a mill in one or two years, and then thrown out to pick up what they can, till God in his mercy shall take them where the weary are at rest."

This will illustrate not only the need of a day of rest, but the dreadful abuse of Sunday. I would remove the dreadful superstition which hangs over it, and make of it a fit day of rest for the weary, or recreation, rejoicing, social enjoyment, instruction, or *labor*, suited to the condition of each human being, as his own bodily and mental wants demand. How much could be made of the Sunday were it not enfolded in the black pall of Superstition. The scientific lecture might profitably be made to take the place of the popular sermon, and people who toil in the shop or in the soil be made better and wiser. In this way thousands could be instructed, by the diligence and mental labor of one man. But to the man of health, who has his affairs well ordered, all days are holy alike. Each day brings its blessed labor and rest. Each day its intellectual and moral instruction. To this man, a Sabbath or Sunday is as superfluous as a sick day, or a day in prison. The man who is not a slave to his passions or to another, has no need of the Christian Sunday or the Jewish Sabbath; God never meant it for him.

Labor must be reclaimed from the curse of Avarice, the curse of the Law, and the curse of the Bible. This three-headed monster is eating up, before their time, the best and the purest of the land. The "Eight Hour System" will help a little, but we will have to look to the common Free schools, and to the Free Press for a wider distribution of knowledge, and to bold patriotic preachers, who will face old Superstition, and drive him from the pulpit, and give to the world Natural Religion. It is strange to see with what wickedness Christians will charge their god. Making him the cruel taskmaster of a cursed and doomed race. It is not God who has cursed labor. He never cursed the ground for man's sake; but he has blessed it, and continually blesses it. He has made labor the greatest blessing to man which has come from infinite wisdom. Without labor, surely the world would be cursed, and no Sabbath or Sunday could save it from irretrievable doom. It is man who has cursed labor. Avarice steals the wages of the Poor. The Strong eat up the substance of the Weak. Cupidity harnesses slave muscles to the plow. Cupidity drives man to toil under the lash. Cupidity drives defenseless women into garrets of want and unceasing labor; into dens of vice and into garnished halls of licentiousness. The beggar, in rags, asking a pittance at the rich man's door, is the effigy of cursed labor; nay, is the literal fact standing there. God will always keep him standing there till mankind remove the curse, which they, themselves, have made. The Sunday of rest cannot clothe or feed him. The Sunday sermon from costly pulpit, preached to costly pews, cannot reach him. The Sunday prayer cannot save him. He is doomed under the curse of labor. Christian! do you believe that God robs the poor man and gives his substance to the rich? Then think not that he has cursed labor. Oh! man, remove this curse you have placed upon labor, and sanctify honest toil with the laying on of holy hands, and baptize it with the sweat of your face. The holiest hours of the life of mortal man are his laboring hours, when he is free and the reward of these are his own. A man who idles on week-day, might redeem himself in some small degree by working on Sunday, and so not curse that day also in idleness.

Here is the theological mistake of Christendom. One day is taught to be more holy than other six days, and that no unholy thing must be done on the holy day. But labor is unholy according to the "Curse." It is the direct result of the "Fall" and the "Curse," and therefore man is not allowed to do the cursed thing on the holy day. This mistake has wrought much mischief in the world, and will ever work mischief till untaught the world. If the honest labor of man be in itself not evil, but good and holy, then why not labor on the "holy day?" But, no! labor is, in the Christian theology, considered a "cursed thing," and would defile the Lord's day. Not even in this Republic will Christians celebrate Washington's birth-day, should it come on Sunday. No one thinks the Fourth of July holy. Yet the holiest act of the centuries was done on that day, 1776. Some years the Fourth of July comes on Sunday. It is the Tyranny of superstition and priestcraft which say: "It must stand aside for Sunday." What! must the Declaration of Independence bow to a Roman decree? Must it skulk aside at the bidding of an English statute made hundreds of years ago? Must the signers of the Declaration of Independence be thought less worthy of our esteem than a body of wrangling bishops at the Council of Nice, who thought they could vote divinity into and out of certain bible manuscripts? Must Jefferson be made to bow at the feet of the most corrupt and licentious of Roman emperors? Must civil liberty in America be thought less holy than pagan worship? If there be aught of divinity in respect paid to great deeds and noble sentiments, it is in our civic honors paid to these on the Fourth of July. Yet some "dry-as-dust" statute or decree of a dead age, which statute or decree ought to have been long ago forgotten for not having the breath of divinity in it, will make a whole nation of men, in sham and mock attitude before high heaven, and in scorn of common sense, go out and play Fourth on some day which is not the Fourth of July, as recorded in a Nation's heart. A nation of men must not only declare Hypocrisy to be legitimate, but they must go out on parade and make Hypocrisy keep step to the music; they must harangue it, and sing it, and pray it, in sham celebration. But it is said we celebrate the act, not the time. True. But if God rested on the Sabbath, and it is celebrated therefor, then it is worship paid to rest, inaction, idleness, weakness. But Jesus rebuked this by saying: "My Father worketh hitherto, and I work." And if Jesus rose from the dead on Sunday, and Christians celebrate it therefor, it is worship paid to the active, working Son of Man who worked every day of the week, and they ought to heed his counsels and put away this Sunday superstition, which never belonged to Jesus or Paul.

The fact is, this Age is the child of the Past. This Age partakes of the Past through the law of inheritance. The Mind of the Past though not alive and active now, has many monuments of thought standing to-day. Like an extinct volcano, though the fire be no longer seen, the mountain of lava is left. So we have our high and low days, our feast and fast days, our saint and secular days, our holy and profane days, all descended from the Past, with its star, and hero, and fire-worship. But these days must be all alike to God. The revolution of the Earth on its axis is no more to him than the tick of a watch in a farmer's pocket. It is not the seventh part of a man's life that can be taken as holy, because he pays respect to some day therein. It is the holy life, which makes worthy the man. It is the aggregate of life which writes Holy or Unholy across the dial plate of Time. We reverence the Past more than we respect the Present. This is why our blind and foolish worship of a day, is thought of more vital importance than a whole life of noble deeds, holy thoughts, and manly and womanly aspirations. This is Religion without Reason; nay, it is worse; it is a solemn sham which we are forbidden to laugh at. It has no authority which this Age is bound to respect. It has for a foundation only the statutes of men, arising from the profound ignorance of the world. The Sunday religion will not do to live by; it is a Phantom which imposes on the mental vision. Be not deceived; the righteous act will always be rewarded of God; the unholy act always be punished. It is your duty to act so well always, that a Jewish Sabbath or Christian Sunday, might blush of its own shame to look over the days of your life. That which thou findest good to do, do quickly and well; and this will make the hour or the day holy to you, be it Saturday or Sunday. All time should be holy to man, as it is to God. Man should pronounce upon each day, "Well done, thou good and faithful servant, enter thou unto the joy of thy Lord." Each day man should labor, live temperately, and rest. Each day feed body and mind, and when from the diversity of employments he is made to neglect some part of the man, body or brain, the day of rest which custom brings should be devoted to restoring as much as possible the lost equilibrium, and thus the day will be honored in mending the man.

In that little cottage, beyond the way, a poor farmer is mending his wife's shoes, on Sunday night. He is not old in years. He was a poor boy, and at twenty-one was set adrift without a dollar, to buffet the world. To share his toils, privations and joys, some kind companion in marriage, such a man nearly always finds. "By the sweat of thy face thou shalt earn thy bread," was lettered all over that face, and blistered into callous hands. He had served his country in the war, saved the remnant of his private's pay, bought him some land, built a little house of his own; and there his early and late hours he consecrated to toil. Necessity, cold and stern, rather than see his little farm mortgaged for taxes, compels him to adopt the old adage of Poor Richard: "A penny saved, is worth two earned." So he devotes the odd hours of rainy days and Sundays to rest, by doing the saving chores about the house. If he has saved a dollar by patching or half-soling his wife's shoes, in a few hour's time, on Sunday eve, how much is God injured thereby? The man and the wife are certainly benefitted; besides, it is a holy and comforting rest to muscles inured to heavier toil. And the good wife shares in the religious exercise of her husband, with a thankful heart, and pays him with a kiss. Where is the injury to God or his government in this? Where is the law of the Almighty and Allwise, that this man has violated? It is not recorded. We find it not in the Flesh or Spirit of man, where God's ordinances are writ. We find it not in the Christian Bible, nor even in the Code of Justinian. He has violated no law of God, it is only a statute of Kansas. He has outraged no divine principle, no holy law, no holy day nor hour. It is only the most debased Superstition, worthy of a dead and heathen age which says: "this man sinned."

Hard by this poor man's house, in a grove, on that same Sunday night, rainy and damp, a meeting of much noise and tumult, of loud preaching, loud praying, of shouting and singing, was protracted into midnight. At a distance, or close approach, one would be reminded of the history of bacchanal revelry among ancient pagans. A curious and enquiring man is always attracted by a great noise or a large multitude; much more so when the noise proceeds from the multitude. Many respectable people are ashamed to be seen at such a meeting in open day. Half covered by the night, curiosity may take them there. What vast themes of speculation and thought are presented to the philosopher, on *Man*, *Monkey*, *Animal;* Reason, Instinct, Sensation, as he looks in upon that herd of bellowing men and women, mingling their groans of devotion with the shouts of gladness, the screeching of frenzy with the songs of praise, and the prayers of the "vile sinner" with the outside curses of hucksters and hack-drivers. What wonder, also, must transfix the philosopher, as he beholds a heaving mass of men and women, in a sort of human pen, promiscuously mixed,—standing up, lying down, falling prone, being held and bound, carried out as though dead, frothing at the mouth, muttering, babbling, uttering extravagant and foolish sentences, striking attitudes of devotion, with eyes uprolling, exhausting breath and body in a wild frenzy! He might pray for some Jesus to come back and cast the devils out of these men and women; for their name is surely Legion here. He would invoke some Power to abolish this relic of barbarism, which is thrown athwart our civilization, in spite of the culture of this age. Shade of Cotytto, with thy followers, come back to us! In thy name, how many deeds are done at camp-meetings, which bring shame in days that follow? And yet, this is called Religion, and a sacred and wise use of this "holy day."

The poor farmer, with his waxed ends and bits of leather, on Sunday night, stitches holy time into his life, because it benefits him and his dear one. And his duty done puts to shame this misguided popular Superstition which wastes the precious hours of human life in that which makes the body worse and the soul no purer.

We have one more scene to present. It may be quickly told, and vividly imagined. On Monday morning, the poor farmer for his evening's labor, is summoned before the "squire" of the township. A camp-meeting "worshiper" had spied this wicked and vain fellow stitching away in good earnest. Christian spite, it was said, wrankled in the complainant's breast, but the farmer is not the victim of that alone. The Religion of the great State of Kansas has been disturbed. He comes in fresh from the prairie with the smell of new mown hay upon him. He had been baptised with the dew of the morning at God's baptismal font, and he feels at peace with God and himself. But the holy rites of labor and love were not sufficient to shield him from man's law, which he had violated. He acknowledges his guilt; he scorns to tell a lie, and Christianity is there vindicated in a fine which the poor man sells his only cow to pay. Christianity, where is thy blush? The world demands a new Religion commensurate to its present growth, and highest civilization. That it will come, and that right soon, is *inevitable.*

LECTURE.

PRAYER,—TRUE AND FALSE METHODS COMPARED.

It is said: "Christ was eternally begotten of God," and the religion which took the name of Christ, is "the everlasting and true religion." It is also said, that "Jehovah is the father of Christ," and "prayer to the Father is prayer to Christ; and, conversely, prayer to Christ is prayer to Jehovah, God, and the Father." It follows legitimately, then, that the Jewish religion was Christianity, and prayer to Jehovah by a Jew, was the same as prayer to Christ by a Christian. Save, perhaps, that the Jew must have lived and said his prayer a day, year, or century before Jesus of Nazareth was born. "Since that period, any prayer," says the Christian, "offered by a Jew, as such, is an abomination in the ear of Jehovah." However this may be, I leave for those who think, to determine.

There is a very ancient story which, perhaps, some Christians have not read. This story I will give, for it contains a moral as well, as shows the ancient method of revenge in prayer. A certain ancient king, ruled over a people at the eastern end of the Mediterranean. He was a great warrior, and enriched himself by pillaging the surrounding tribes, less strong in arms than his own people. This made him enemies at home and abroad. Besides he did some foolish things, as well as very wicked things, which brought upon him derision and contempt. For example, he danced naked before a great multitude of men and women, upon a celebrated religious occasion, and, because upbraided by the queen, his wife, debauched himself, so that he even became base in his own sight. He afterwards murdered a man for the sake of adultery. It was therefore quite natural that this king should have enemies, and when he could not sufficiently punish them for their hatred, and satisfy his own revenge; when no word or act of his own would suffice, he goes down in prayer to his god, as follows: "Set thou a wicked man over him; and let Satan stand at his right hand. When he shall be judged let him be condemned, and let his prayer become sin. Let his days be few; and let another take his office. Let his children be fatherless, and his wife a widow. Let his children be continually vagabonds and beg; let them seek their bread also out of their desolate places. Let the extortioner catch all that he hath; and let the stranger spoil his labor. Let there be none to extend mercy unto him; neither let there be any to favor his fatherless children. Let his posterity be cut off; and in the generation following let their name be blotted out.

Let the iniquity of his fathers be remembered with the Lord; and let not the sin of his mother be blotted out. * * * * Let this be the reward of mine adversaries from the Lord, and of them that speak evil against my soul. But do thou for me, O God, the Lord for thy name's sake; because thy mercy is good, deliver thou me."

According to the popular rendering of the word Christian, this man was a Christian. Not only this, but he was the great progenitor of the god-man Jesus Christ, from his lustful and murderous wedlock with Uriah's wife, according to Saint Matthew.

There are some who would be ashamed of such a genealogy. This arises from ignorance. Jesus of Nazareth need not be ashamed, for doubtless we all have sprung from beings as low in moral type as David, and David from still lower than himself. I think, however, the step is too short in time to develop so good a man as Jesus out of so base a man as David. It could only have been by the "saving grace" of several generations of mothers. The contrast in the two men is brought out most strikingly in comparing this prayer of David with what Jesus said. Here it is: "Ye have heard that it hath been said: Thou shalt love thy neighbor and hate thine enemy. But I say unto you: Love your enemies; bless them that curse you; do good to them that hate you, and pray for them which despitefully use you and persecute you, that ye may be the children of your Father which is in heaven;

for he maketh his sun to rise on the evil and on the good, and sendeth rain on the just and on the unjust. * * * And when thou prayest, thou shalt not be as the hypocrites are; for they love to pray standing in the synagogues, and in the corners of the streets, that they may be seen of men. Verily I say unto you: They have their reward. But thou, when thou prayest, enter into thy closet, and when thou hast shut thy door, pray to thy Father which is in secret; and thy Father, which seeth in secret, shall reward thee openly. But when ye pray, use not vain repetitions, as the heathen do; for they think they shall be heard for their much speaking. Be not ye, therefore, like unto them; for your Father knoweth what things ye have need of, before ye ask him." The contrast is so great, that the one is the contradictory of the other. The one says: "Love your enemies," and "pray for them which despitefully use you and persecute you;" the other prays to his god not only to curse his personal enemy, but to make the curse extend back to his mother, and forward to his children yet unborn. This is a curse with roots, trunk, and branches, and is the outgrowth of barbarism; whereas, Jesus expresses a high degree of moral attainment and philanthropic culture. The one makes his god a partaker and an assistant in his crimes, curses, and follies; the other says:

> "He prayeth best who loveth best
> All things, both great and small."

It has been argued in favor of prayer, that "It was and is; therefore, means something." True. Just so war, theft, murder, slavery, lust, were and are; therefore, mean something. There is a terrible meaning to them all. They mean undeveloped manhood. Some day we will outgrow them. The fact is, we are all dependent beings. We are immediately dependent on all nature about us: the air we breathe, the earth we tread, the sun that shines. We are dependent on each other, but mostly on ourselves, for immediate aid.

And in acknowledgment of this dependence, man has to look two ways from the conscious self, outwardly or distributively into Nature, and centrally inward through the conscious self upon infinite Mind.

In this dependence we are not unlike many of the lower animals. Birds congregate in flocks, fishes in shoals, cattle and horses in herds. These animals and also the lower types of mankind are all gregarious by instinct. I do not affirm they congregate for the sole purpose of protection, having the idea or conscious knowledge of self-defense as a formative cause for this gregariousness; yet self-defense, no doubt, is one of the principles whether conscious or instinctive, lying at the base of all associations, both of man and lower animals. The grazier of our Western prairies must have noticed, that a herd of cattle, if attacked by a dog, will often stand a wall of horns about the young of the herd, to protect them from harm. There is, also, much intelligence or intellect, if you please, exhibited in the animal creation below man; especially in those animals, the companions of man; the horse, the ox, the dog. We have the experience of man, and also, the Bible for authority, that "The ox knoweth his owner and the ass his master's crib." These animals, the associates of man, daily ask of him their daily bread. If fed they follow him, and abide by him, and cheerfully return the thanks of labor therefor; if not, they go elsewhere, and depend on their own art, or cunning, or knowledge for their daily support. It is much the same with rude, savage man. The Indian comes to the white man, and asks for bread. If fed, he comes again. The lazy, the weak-minded, the helpless; made so before birth through the ignorance of parents, or after it, by false education, unjust laws, or oppression, form an army of beggars in the world. These pray daily for bread, shelter and clothing; pray to man and pray to God.

For the purpose of this discussion, Prayer may be divided into three classes: 1. Petitioning God to give, or do something. 2. The striving to get, or do something legitimately ourselves. 3. The silent communion with God.

1. Petitioning God to give or do something.

This form of prayer is that which now generally prevails throughout the world. In this regard, there is no difference between the American Indian, the

New-Zealander, the Hottentot, Greek, Jew or Christian; they all beg God for something, or to do something for them. There is a seeming difference in the character of the gods they worship, and in the manner of petitioning for divine acts and gifts; but the form of the prayer is the same, and the supposed relation of man to God is the same.

It may be laid down as a proposition: The less the mind's capacity, or the more ignorant the person, the more debased will be the conception of God. From this we conclude the more fervent and frequent the prayer, the lower the development will be.

If you look at the history of those people who think God embodied in a stick, or stone, or animal; who observe a fetich worship, they are of all people the most constant in prayer, the most devout in worship, the most aggrieved and exasperated when their object of worship is taken away or destroyed. Their history seems to be summed up in that wail of holy agony which has come down to us, and which is yet heard among the most debased of earth: "Verily, ye have taken away our gods." The Roman soldier who, through ignorance, or willful folly, killed an Egyptian cat, was quickly dispatched, in the people's fierce fury. He had destroyed a god in this consecrated cat, or at least the abode of a god. In this low stage of human development, people prayed to what they supposed contained, or concealed a god, who must be thus present to hear their petitions. This gone, there was nothing to pray to.

Whom would those rude Egyptians ask, with face bowed down to earth in holy reverence, to bring back the great waters of the Nile to water the land and sprout the seed-corn? Whom would they implore to save them from pestilence or visit vengeance on their enemies? Verily, their prayers would be wasted in empty sound; their loud wailing and fervor of words would echo over plain, in palm grove, and grotto, all in vain. How often and how fervently these fetich worshipers pray aloud, wailing and agonizing to God.

So also from mental darkness, not comprehending the physical and warring forces of Nature, which produce their varied manifestations to eye and ear, often bringing pain and death to man, he has learned to worship what he fears. Thus the tiger is worshiped by many tribes, and its nose used as a charm. In Abyssinia the hyena's skin is prayed over, and exorcised by a priest, before the inhabitants dare touch it. In Siberia great and reverential respect is paid to bears. Snakes have been worshipped from the earliest historic period. The Hindus worship Siva, the Destroyer, who is represented with a deadly serpent hanging over his left shoulder. Allied to this was the worship of the Esculapian serpent of the Greeks, and the Brazen serpent of Moses. Even the Devil, in our popular mythology, is worshiped by some as the Old Serpent. In this worship, prayer may be addressed to the god incarnated in these animals; or who is exterior to them, and using them as instruments of punishment.

The American indian has a great Indian Spirit to worship. To this Spirit he often prays long, and loud, and earnestly. A few years ago, a few companies of Osage indians were enlisted for the war. For two months I studied their character and habits of worship. An aged Indian, I soon found, they had as a spiritual adviser, or priest. Every morning, at about four o'clock, he would begin his divine ejaculations, making the whole camp ring. No bugler need sound the reveille while he was with us. I had recourse to an interpreter, who translated, on several occasions, the prayer of this Indian priest; and it is curious to know how earnestly he besought God to discover to him, and his Indian associates, the place of very many, "heap" ponies, and to aid them to steal them, and *to steal them easy;* which prayers were literally fulfilled on two occasions. The last time they all deserted in a body, taking with them about five hundred stolen horses. Nothing could make the Indian believe the divine agency was not the ruling cause of this success. Such is their faith in prayer, I was assured by the half-breed interpreter, they would never engage in any hazardous undertaking, in any great thefts, without imploring divine aid. Now, it is a fact, that Christianity has tried in vain to teach these savage people any higher conception of God, any more Christian form of prayer.

For the last thirty years has the Government, through schools and missions, tried in vain to convert a single Osage indian to Christianity, or to civilized life. Half-breed Christians we sometimes find. So that Christianity may be promulgated, among them, only by infusion of Christian blood. Their religion, their prayer, is a part of their rude spiritual development. They believe that God is fond of bear-meat, as the ancient Hebrew believed Jehovah loved the smell of the burnt flesh and blood of bulls and goats; and they ask with child-like confidence any favor their hearts desire.

One-third of the praying population of the world bows down to images of Buddha. Those people have lived and died for ages, without any knowledge of the Christian god; without any knowledge of the practical workings of Christianity; and so they still live, standing amongst the most devout and prayerful people on the face of the globe. At this day one hundred and sixty million Mahometans profess the Islam, and worship (to them) the only true God. Five times each day they turn their faces towards Mecca, and offer up prayer. The most noticeable feature in their worship is prayer. In this their zeal is unbounded; no impending crisis in their affairs, neither death of friends, fire, pestilence, famine; nothing but the fierce heat of a holy battle, can withdraw the devout Moslem from prayer. "In every town a public crier awakes the inhabitants, and calls the faithful to prayer." As the sun begins to streak the eastern horizon, awakening the world from slumber, the faithful crier is heard to sound forth: "Prayer is better than sleep;" or: "Awake to the best work." And then these children of Islam, to whom the only true prophet had given the hope of Paradise, pray, as with one voice, to the god who has chosen them a special people. Thus, at daylight, at noon, in the afternoon, at sunset, and one hour and a quarter after sunset, their voice may be heard imploring God to give divine aid, and to answer prayer.

The Hebrews were very earnest in prayer. The twentieth chapter of Genesis shows how Abraham, a prophet, leagued with Jehovah to impose on Abimelech, to defraud and fleece a man of better integrity than the prophet or his god. Moses, in the thirty-second chapter of Exodus, is recorded as standing in the breach between the children of Israel and Jehovah, to turn away his fierce wrath and prevent a total destruction; which is accomplished by appeals to his vanity and pride; working a positive change in the designs of Jehovah. Only a man like David, with a rude spiritual nature, living in low, animal gratification, who could murder for the sake of adultery, would be found guilty of praying the prayer of the one hundred and ninth psalm.

The Feejees pray that God will deliver the bodies of their enemies into their hands, that they may feast on them. They pray with more fervor for the wives of their enemies; for the Feejee epicures prefer to eat the flesh of women to that of men. There is but a short step, in spiritual development, from the Feejee, asking God to deliver his enemy's wife into his hands, that he may have a feast of good things, to that of David, who prays against his personal enemy, as follows: "Let Satan stand at his right hand; when he shall be judged let him be condemned, and let *his prayer* become sin. Let his children be continually vagabonds and beg; neither let there be any to favor them."

David stands in much closer relationship, spiritually, to the Feejee than to Jesus of Nazareth. The Osage indian, who asked his god to help him steal ponies, and the Jewish king, who asked his god to help him curse his personal enemy, stand on the same religious plane.

Now God, in his own good way, permits all these prayers of the heathen. He permitted the very wicked prayer of David, no less than he permits the prayer of the blind fetich worshiper, who bows down to "stock and stones." He also permits worshiping, praying cannibals to exist; and hears every utterance, and every heart-felt emotion. He has his own good way in developing the race. There is an infancy of religion and worship as well as an infancy of intellect and good manners. The form of prayer serves to express the soul's development. In prayer we see the spirit of man revolving about the axis of his own selfishness, not God, who swings round daily to be advised about matters and things in the world. I do not say the Feejee-Islander sins in prayer, though rude and barbarous, praying to gratify a desire for human flesh; neither do I say David sinned in the curse of his prayer. He knew no better. He told to the world the degree of his own spiritual development. There is no fact so plainly stamped on the face of the world's history, as this constant, ever progressive change of the world's worship. The religious faculty of man is not undergoing any change, but Reason is guiding it onward to Truth and Knowledge. In the lower orders of mankind how rude and selfish are their prayers; how vain their appeals must be; praying for the basest gratifications; praying through the spirit of revenge, jealousy, appetite, lust. We need not go out of our own age to find every possible form of prayer that ever mouth uttered; the prayer of the cannibal, the pirate, the thief; the prayer of David and the hypocrite; the prayer of the slave for freedom, and the prayer of the master; the prayer of Pagan, and Jew, and Christian, to the god of Mahomet, and Moses, and Jesus. Yes, all are going up this very hour, and all are earnest and honest, except that of the hypocrite; and God hears them all. Omnipresence can not turn a deaf ear; besides he would be unfaithful to the race if he did; not that God answers every fool's babbling that is heard in prayer, yet the pirate's prayer does not grieve him. Once a child three years old, cried and prayed his father to go and bring the new moon to him, he wanted it for a cart-wheel. This prayer of the child did not grieve the father; he rejoiced at the genius of the child. Uneducated brains prayed for the moon; educated brains might laugh at the folly.

In my early religious reading, a copy of the Spectator fell into my hands, and I never shall forget the impression which the following fable made upon my mind. I transcribe it, because the Spectator is now so seldom read. The beauty of the fable is, the name of any other great national god will answer just as well as Jupiter:

"Menippus, the philosopher, was a second time taken up into heaven by Jupiter; when, for his entertainment, he lifted up a trap-door that was placed by his footstool. At its rising there issued through it such a din of cries as astonished the philosopher. Upon his asking what they meant, Jupiter told him they were the prayers that were sent up to him from the earth. Menippus, amidst the confusion of voices, which were so great that nothing less than the ear of Jove could distinguish them, heard the words: 'riches,' 'honor,' and 'long life' repeated in several different tones and languages. When the first hubbub of sounds was over, the trap-door being left open, the voices came up more separate and distinct. The first prayer was a very odd one. It came from Athens, and desired Jupiter to increase the wisdom and the beard of his humble supplicant. Menippus knew it, by the voice, to be the prayer of his friend Licander, the philosopher. This was succeeded by the petition of one who had just laden a ship, and promised Jupiter, if he took care of it, and returned it home again full of riches, he would make him an offering of a silver cup. Jupiter thanked him for nothing; and bending down his ear more attentively than ordinary, heard a voice complaining to him of the cruelty of an Ephesian widow, and begging him to breed compassion in her heart. 'This,' says Jupiter, 'is a very honest fellow; I will not be so cruel to him as not to hear his prayers.' He was then interrupted by a whole volley of vows, which were made for the health of a tyrannical prince, by his subjects, who prayed for him in his *presence*. Menippus was surprised, after hearing prayers offered up with so much ardor and devotion, to hear low whispers from the same assembly, expostulating with Jove for suffering such a tyrant to live, and asking him how his thunder could lie idle. Jupiter was so offended at these prevaricating rascals, that he took down the first vows, and puffed away the last. The philosopher, seeing a great cloud mounting upwards, and making its way directly to the trap-door, inquired of Jupiter what it meant. 'This,' says Jupiter, 'is a whole hecatomb that is offered me by the general of an army, who is very importunate with me to let him cut off a hundred thousand men that are drawn up in array against him. What does the impudent wretch think I see in him, to believe that I will make a sacrifice of so many mortals as good as himself; and all this to his glory, forsooth? But hark,' says Jupiter, 'there is a voice I never heard, but in time of danger. It is a rogue that is shipwrecked in the Ionian sea. I saved him on a plank but three days ago, upon his promise to mend his manners. The scoundrel is not worth a groat, and yet has the impudence to offer me a temple if I will keep him from sinking. But yonder,' says he, 'is a special youth for you. He desires me to take his father, who keeps a great estate from him, out of the miseries of human life. The old fellow shall live till he makes his heart ache; I can tell him that for his pains.' This was followed up by the soft voice of a pious lady, desiring Jupiter that she might appear amiable and charming in the sight of her emperor. As the philosopher was reflecting on this extraordinary petition, there blew a gentle wind through the trap-door, which he at first mistook for a gale of zephyrs; but afterwards found it to be a breeze of sighs. They smelt strong of flowers and incense, and were succeeded by most passionate complaints, of wounds and torments, fire and arrows, cruelty, despair, and death. Menippus fancied that such lamentable cries arose from some general execution, or from wretches lying under the torture; but Jupiter told him that they came up to him from the isle of Paphos, and that he every day received complaints of the same nature from that whimsical tribe of mortals who are called lovers. 'I am so trifled with,' says he, 'by this generation of both sexes that I find it impossible to please them, whether I grant or refuse their petitions, that I shall order a western wind, for the future, to intercept them in their passage and blow them at random upon the earth.' The last petition I heard was from a very aged man of near a hundred years old, begging but for one year more of life and then promising to die contented. 'This is the rarest old fellow,' says Jupiter. 'He has made this prayer to me for above twenty years together. When he was but fifty years old, he desired only that he might live to see his son settled in the world; I granted it. He then begged the same favor for his daughter and afterwards, that he might see the education of a grandson; when all this was brought about, he puts up a petition that he might live to finish a house he was building. In short, he is an unreasonable old cur, and never wants an excuse. I will hear no more of him.' Upon which he flung down the trap-door in a passion, and was resolved to give no more audiences that day."

It is, perhaps, useless to say, the above fable is the short history of the praying world to-day, and it matters not whether the petitions are sent up to "Jehovah, Jove or Lord." But "prayer was and is; therefore means something." Who shall answer what it means?

To-day let us listen a moment to the prayers which are ascending and descending from the great throat of mankind, all over the earth. Imagine one-third of the praying population asking Buddha for bread. Many million Mahometans bowing towards Mecca, asking Allah to extend their holy religion over the heathen Christian lands. Imagine the Christians imploring God, as with one voice, to extend Christianity over the heathen Mahometan land, each professing to worship the true God and in the true spirit. See the Catholic, with earnest fervor, praying some soul out of purgatory; pleading with Christ to overcome God, and make his wrath relax. See the Protestant asking god to open the poor Catholic's eyes, and show him the true Christianity. See the Baptist and Campbellite praying in the wintry water waist deep, in the name of the Father, Son and the Holy Ghost. See the more comfortable Congregationalist, sprinkling his prayer in the face of Heaven. Hear all the denominations of the popular faith in America, teasing God to " come down and show his great power in converting sinners; to come miraculously, and make his power felt, for his glory, and for Christ's sake." Hear the teasing for rain, for large crops, for temporal and spiritual prosperity; begging God to do the work he designed man to do, both of hand and head. Hear the teasing to save from the perils of storm and pestilence; to save from their enemies; and to miraculously save the souls of sinners, by getting them into the Church. Go back a few years, and hear the earnest petitioners of the North, praying the "God of mighty battle" to give victory to the boys in blue; and also the earnest petitioners of the South praying the same god to give victory to the boys in grey. See with what bloody sweat the prayers ascended from many a battle field to the "God who heard and answered prayer." The one prayer the very opposite of the other. Not, however, would he answer, till fiery words of prayer from the cannon's throat had sent thousands to their graves; and the steady tramp of boys a-marching four long years, 'mid the rattle of musketry and the clashing of sabres brought victory to our arms. Then he deigned to answer.

It is said, Jefferson Davis is a Christian, and a praying man. Certain we are that many a Christian, under him, in the Rebel army, prayed to the Christian's god to destroy the Union, and especially, to remove Abraham Lincoln. Did the Christian's god kill Lincoln by the hand of Booth? Was it done in answer to prayer? or was it done in vengeance, because he was not a Christian, nor believed in the Christian's god? Let Christianity, both South and North, answer. These are questions which Christians have already discussed.

One fact well understood would put an end to all the special prayers of Christendom, viz: God is no respecter of persons. The rain will fall upon the farm of the infidel as well as on that of the Christian. The atheist, even, who believes in blind fate, and the fortuitous occurrence of things, if he plant his corn in as good soil in the spring time and not in August; if he plant the best varieties of seed; if he till the ground as well, and obey the natural laws of the corn and seasons, will raise just as good corn on a Kansas prairie as the Christian deacon will. The material universe is arranged to accommodate all God's children alike. There is no such difference in the physical structure of men, that a doctor, in dissecting the body or brain of an infidel, could distinguish him from a church deacon, and point out the peculiar theological tenets of each. Both are made on a general plan. The one feels pain and pleasure, loves food and society, property and children, laughs and weeps, walks and talks, the same as the other; is born the same, grows the same, lives on the same air and substance as the other, coils up his feet in death and goes back to his God the same, "the dust to dust and spirit to spirit." God watches over and provides for the Christian, Greek, and Jew, the Pagan, Atheist, and Infidel, all the same. We are all children of the same impartial God, brothers and sisters to Mary, and Judas, and Jesus. Lobelia will vomit, and strychnine will poison the devout Christian, as well as the devout Moslem, or Infidel. Fire will burn, water drown, and lightning kill; the one as readily as the other. The Sun does not withhold his light and heat, the Moon does not veil her face, the Rain does not fail to fall, the Night to distill her dew, the Corn to grow, the Flower to bloom, because a devout Christian and a bigoted Infidel disagree about the nature of

God, nor because a devout Infidel and a bigoted Christian fail to agree about miracles. Nothing is withheld or given to one of God's children, because of any special reverence one may have for him, more than another; nor because of any special prayer put up by saint or sinner. He is unchangeably the same impartial God, the same yesterday, to-day, and forever, developing Earth, plant and animal, by and through general Laws. Hence, when a rock is loosened from the mountain top, by the denuding action of a storm, and is hurled down by the force of gravity, it may tear off the limb of a tree, and a man, in its course, for which cause the tree is rendered imperfect, and the man goes limp the rest of his days. In order to save the man's limb, God would have to suspend the force of Gravity, whereby he sustains a universe of worlds, and whereby he gives sure footing to whole races of men. So, also, hard by, in the same storm which loosened the rock from the mountain's peak, a man and tree were felled by the lightning's stroke. In order to save the man and tree, God would have to suspend the electric force, which, doubtless, is of much more value than the lives of whole nations of men. Nor does it make any difference whether the man be very pious or wicked, still, the lightning would strike the one as readily as the other.

A man of much nobility of life and religion was killed by lightning in the harvest field; while his neighbor, an impious man, cursed god for sending the rain on his unstacked grain and was spared; whereupon the wife of the deceased, in her prayer, said, God was unjust, for "he should have stricken down the wicked and spared the good man." No doubt, God looks alike upon the pious scolding of the wife, for her husband's sake, and the impious zeal of her neighbor, for his harvest's sake. They both mistook the Perfect and Absolute God for a partial and capricious person who dealt out the thunderbolt to suit his fancy.

A mother got angry at her mischievous child; she raised her hand and struck it; whereupon the mother was hurt as badly as the child. This exasperated the mother still more, and she exclaimed: "I wish to God my hands were iron that I might crush you!" Suppose God had granted her prayer; iron hands would have annoyed her more than the mischief of her child. This prayer was foolish, thoughtless and selfish. So, also, have been nearly all the prayers of the world from Joshua down to Brigham Young, and would never have been offered up, had not the petitioner projected, in conception his own image on the infinite back-ground, and worshiped *that* as his god; who is supposed to nod assent to man's spiritual yearning, which revolves about the axis of his own selfishness.

The Christian, whether Catholic, Protestant or Mormon, beholds God and heavenly visions through the mental lenses of small or great magnifying power, as they have been given him, or he has made them. He may be deceived as he looks through his little spy-glass, because ignorant of phenomena and the laws relating thereto; false notions may obscure his object glass; it may be covered with dust, incident to the material world; it may be warped by passion, or dimmed by lust; it may be darkly spotted by crime; it may be dwarfed and narrow, unfitted to take in a large scope of earth, much less to sweep the heavens. All these things incident to the finite man, limited and controlled by time and circumstances, will warp his judgment and obscure the mental vision. Thus, God shines in through the imperfect mental spy-glass, and he is dwarfed and distorted into a partial and selfish creature. We forget that man was not born into the world like fabled Minerva, fully armed and equipped from the brain of Jove, but was born a great babe and made to grow. We forget that in his growth the *Unseen Force*, in a wide, wise, and universal providence has brought him up from a low estate, gradually on to higher and holier life, step by step, in mighty human heart-throbs of improvement; one great movement of reform succeeding another, like the waves of ocean breaking on the shores of Time; the ocean now ebbing, to be followed by the rising tide, and the waves rolling upward and onward forever.

In all this onward movement, the vision of man is limited by the horizon of his own ignorance, and when his corn-crop suffers from the drouth, and his potatoes are eaten up by the rot, or his winter wheat by the grasshoppers, he thinks the machinery of this world quite imperfect and worn out; so he goes down in prayer to his god, asking him to send the rain, and heal the potato and sweep out the grasshopper. Not long since, in Kansas, we had grasshoppers. Special petitions were sent up for the squelching or driving out of these little pests; as much as to say: "God, you don't know your own business, let us teach you." Even a pressure (though failing in its object) was made by godly men, on the Governor, for a general day of prayer, when all voices could concentrate at one hour and moment, and so as by much noise, storm the citadel of God's throne, and strike the great tympanum of his ear in one vast spasmodic effort; compel him to hear, and order him down with his besom to sweep out the grasshoppers. But the little grasshoppers hatched out, and millions of them died of the uncongenial clime; many were eaten up by birds, and consumed by parasites; and at last when God had completed their mission, he led the remainder back through the air on their own wings. The reason why God would not answer all these pious prayers against the grasshopper, is because he is the God of the grasshopper as well as the Christian. When the Irish were starving from the potato rot, what thousands of prayers were sent up for the potato and the Irish. Yet this was the only method God had of teaching men how to raise potatoes, and to improve the seed. God has appointed the rain its season, has made the plant to grow, and improve, and die by fixed laws, has produced each animal for the sphere of its own operations, and when man complains at the annoyance of insect, animal, flood, drouth, he only scolds because of his own ignorance. And his prayer to God, because of these, is no more answered than the prayer of a mosquito, thirsting for blood. The good housewife, at her pastry cooking, in the summer time, is tormented and nearly provoked to swearing by flies, which are preying on her sweetmeats. She wishes to God flies had never been made. How thoughtless is her prayer! Those little scavengers are connected with the causes of the bloom of health on her cheek; while she is fretting and scolding, and charging God with foolishness, he is watching over the health of a whole people, by sending these countless insects to eat up the pestilence which is breeding around her. Suppose it were possible for the fly and mosquito to pray, the fly would pray for sugar, the mosquito for blood. Not one in a hundred million, of these, get what they would pray for; and thus it is of all the prayers that are offered up; perhaps not one in a hundred million is answered. The reason is plain. God knows best how to take care of and develop the race. Could he be importuned by man, in his finite weakness and blindness, very soon the great harmony of creation would be repealed at the altar of prayer. Men would pray for what they supposed great blessings to mankind, but only the worst results would follow. God would kill at one fell-blow the great Doubting Heart, which goes out in unbeaten paths, searching after Truth. The pioneers in religious and political reform would be cut down as vile cumberers of the ground. Many a bold tongue, uttering God's oracles, would be silenced, and many an ear deafened.

We have fast and prayer days for the whole land, or for whole communities, when men congregate to pray at a mark; so as to direct the divine arrow in a centre shot, to knock the heart out of some real or imaginary evil. Prayers are offered up for rulers, and legislators, and "all others in authority," as though praying for men who are in authority, will do the whole business, and make them wise, efficient and honest. Wisdom, however, comes by the prayers of birth and education, and many a toilsome hour in study and discussion, and inward thought and outward act. If this is to be obtained by some minister praying wisdom into these rulers and men in authority, we had better elect the softest and most passive pieces of human flesh and spirit possible, and set them up at a certain time and place for everybody to centre the prayerful shot at them; so that they may be imbued with knowledge, by a sort of super-induction, miraculously through prayer, moving God to do something for them he had failed to do. If this method of prayer is at all efficacious and not blasphemous, we ought to dispense with our school-houses and colleges, and only have recourse to the pulpit and prayer-meeting. Now, praying for a ruler does not make him better, wiser or worthier. Unless he prays himself, and strives to reach the good, and to be wise by a daily and hourly striving of labor and industry, in the practice of righteousness, the devoutest prayer for him is only empty noise. As well pray to raise the dead.

Then, also, to pray in the popular method, and keep truth within the prayer, either the minister offends his hearers, or asks God to do what he must know he never will do. Hence, he babbles to God rather than offend his hearers; *e. g.:* I pray that God will "bless my whole congregation," or "bless a dying world." Now, suppose in my congregation there are women with deformed waists from tight lacing; others with dyspeptic stomachs from intemperate eating; others with nervous affections from the use of narcotics and living an improper life; as many men who are intemperate in various habits; use tobacco, get drunk, lie and cheat; and without singling out the good, and specifying those whom God would naturally bless, because they had lived in harmony with his laws, I indiscriminately say: "Oh! God, bless this entire congregation;" and I send the petition up with earnestness and closed eyes. Imagine a spiritual finger tenderly tapping my shoulder in the midst of my devotional exercise, and a voice, audible to my spirit, saying: "Stop! unfaithful servant; not so fast. Have you taken a list of your congregation, and an inventory of their sins, errors, and follies? Stop a little; you are going it blind. Open your eyes, and see the ruin and curse many of these people have brought on themselves by not harmonizing their life with my holy and unalterable laws. These I never repeal, to accommodate the most favored child of Earth or Heaven. No prayer can annul the effect of violated law. I can not, and will not, bless these deformed and sickly bodies. I will not send blessings upon intemperance, fashionable folly, and sinful manners. This is contrary to my way of doing business; always and forever. Your prayer is useless; your words are nonsense, if you did but know it, spoken in dreadful ignorance of my modes of operation; or else meant only to tickle the ear, and please the vanity of your hearers. Either unfits you for my ministry. Stop your babbling; go, seek other labor. I have never 'called' you to teach, when you ask me to violate my own laws, while you make an eloquent prayer to please your congregation." These are reflections which must naturally arise before the honest expounder of God's laws, when he thinks of petitioning God to do something for some particular people, at some particular time and place.

Then the effect on the minister must be bad. It makes a praying machine of him, which on certain days of the week, at fixed hour and minute, repeats, year in and year out, the same petition, to the same

God, for the same purpose, without ever being answered. Like a clock, made to strike the hour of the day, he strikes off the daily or weekly prayer. Hypocrisy must only be the result to the human soul from such a practice.

And thus it has come to be a fact. The Church hides, unwittingly perhaps, all the vices, tyrannies, wrongs of the world behind the pulpit. Suppose the whole Christian world would now stop praying in the pulpit, what would be the result? Instead of asking God to cure these vices, destroy these tyrannies and right these wrongs, the praying world would set about the work itself, and more would be accomplished in a twelve-month than now can be done in twelve centuries.

Now, I do not mention these special prayers to bring ridicule upon them. Far be it from me to speak lightly of any form of devotional exercise; but only to let you see the foolishness of these old methods, and lead you out to a higher, and wiser, and saner worship. Far be it from me to deride; I would only be mocking at the child that cried to have the moon for a cart wheel. I would not laugh at, nor scold the babe that fell more times than it had fingers, in walking the first time from father to mother; no more would I throw stones at the oldest orthodox child that ever stumbled over Trinity or the Devil. The savage who bows down to wood and stone, and devoutly prays, I would not deride. He is full a step lower than the Mahometan and Christian, and is fully as sincere as they. He is feeling out, in prayer, after God, and the weakness of his intellect, and his meager knowledge, make his mouth to utter folly. Yet, the Father of the savage and Jesus looks the same upon the prayer of each.

II. The striving to get or do something legitimately ourselves.

I, also, believe in prayer. Not asking God to come down from Heaven, or striving to conjure him up from the earth, for he is already here, close to us all. *He* needs no prayer, uttered or voiceless. We need not call aloud, for he hears the silent murmurings of the life rushing in our bodies. He hears its stillest thought whisper. I do not believe in prayer, asking or imploring God to do something for us. He has done already all that is needful, and the work to be done is on our part. When God formed us in his all comprehending wisdom, every want of man he took into consideration, and provided for it in act and knowledge, far back in the lap of Time. The mysteries of our life, the development of our bodies, the secret workings of our spirit, he smiled upon, away back in the thoughtless ages. He knew every stumble of the world's children in stepping towards the spiritual light. He knew all the pains, the sorrows, and sufferings, of the mortal life of ages of people. He counted all the happiness, and numbered all the holy and unholy prayers and oaths, that should come from the lip of mankind. He was not taken by surprise when David murdered Uriah for the sake of adultery, and prayed the wicked prayer against his enemy, and asked God to curse innocent children. And he knew long ages ago, when the world was unborn in time, that Jesus, who had the true idea of prayer, would teach a higher conception of God, and a holier religion than modern Christian has yet found. But there is a practical prayer we all need. We want to pray with muscular energy; with axes and saws; with plows and hoes; with reapers and mowers; with horses and cattle; with steam and lightning, for the salvation of the bodies and souls of men. Ministers pray for the salvation of souls, in the pulpit. How vain the petition! The soul's development is its salvation. Its development is a growth from an inward force, a continual prayer of upward striving. Praying for rain, for dear life, for health, for harvests, for souls, by word of mouth, is all the weakness of undeveloped brains. Such prayers are never answered. But if the sturdy farmer goes forth in the springtime, planting the seed-corn, even though it be in toilsome and prayerful sweat, he anticipates the rain which the good God sends on the just and the unjust; and thus, at length, his prayer is answered in developed muscles and ripened harvests. This prayer puts to shame the most fervent petitioner doing lip service to God, asking for temporal blessings. Temporal blessings are ours only through the prayer of head and hand. They come by obeying God's laws, never by verbal praying. So, also, if the father and mother pray for sound children, in mind and body, they search out God's laws of pro-creation, in severe and arduous study, and apply wisdom to themselves, with wise intent and hopeful trust, long before the child is born. God never fails to answer such people's prayers, in hale and happy children; who are born heirs of God, and joint heirs with Jesus, and every other god-like soul that has come into the world to adorn and bless it.

The attention of the masses must be directed to the facts of Science: life, thought, being; the body, and its development; the mind, and its unfolding. Public prayer, whether at church or camp-meeting, never saved a soul before or after it was born. To this end people must pray at the family altar of a holy marriage, whose inner courts are sacred to God and man.

III. The silent Communion with God.

Let us look at the teaching of Jesus in regard to prayer. The more I study the character, teachings, and times of that noble Nazarene, the more I admire him. Even encrusted with the teachings of the churches of to-day, falsified and abused in many a creed; yet if we read with a half-eye open to truth, we can find more than all the churches contain. Here is what he says about prayer: "And when thou prayest, thou shalt not be as the hypocrites are; for they love to pray standing in the synagogue, and in the corners of the streets, that they may be seen of men. Verily I say unto you, they have their reward. But thou, when thou prayest, enter into thy closet, and when thou hast shut thy door, pray to thy Father, which is in secret, and thy Father, which seeth in secret, shall reward thee openly. But when ye pray, use not vain repetition as the heathen do; for they think they shall be heard for their much speaking. Be not ye, therefore, like unto them; for your Father knoweth what things ye have need of, before ye ask him." This is the whole story. Volumes could not make it plainer. True prayer is the secret, silent communion with God. It is so secret, that it is best and sincerest when alone. No hypocrite goes into his soul's closet to pray. You want to go away alone, lock out the world, turn the eyes within, commune with God; who knows better than you what you want; who knows your most secret thought. How useless are words, then. This prayer will make you pure in spirit; and the pure in spirit shall see God. I have often thought, if Jesus were here on earth, he would cry out: "Stop this begging in public; away with your hypocritical nonsense; enter your soul's closet; there you will find God."

If we cast aside the spurious Fourth gospel, and take Matthew's account of Jesus, we find he never prayed in public. He would not even let Peter, and James, and John, when alone with them, agonizing in Gethsemane, hear him pray. Three times he went away, alone, to pray; and then he asked nothing which was not in accordance with the Father's will.

In this sense all things pray, and God always answers. Man feels hunger; he desires food; he reaches forth his hand and partakes. This is the fact in regard to God's providence; he does not feed his grown-up babes with a spoon. They must themselves not only handle, but make the spoon. They must make their clothing and shelter, and gather the fuel for warmth. There is not a beast of the field, or bird of the air, but prays; not a tree, or flower, or blade of grass, but prays; nay, old earth itself prays, and the Sun responds with the coloring, warming, and vivifying ray. But this only means: God answers prayer.

People go to prayer-meeting as though God would be easier moved by a concert of verbal action. Such prayer never reaches beyond the church door; never gets behind the counter; never takes hold of the plow handles, looking not back; never carries the hod of mortar up the mason's ladder, even while erecting churches to God. If such prayers are merely a social repast, they may be well with some, but to me as with Jesus of Nazareth, it would be better in silence and alone. The sweet hour of prayer comes silently, cheerfully, hopefully, like the sun rising out of the ocean, bringing the day-spring from on high to the mariner on life's sea. So prayer may become the outpouring of a thankful heart, the psalm of praise to the Giver of life and light, and the earnest endeavor by head and hand force, to develop the outer and inner man, so as to live wisely and act righteously, growing up to the full stature of noble men and women. Thus the spirit developed into the higher man, puts away the begging prayer and communes with God.

> "As down in the sunless retreats of the ocean,
> Sweet flowers are springing no mortal can see;
> So deep in my soul the still prayer of devotion
> Unheard by the world, rises silent to Thee,
> My God! Silent to Thee. Pure, warm, silent to Thee."
>
> "As still to the star of its worship though clouded,
> The needle points faithfully o'er the dim sea;
> So dark, when I roam in this wintry world shrouded,
> The hope of my spirit turns trembling to Thee,
> My God! Trembling to Thee. True, sure, trembling to Thee."

This communion with God, the best and truest prayer, is the unutterable. We feel it; words can not express it. It breathes forth in pure emotions; in godlike aspirations. Our spirits flee away from this body of earth, and are born children of heaven and heirs of God. It is when the soul rushes out to meet the Infinite, that true prayer passes over the face of the Spirit. We seem to enter within the vail and tread the confines of other worlds. It is a realm of feeling and thought, which words have no power to portray. "It is a realm where presumptuous man had better not take plumb lines and levels." An ocean, he is foolish to attempt to fathom. In contemplating the Infinite, the soul is soon lost in the inner depths of conscious existence, and the mightiest thought is soon spent in the feeble effort to comprehend either the power that sustains us, or the thought itself that adorns. Like some rocket at night sent up from earth, it soon vanishes in mid-air.

But the communion of the spirit with God, is the true prayer; the highest and noblest thought. Man stands alone with God, and the sunlight of the Infinite shines in upon his little bodily garden, and unfolds the petals of many a spiritual flower. His mind revels in ideas in scientific and spiritual truths, and the vain babbling of words is dropped for an ineffable experience.

Not in words or rapturous shout,
But voiceless and joyous, the spirit goes out,
And stands in the presence of God
A child of heaven, new born;
Like some flower opening out of the sod,
Greeting the sunlight of morn.

www.ingramcontent.com/pod-product-compliance
Lightning Source LLC
LaVergne TN
LVHW010200110826
845151LV00002B/568

* 9 7 8 1 4 2 5 5 3 6 7 6 3 *